VIETNAM
TRIALS AND TRIBULATIONS OF A NATION

VIETNAM
TRIALS AND TRIBULATIONS OF A NATION

D.R.SarDesai

NEW DELHI
PROMILLA & CO., PUBLISHERS

LONG BEACH PUBLICATIONS
POST OFFICE BOX 14807
LONG BEACH, CA 90803

4P

First published 1988 in India by Promilla and Co.,
Publishers, 'Sonali,' C-127, Sarvodaya Enclave, New Delhi 110 017
ISBN 81 85002 09 6

SarDesai, D. R.
    Vietnam, trials and tribulations of a nation / D.R. SarDesai.
1st ed. — New Delhi : Promilla, 1988.
    x, 213 p., [4] leaves of plates : ill., maps, port., 23 cm.
    Bibliography: p. [192]-202.
    Includes index.
    ISBN 81 85002 09 6

    1. Vietnam—History—20th century. 2. Nationalism—Vietnam.

LONG BEACH PUBLICATIONS
POST OFFICE BOX 14807
LONG BEACH, CA 90803

ISBN 0-941910-04-0
LC: 88-080065

Printed in India by Gayatri Offset Press, NOIDA, Ghaziabad
Phototypeset by The Word, New Delhi

8/17/90

Contents

Preface   ix

1. THE HISTORICAL SETTING   1

2. A MILLENNIUM OF FREEDOM   26

3. THE FRENCH CONQUEST OF VIETNAM   44

4. DONG MINH HOI—THE NATIONALIST
   MOVEMENT   60

5. THE SECOND INDOCHINA WAR—
   THE ROOTS   90

6. THE INDOCHINA IMBROGLIO   115

7. THE NEW VIETNAM   133

8. VIETNAM'S INTERNATIONAL
   RELATIONS   160

   BIBLIOGRAPHY   192

   INDEX   203

MAPS

Geography of Vietnam and its neighbors.

North and South Vietnam showing principal places of conflict — Dien Bien Phu, Hanoi, Haiphong, Gulf of Tongking, Saigon ...

PLATES

Ho Chi Minh.

General Giap, the hero of Dien Bien Phu, at his Command Post.

National Liberation Army on the march.

Vietnam army's bicycle transport!

The fall of Dien Bien Phu (10,000 French prisoners).

Vietnam People's Army militia girls.

Women workers' political education at Viet-Tri electrochemical complex.

"Before, our life was good. There was peace. We had to work very hard, but we were not afraid of anything."

Rural Vietnam: ricefields, buffaloes ...

Buddhist monks in procession.

Nguyen Trai (1380-1442).

Preface

Vietnam has evoked more interest internationally among scholars and statesmen, militarists and peaceniks, journalists and common readers than most other countries in recent times. The spectacle of a small nation with far less sophisticated weaponry than its opponents, with hardly any use of air-power, immobilizing the most advanced, militarily best-equipped nation, moved people across the globe. The Vietnam conflict, in all its brutal manifestations, was brought, for the first time, to the living rooms of millions by television stirring the depths of human conscience day after day for several years. What is it that motivated the Vietnamese people—men, women and children—to make such supreme sacrifices? Was it communism or nationalism? Or a combination of both?

My interest in Vietnam was further aroused by numerous Vietnamese students who immigrated in the wake of the "fall" of Saigon in 1975 and thereafter as "boat people" to Southern California and enrolled themselves, in due course of time, at UCLA. Their plaint about a persistent bias in most of the Western accounts about Vietnam and the plea to write an objective history of the modern period in the perspective of its long historical past has been primarily responsible for this book. I have profited most from discussions with them, in particular, Nguyen Đao Phan, who completed a thesis on the National Liberation Front under my supervision. My thanks are also due to Dr. Pham Cao Duong, whose scholarly insights into the agrarian policies, successes and failures of successive governments in Vietnam, have benefited my understanding of rural Vietnam. For the recent period, I have extensively drawn from the most well-informed and fairly objective and analytical reports of Nayan Chanda, Special Correspondent and expert of the *Far Eastern Economic Review* on Vietnam.

I should acknowledge my debt of gratitude to Ms. Charlotte Spence, the recently-retired Indo-Pacific Bibliographer of the University of California, Los Angeles, for her unfailing assistance in locating materials and to Mrs. Ingelise Lanman, my research assistant and doctoral student for helping, in a variety of ways, in the writing of the book. I am very grateful to Ms. Jane Bitar, Manager, Word Processing for Social Sciences and Humanities, and Ms. Nancy Rhan at UCLA for their professional expertise in the preparation of the manuscript. I am most appreciative of the young and dynamic Ashok Butani for his exemplary zeal in maintaining high production values in his publications including, of course, this one. Lastly, as always, I am beholden to my wife for providing consistent encouragement and inspiration in all my scholarly and writing endeavors.

D. R. SarDesai

1
The Historical Setting

The Southeast Asian littoral, the promontory at the extremity of mainland Southeast Asia, constitutes Vietnam. It extends from about the 9th parallel to the 26th. The long coastline of Vietnam uncoils like a mighty serpent in the shape of an "S" running from China's Southern border to the tip of the Indochina peninsula. Nearly 1,240 miles (1995 km) long, the country extends unevenly with widths ranging from 31 (50 km) to 310 (499 km) miles covering an area of 128,405 square miles (33 million hectares). Vietnam is as large as the British Isles, smaller than Burma or Thailand, with a population estimated at 50 million in 1980. It is bordered on the North by China, to the West by Laos and Kampuchea, to the East and South by the South China Sea.

Vietnam's two fertile alluvial deltas—Tongking in the North and Mekong in the South—have inspired an image of a typical Vietnamese peasant carrying two rice baskets suspended at the ends of a pole. Connected by a chain of narrow coastal plains, the deltas produced, before the recent long drawn-out war, abundant rice enough to feed the population and to export. Although these delta regions constitute only about a quarter of the country's area, they support almost 80 percent of its population. The rural population density in some of the provinces of the Tongking delta is as high as 1,000 per square mile (3.86 per hectare). The Mekong delta is the richer of the two and extends well into Kampuchea. Both the deltas are known for their intensive agriculture; the Tongking delta has long reached the point of optimum agricultural expansion. The country's historical, political and economic development has taken place in these two separate areas partly because of a mountain range dividing the country. The Annamite Cordillera runs approximately north and south along the border of Laos and Vietnam cutting the latter almost half-way and also extending along the Vietnamese-Kampuchea border. At certain points, the mountain ranges have elevations of up to ten thousand feet.

Communications between Vietnam and Laos or Kampuchea are possible through certain strategic passes. Of these, the more difficult ones are located in the North at an altitude of more than 3,000 feet (915 meters) at the head of the valleys of the Song Da, the Song Ma and the Song Ca. Further south, the communications are, by comparison, not as difficult. Thus, the Tran Ninh area can be reached through Cua Rao while the Cam-mon plateau can be reached from the Nghe An area through the Ha-trai and Keo Nua passes at an altitude of more than 2,000 feet (610 meters) or further south through the Mu Gia pass at a somewhat lesser altitude. From Quang Tri one can traverse just north of the Kemmarat rapids through the Ai Lao pass (at an altitude of about 1,300 feet or 396 meters), regarded as the gateway to Laos. As for communications between the Tongking delta and Central Vietnam, there are several passes and corniches at Hoanh Son, the gateway to Annam at elevations of between 1,300 (396 meters) and 1,500 feet (457 meters). The geographical configuration and the varied accesses are extremely significant for understanding the movement of people and armies in the military encounters in ancient as well as recent times.

Vietnam — The Nomenclature

For most of their history, the Vietnamese habitat was limited to the Tongking delta. During the first millennium

of the Christian era, from 111 B.C. to 939 A.D., it formed a
directly-ruled province of the Chinese Empire. South of its
border in Central Vietnam lived the Chams in the kingdom
called Champa, until in 1471, most of it was overrun by
independent Vietnam. The remnant of Champa was
absorbed by the Vietnamese in 1720. Thereafter, taking
advantage of an extremely weakened Khmer Empire, the
Vietnamese gradually expanded into the Mekong delta
completing the conquest by the middle of the 18th century
and reaching the modern borders of Vietnam.

Vietnam was known by different names at different times
in its history. The Chinese called it Nan-Yueh and the
Tongking area as Chiao Chih. In the seventh century, the
Chinese renamed it Annam meaning "pacified south" after
attempting to put down a series of revolts by the Viet-
namese. A little after the Vietnamese overthrew the direct
Chinese rule in 939 A.D., the kingdom was called Dai-co-
Viet (Country of the Great Viet People). As the kingdom
extended its borders, the three natural divisions of Vietnam
—North, Central and South—came to be known to the
Vietnamese respectively as Bac Viet, Trung Viet and Nam
Viet. Politically, the territory was divided into two separate
kingdoms in the 16th and 17th centuries through China's
mediation and ruled by two different dynasties. The
country was unified for the first time in 1802 by Emperor
Gia Long and was named Vietnam. Because France conquered Vietnam in three different stages and later tried
through official policies to submerge the nationalist identity
and spirit of the Vietnamese people, the French never called the country by its real name Vietnam, instead calling
the three regions by their administrative units insisting also
that they corresponded with three separate cultural entities.
In the South, Cochin-China (a term originally coined by the
Portuguese from the Chinese Chiao-chih) was a French
colony; Annam or Central Vietnam, with its imperial capital of Hue, a protectorate; and Tongking with Hanoi as
capital, was regarded as a separate protectorate. The arti-

ficial vivisection of their country by the French was regarded an insult by the Vietnamese nationalists, who vowed its liberation from the French and later from the Americans, and to bring about its reunification as the single nation-state of Vietnam. That was accomplished in 1976 after a relentless struggle of several decades that ended in the previous year.

The Human Fabric and Languages

The Vietnamese

The Vietnamese, who form 85 percent of the population, were a mixture of non-Chinese Mongolian and Austro-Indonesian stock inhabiting the provinces of Kweichow, Kwangsi and Kwantung before the area was brought under Chinese rule in 214 B.C. The ancient Chinese called the Vietnamese pai-Yueh or a hundred Yueh. There possibly took place a further racial intermixture through marriages between the Vietnamese and a Tai tribe much after the Vietnamese had moved into the Tongking delta.

The mixed racial descent of the Vietnamese is reflected in their language, which is both monotonic like the Malayo-Indonesian and variotonic like the Mongolian group of languages. It is also influenced in its grammar (no declension or inflection) and even more so in its vocabulary by the Mon-Khmer languages to the extent of 80 to 90 percent of words of every day usage. It owes its multi-tonic system as well as substantial repertoire of words to the Thai language. By the time the Vietnamese came under the Chinese rule in 111 B.C., they had already a well-developed language of their own. Thereafter, the Vietnamese language drew heavily on the Chinese for administrative, technical and literary terms.

The Vietnamese language is monosyllabic. For most of their history, the Vietnamese used Chinese ideographs for writing purposes. In modern times, a system of writing cal-

led *Quoc-ngu* has been employed, thanks to the invention
of Alexandre de Rhodes, a French Jesuit missionary of the
17th century. Like many other missionaries in many other
non-Western parts of the world, his purpose was to be able
to translate the Bible in local languages and train a number
of missionaries to reach the masses. The differing levels of
pitch as well as vocal consonant elements are shown in
Quoc-ngu by diacritical marks.

The Tribals

In the extensive mountainous country of the North and
West of the Red River delta live several groups of which the
Meo, the Muong and Tai tribal people, all of Mongolian
origin, are the most important and numerous. Together, all
the tribals account for about two million people. The Tai
speak languages closely allied to those of Thailand and
Laos. The other tribes speak dialects of Tibeto-Mongolian
origin except the Muong, numbering about 20,000, who
speak a language akin to the Vietnamese. The vast plateau
and hilly areas of Central Vietnam are inhabited by a
number of ethnic minorities, numbering nearly a million
people, collectively called the Montagnards by the French.
Six of the larger tribal groups account for nearly half of the
tribal population. These are the Rhade, Sedang, Jerai,
Tho, Bahnar and Roglai, certainly a heterogenous people,
whose skin color ranges from brownish white to black.
Their languages are drawn both from the Malay-Polynesian
and the Mon-Khmer groups. They were pushed into the
mountains by the Vietnamese moving South.

Traditionally, there is not much love lost between the
tribal people and the plains people. The tribals have been
renowned as warriors and as masters of the strategic passes
able to move swiftly across the borders of Vietnam into
Laos and Kampuchea. They may be fewer in numbers and
their weapons far less sophisticated than those of the Vietnamese. Yet, they were never completely subdued by the

Vietnamese. Because of their bravery, skills and knowledge of the terrain, they were wooed by the Chinese considering an invasion of Vietnam, later by the French and in the recent long drawn-out war in Vietnam, by both sides in the conflict. The tribals have held all outsiders including the ethnic Vietnamese in contempt and have regarded them with strong suspicion. They do not have the Vietnamese enthusiasm for wet rice cultivation, preferring instead to burn the brush on the mountain slopes and resort to dry rice cultivation. Their ways of life, languages, dress, social organization, and house structures have been all so distinct from those of the Vietnamese. Generally speaking, the Montagnards have never displayed a high regard for law and government of the plains people.

Despite governmental efforts to improve their lot, the tribal population of Vietnam still follows primitive ways of life eking out a miserable existence exploiting the infertile and inhospitable terrain constituting four-fifths of the country's area. After 1954, the North Vietnamese Government was kind to them. This was perhaps because of the valuable assistance given by them during the underground struggle against the French to the Viet Minh, who had operated for years from their hideouts in the mountainous territory of the North-West. The present government of Vietnam has a twofold policy toward the tribal population. On the one hand, it allows them autonomy, thus helping them to maintain their ethnic identity through retention of age-old social institutions and practices. On the other hand, it encourages assimilation through education and common participation in the life of the lowlands.

The Chams

Also in Central Vietnam are the Chams, numbering about 40,000. They are the unimpressive descendants of a former dominant and highly civilized people who controlled Central Vietnam for nearly fifteen centuries. They are

brown-skinned people of Indonesian stock, who have sunk
almost to the level of the other tribal people in Vietnam.
Their kingdom was called Champa or Lin-yi in Chinese
records. It was founded in 192 A.D. by a local official
overthrowing the Chinese authority. Taking advantage of
the weak Chinese control over Tongking in the declining
days of the Han dynasty, Champa extended northward. Although the Chams controlled portions of Annam at various
times. Champa proper extended from a little south of Hue
to the Cam Ranh Bay and westward beyond the Annamese
mountains into the Mekong valley of Kampuchea and
Southern Laos. The history of the relationship between
China and Champa was one of alternating hostility and
subservience on Champa's part. With the re-consolidation
of China under the Tsin dynasty, Champa sent the first
embassy to the Chinese Emperor's Court in 284 A.D. But
whenever the Chinese authority in Tongking slackened, the
Chams seized the opportunity and raided the northern
province. During this early period, the center of the
Champa Kingdom was in the region of Hue.

Champa came under Indian influence in around the mid-
dle of the fourth century A.D., when it absorbed the
Funanese province of Panduranga (modern Phan Rang).
Funan was an early kingdom based in Kampuchea
extending its authority over the Mekong delta, Southern
Laos. Kampuchea and Thailand from about the first
century A.D. Tall towers of kilned brick in Phan Rang,
Nha Trang, Qui Nhon, Quang Tri and Da Nang in South
Vietnam are surviving vestiges of the once-powerful Cham
Kingdom. The first Sanskrit inscription speaking of
Champa also belongs to this area and dates back to the
fourth century A.D. The political center of Champa had,
by then, moved from near Hue to the Quang Nam area.
The Kings of Champa assumed the South Indian Pallava
style, their names ending with *varman*, as in Bhadra-
varman, who built the first temple of the Hindu god, Siva.
The famous Cham archaeological sites of Tra Kieu and

Dong Duong in the Quang Nam provinces of southern Vietnam indicate profound Pallava impact of the Amaravati
school of art. In the same area, the most notable archaeological site is that of My-son, a holy city, whose art represents Gupta influence as well as that of indigenous pre-
Khmer artistic concepts of Kampuchea. On this site, the
Chams built in the fourth century a temple for Bhadreshwara, the guardian god of the kingdom. The materials they
used must not have been of an enduring nature because
records indicate that the Chams rebuilt the temple several
times in the following ten centuries. Later, when the center
of Cham activity moved south to Panduranga or Phan-rang,
the South Indian influence increased as is seen, for instance, in the towers of Hoalai. On the top of the oldest of
these towers, a horseshoe style structure resembled *Kudu*
in the Dravidian art of the time. In the opinion of an eminent French scholar, Georges Coedes, it was the Indianiza-
tion of Champa that lent it strength against its Sino-
Vietnamese enemies.[1]

Despite the fact that the kingdom was divided into several units, separated from each other by mountains, the
Chams rallied dozens of times in the defense of freedom
against attacks by the Chinese, the Vietnamese, the
Khmers and later, the Mongols. In such conflicts Champa's
mountainous terrain and easy access to the sea provided
considerable scope for military maneuver. At last, after a
millennium and a half of survival as an independent state
the Chams suffered a severe defeat at the hands of the
Vietnamese in 1471. More than 60,000 Chams were killed
and about half that number were carried away into capti-
vity. Thereafter, Champa was limited to the small area
south of Cape Varella around Nha Trang. The remnant
state lingered until 1720, when it was finally absorbed
by the Vietnamese, the last Cham King and most of his
subjects fleeing into Kampuchea.

The Cham society was, and is, matriarchal with daughters
having the right of inheritance. Following the Hindu tradi-

tion, the Chams cremated their dead, collected the ashes in an urn and cast them into the waters. Their way of life resembled that of the Funanese. Men and women wrapped a length of cloth round their waists and mostly went barefoot. Their weapons included bows, arrows, sabers, lances, crossbows of bamboo. Their musical instruments included the flute, drums, conches and stringed instruments. Today about 40,000 southern Vietnamese and about 85,000 Kampucheans claim Cham ancestry. Their social organization, marriage, and inheritance rules have not changed despite their later conversion to Islam.

The Khmers

Not far west of Saigon and south of the Mekong, there live about 500,000 Khmers in what were once provinces of the Khmer Empire (founded in the 9th century A.D.) and its precursor, the kingdoms of Chenla (7th-8th century A.D.) and Funan (1st to 6th century A.D.). The Funanese were, like the Chams, of Indonesian race while the Chenlas and the Khmers were kindred to the Mons of Burma. The Khmer Empire at its height extended over the southern areas of mainland Southeast Asia including the Mekong delta. The Funanese and the Khmers were extremely active as a maritime commercial power serving as intermediaries in the trade between India and China. Both were Indianized kingdoms adopting Sanskrit language, Indian literature and religions as well as grafting Indian concepts of art and architecture to indigenous forms producing, among others, the world-renowned monuments of Angkor. After the sack of Angkor by the Thais in 1431 A.D., the Khmers became subservient to them but still retained control of the Mekong delta. With the Vietnamese conquest of Champa in 1471 A.D. and the absorption of the remnant of the Champa kingdom finally in 1720 A.D., the Mekong delta portion of the Khmer kingdom was exposed to the Vietnamese aggressive policies. The present-day Khmers of

Vietnam are descendants of the population that chose to stay on in the Mekong delta after its conquest by the Vietnamese in the 8th century. An indeterminately large number of them were used by the Vietnamese as an advance column in their recent march into Kampuchea in December 1978.

The Chinese

And finally, there were until the recent exodus, over a million Chinese in Vietnam, mostly in the South, more particularly in Cholon, the twin city of Saigon (now called Ho Chi Minh City). Some of them are descendants of very old families while ancestors of most others migrated in the wake of the French colonial rule in the 19th century, principally from the Canton area. As in most of the other countries of Southeast Asia, the Chinese dominated the economic life of the country of their adoption as traders, bankers, moneylenders, officials and professionals. They maintained close ethnic ties with their homeland. Because of their economic power, they invited hatred and distrust of the Vietnamese people and governments including the present Communist government. More recently, they became the target of official persecution in 1978-79, resulting in their large-scale migration to China and as "boat people" to other destinations. A large number perished on the high seas.

One of the most persistent themes throughout Vietnamese history is a love-hate relationship between China and Vietnam. While the Chinese culture was appreciated, admired and adopted, Chinese political domination was despised, dreaded and rejected. Such a mixture of envy and hostility is seen in the contemporary Vietnamese attitudes towards the ethnic Chinese in Vietnam, who have been by far superior to the Vietnamese in trade, commerce and finance. Historically, Vietnam was the only country in all of Southeast Asia with close political and cultural ties to

China, all the other Southeast Asian countries being heavily influenced by Indian culture at least in the first millennium of the Christian era. As David Marr has observed, there is "the subtle interplay of resistance and dependence which appeared often to stand at the root of historical Vietnamese attitudes toward the Chinese."[2]

The long history of Sino-Vietnamese relations was marked by significant Vietnamese absorption of Chinese culture both through imposition and willful adoption by the Vietnamese themselves. Vietnamese intellectuals through the centuries have regarded their country as the "smaller dragon" and a cultural offshoot of China. On the other hand, their history was punctuated by numerous valiant efforts to resist against the deadly domination of their fair land by their northern neighbors. The Vietnamese nationalism took a virulent form whenever fear of Chinese takeover loomed large on the horizon. Some of the greatest Vietnamese legends have been woven round the exploits of their heroes who led the struggle against the Chinese. It is, therefore, no surprise that a significant section of the Historical Museum in Hanoi is dedicated to "The Heroic Struggle of the Vietnamese People Against Chinese Feudal Invaders." Even in terms of culture, the Vietnamese never allowed their culture to be totally overwhelmed by the Chinese, taking care periodically to review, to rearticulate and maintain their identity as a people distinct from the Chinese. The hostility born of Chinese domination for long centuries helped sharpen into a militant nationalism against any alien rule.

Early Vietnamese History

The Vietnamese have attempted to give their country a history as hoary as China's. According to one of the numerous legends concerning the origin of their state, a Vietnamese prince named Lac Long Quan came to Northern Vietnam from his home in the sea. He married a princess from the mountain, Au Co, who is also described as the wife of a Northern (Chinese?) intruder, on the top of Mount Tan Vien, sometimes around 2800 B.C. Instead of the commonplace results of a union, the princess laid 100 eggs; when they hatched, a son emerged from each of them. For some unknown reason, the parents separated, the mother leading half the progeny across the northern mountains—and became the ancestors of the Muong— while the remaining fifty followed the father to the sea and became ancestors of the Vietnamese. The most valiant of the sons was chosen to be the first of the eighteen Hung Kings. Lac Long Quan, a prince of the sea, and Au Co, a princess of the mountains, are regarded by the Vietnamese as their primal ancestors. Does this imply that the Vietnamese were originally of the Malay-Polynesian, sea-oriented race coming to terms with the Mongolians of the Southern Chinese plains?

The Dong-Son Culture

The earliest name for Vietnam was Van Lang, founded by King Hung. Seventeen kings or generations succeeded him, all styled Hung, covering the Bronze Age from Phung Nguyen, in the Hong River alley (site of Early Bronze Age, 3rd millennium B.C.) through Dong Dau (site of Middle Bronze Age in the middle of the second millennium B.C.), Go Mun (peak of the Bronze Age, 1200–800 B.C.) to Dong-Son, the most famous site of the Late Bronze Age (800–300 B.C.). Although the archaeologist's spade had discovered substantial quantities of bronze arrowheads in Dong Dau and Go Mun, the real emergence of a fairly centralized state must be ascribed to the Dong-Son period. The "Hung Era" is rightly termed "legendary" by most historians inasmuch as no eighteen kings or generations could have spanned the nearly two millennia of pre-historic development in the Tongking delta. Possibly, the rule of the eighteen Hung monarchs relates to the Dong-Son period, which marked the displacement of the economic and social leadership of primitive agricultural practices by a monarchical apparatus responsible for the building and maintenance of an irrigation system of dykes and canals, providing against nature's vagaries of drought as well as floods caused by excessive rise in the water level of the rivers.

The new state based on the irrigation system in the region of the three rivers in Upper Tongking must have produced excess wealth, requiring protection against predatory enemies from the exposed borders to the North and the South. Hence the need for extensive use of bronze technology for varied weaponry. By the Dong-Son period, the kingdom of Van Lang extended to Hunan in Southern China. The capital was moved to Vinh Phu where the three rivers—Song Da (Black River), Song Ma (Red River) and Song Chay meet.

The evidence of the bronze-using Dong-Son culture is spread not only along the Northern and Central Vietnamese coastline but also as far away as Yunnan and Szechuan in China and in Malaya and Flores in the Moluccas. A large number of ornate bronze drums as well as hoes, axes, knives, spears and plates of armor, among other archaeological artifacts speak of a flourishing culture noted for agriculture, handicrafts, pottery, silk, music and maritime activity on a substantial scale.

The Dong-Son people were undoubtedly sea-farers, who built their own canoes, for domestic communications but also modest sized ships for distant trips, guiding their navigational movements with some knowledge of astronomy. Their trading contacts with the outside world must have brought them the knowledge of metallurgy. The discovery of the Dong-Son culture demolished the earlier theory that bronze was introduced by China (where iron was not used until the third century B.C.) and iron by India. As for religion, the Dong-Sonian art demonstrates their practice of ancestor worship and animism. Gods were related to

agriculture; temples were built on hills or elevated plat-
forms. The ashes of the dead were buried in jars or in
megalithic dolmens, although the people seemed to believe
that the dead "sailed away" to some place westward in the
direction of the sinking sun. Lastly, there was an elaborate
cosmologically oriented mythology in which the dualistic
element of mountain and sea, winged beings and water
beings, mountain dwellers and plains people, provided the
core themes. A substantial part of the Dong-Son culture
eroded among the Vietnamese during the subsequent long
period of Chinese rule. Essentials of the proto-Vietnamese
language of the Dong-Son people have survived among the
Muong tribal people, including the Dong-Son title for
princes— *quan lang*—used by Muong hereditary chiefs.

What led to the fall of the Hung rulers of Van Lang,
known to us partly through the Dong-Son cultural remains,
cannot be established by historical evidence. By 300 B.C.,
it seems the people in the region of Kwantung and Tongking were divided into Au Viet, namely, Vietnamese of the
highlands and Lac Viet, Vietnamese of the plains. They
were politically united into the kingdom of Au Lac by An
Duong Vuong, about whom also not much is known. It is
not clear whether the Au Lac people were partly descendants of Van Lang or Dong-Son or whether they were the
Viets, "real" ancestors of the Vietnamese people, migrat-
ing from their habitat in Lower Yangtse around 300 B.C.
under pressure from Han Chinese southward into Tongking
delta.[3] It is, by now, accepted by most scholars that the
Vietnamese are not descended from one single racial group,
that they are instead a racial mixture of Austro-Indonesian
and Mongolian races.

The capital of the new kingdom of Au Lac was built
further along toward the delta, at Co Loa, about twenty
miles north of Hanoi. It was a fortified city, a model for
later capitals, with three walls, the outer one nearly 9000
yards (8230 meters) long. Au Lac followed both land-based
and water-based techniques of warfare in which the Au

Viet and Lac Viet respectively specialized. Co Loa must have been involved with some very heavy fighting in its early days judging from the thousands of bronze arrowheads found in the Iron Age layers, under its ramparts. By the time Au Lac was overthrown by the Chinese general, Trieu Da, it was already well into the Iron Age.

Vietnam Under Chinese Rule

With the first consolidation of the Chinese Empire by Shih Huang Ti, the builder of the Great Wall, in the third century B.C., the Vietnamese living in the Kwangsi, Kwantung and Tongking areas came under increasing pressure of the Chinese. In 207 B.C., Trieu Da, a Chinese general commanding the Kwantung and Kwangsi provinces, brought the Red River delta also under his jurisdiction, carving out a wholly independent kingdom called Nan-Yueh or Nam Viet (Nam meaning South). The capital of the new state was near modern Canton. Nam Viet was thus, ethnically speaking, a composite Sino-Vietnamese state. Trieu Da encouraged local customs of the Vietnamese, promoted intermarriage between the Chinese and the Vietnamese people. The Kingdom retained its independence for roughly a century.

In 111 B.C. the expansionist Han Emperor, Wu Ti (140–87 B.C.) sent his forces against Nam Viet, liquidating its independence and turning it into a province of the Chinese Empire. It took a long time, however, for the outlying provinces of the Chinese Empire to be absorbed into the Chinese central administration. In fact, it was after the Trung sisters' rebellion in 43 A.D. that the Chinese seriously undertook to impose their culture on the Vietnamese. Nan Yueh or Nam Viet remained a province of the Chinese Empire for the next millennium until the ouster of the Chinese rulers in 939 A.D. For administrative purposes, the Han Emperors divided Nan Yueh into three commanderies: Chiao Chih or Tongking, Chiu Chen (Than Hoa) and Jenan (North Annam).

The two essential elements that contributed to the moulding of the early Vietnamese social organization have been the struggle against nature and against the mighty neighbor to the north. In the process, the Vietnamese developed into one of the most determined, persistent, and tenacious peoples anywhere. The vagaries of nature— frequent flooding of the Red River as well as disastrous droughts—compounded the misery of the people of the Red River delta. In a dry year, water may drop by five-sixths, while in a year of heavy monsoon the floods may raise the water level to forty times the normal height of the Red River. Early in Vietnamese history, possibly before the Christian era, the Vietnamese developed an elaborate system of dykes and canals and the rudiments of governmental authority to control and channelize the supplies of water. The dykes cover an area of more than 1,500 square miles (388,500 hectares) in the Tongking delta today, assuring the peasant his sustenance but exposing the people to the risks of an avalanche if the hydraulic installations are damaged. According to some scholars, the collective work on the building of dams and the regularly compartmented field system which provided protection against flooding were Chinese techniques introduced by Chinese rulers. They may have also brought water buffalo and plough to Vietnam and taught the Vietnamese how to use human excrement as field manure. The Chinese may also have introduced the Vietnamese techniques of intensive pig-rearing and market-gardening which have contributed substantially to the alleviation of the peasant's financial woes in China and Vietnam to this date.

The long period of direct Chinese rule extending over a millennium accounts for numerous Chinese traits in the Vietnamese culture. Even before the Chinese rule began, as inhabitants of the composite state of Nan Yueh or Nam Viet, the Vietnamese had come into contact with the Chinese culture. A modest amount of deliberate Sinicization of the Vietnamese culture came after the imposition of direct Chinese rule in 111 B.C. The governors and county chiefs were Chinese. Further intensive and extensive intro- duction of Chinese culture came about later in the first century A.D. when floods of Chinese refugees poured into the Red River delta. These were not needy peasants, but well-accomplished scholars and officials who had fallen out with the Chinese Government under the usurper, Wang Mang (9–23 A.D.). They became agents of intensive spread of Chinese culture through the introduction of Chinese classics, Confucian ethics and, indeed, Chinese ideographs. Until the adoption of the Romanized *Quoc-ngu* in the seventeenth century A.D., Vietnamese was the only lan- guage in Southeast Asia which used the Chinese characters and was, therefore, not alphabetical. Beginning from the fifth century A.D., the Mahayana form of Buddhism was introduced to Vietnam through China by Chinese scholars and preachers, some of whom passed through Vietnam on their way to India for higher studies in Buddhism or for pilgrimage to Buddhist holy places. The Chinese traveller, I–Ching, attests that Hanoi had become a great intellectual center of Buddhism by the seventh century.

Early Nationalism

The Chinese rule of a millennium was punctuated by several violent expressions of hostility on the part of the Vietnamese subjects. Resentment against Chinese rule was first expressed by members of the old feudal class, whose positions had been endangered and, in many cases, abol- ished by the Chinese officials. Vietnamese revolts occurred not coincidentally during periods when the central govern- ment in China was weak and its authority consequently less effective in the outlying province of Tongking. The first of these uprisings took place in 39 A.D. and is notable for giving Vietnam two heroines remembered for their bravery and patriotism. A number of factors led to intense Viet-

namese resentment of Chinese rule. The influx into Nam
Viet of a large number of mandarins in the wake of Wang
Mang's usurpation of power in China has been mentioned
above. They usurped and occupied lands previously owned
by high Vietnamese officials. The Chinese also made heavy
demands in the form of tribute in addition to maintaining a
monopoly of salt and iron. The new Chinese mandarins also
embarked upon a program of Vietnam's rapid conversion to
Chinese culture. A powerful local chieftain, Thi Sach,
violently resisted that Chinese policy. Thereupon, he was
executed at the orders of the Chinese governor, Su Ting,
who wanted the event to serve as a warning to other recalcitrant chiefs. The Vietnamese reaction was exactly the
opposite of what the Chinese intended. The chieftain's
widow, Trung Trac and her sister, Trung Nhi, raised
troops, pushed the Chinese out and proclaimed themselves
joint queens of all of Nam Viet, for a brief period of two
years. It proved a short-lived liberation but was noted for
support not only of the nobility but also of the peasantry.
When the Chinese retaliated and crushed the "revolt," the
two sisters jumped into a river and committed suicide. A
comrade in combat of the two sisters was Phung Thi Chinh,
the pregnant wife of a nobleman from Sontay province. She
was in charge of the army of the center, leading her troops
against the redoubtable Chinese general, Ma Yuan. She is
believed to have delivered at the fighting front and then
placing the child on her back and "brandishing a sword in
each hand, opened a bloody route in the ranks of the enemy
and escaped." When she learnt that the two sisters had
committed suicide, she too took her own life.

The Vietnamese later deified the two martyred sisters;
many heroic legends came to be woven in their memory as
they continued for centuries to inspire the Vietnamese in
their resistance to alien domination.

The widowed Trung Trac is believed to have set aside her
personal grief, not even wearing the traditional mourning
head-dress. Her oath raised the morale of her troops:

I swear, first, to avenge the nation;
Second, to restore the Hungs' former position;
Third, to have revenge for my husband;
Fourth, to carry through to the end our common task.[4]

Many pagodas were built to honor the two sisters, the most notable being the Hai Ba pagoda in Hanoi and the Hat Mon pagoda in the Sontay province. The Government of Vietnam has proclaimed them national heroines. To this day, Vietnamese girls honor their memory on Hai Ba Trung day in March, while troops marching to the battlefield have been known to take along pictures of the two sisters to inspire them in their war effort.

The Trung sisters' revolt was followed by a campaign of severe suppression of the Vietnamese, physically, psychologically and culturally. Ma Yuan, the Chinese general in charge of the operation, pillaged and broke up Vietnamese feudal estates, executed hundreds of noblemen who were even remotely linked with the revolt, humiliated the others, and exiled several others to South China. Chinese garrisons were set up at numerous strategic points to eschew the possibility of future revolts. Nam Viet was divided into three prefectures (quan) and fifty-six districts (huyen), all under the control of Chinese mandarins. A vigorous campaign was launched to further assimilate the Vietnamese into the Chinese culture through more intensive adoption of the Chinese script and educational system, subordination of Vietnamese laws to the Chinese jurisprudence and above all, enforcement of Confucian ethics of submission of subjects to Emperor, son to father, wife to husband.

The Vietnamese proved diligent pupils, mastering the Chinese classics and quickly demanding posts in the civil service. Their industry and intelligence were not readily nor adequately rewarded. For one thing, the Chinese never intended to treat them on a footing of equality. Moreover, they resented the fact that the Vietnamese scholars, despite all the external trappings of Chinese culture, in fact, managed to retain Vietnamese cultural traditions. Among the old Vietnamese traditions that persisted even among the sinicized Vietnamese elite during the period of Chinese domination were tatooing the body, coating the teeth with black lacquer, chewing betelnut and giving a high place to women in society. While such customs were looked at by the Vietnamese as proud symbols of their cultural national-ism, they were regarded by the Chinese as "barbarous" practices which justified keeping them out of the Chinese civil service for a long time. The numbers of Vietnamese who managed to enter the civil service remained small until the T'ang dynasty (618–906 A.D.) when a larger number was admitted to the mandarinate.

Such "collaborators" were far fewer than those who con-sistently hated the Chinese rule and spared no opportunity to demonstrate the sentiment. Rebellions against Chinese domination were staged by nobility and peasantry and even by those Vietnamese who were conscripted into the Chin-ese army of occupation. The Vietnamese have recorded in extensive verse the exploits of their heroes and heroines against the Chinese rule. The Socialist Republic of Vietnam has enshrined the memory of such deeds in a special museum in Hanoi.

Among such revolts or "wars of independence" the Trung sisters' rebellion was, indeed, the most notable. But there were others too which held down Chinese troops for long periods of time. Some of the more notable uprisings were: the rebellion of Chu Dat in 157 A.D., the rebellion of Luong Long in 178 A.D. and the rebellion of Si Nhiep, which made Nam Viet virtually independent from 187–226 A.D. In the middle of the third century A.D., a major rebellion was led again by a woman. This was in Cuu Chan in 248 A.D. led by Ba Trieu, a 19-year-old sister of a headman in Thanh Hoa, who along with her brother raised an army of more than a thousand persons for guerrilla train-ing in the neighboring mountains. They killed the Chinese governor of Chiao Chih (Tongking) and resisted Chinese reinforcements for several months. In the end, the resistance was crushed by superior Chinese forces, Ba Trieu committing suicide on Tung Mountain, where a tomb and a temple have perpetuated the inspiring memory of her sacrifice to this date.

In the 6th century, Ly Bi, a Vietnamized Chinese of the seventh generation, led a revolt in Thai Binh province. With considerable help from Vietnamese aristocracy and peasantry, he brought the country from Thai Binh to Lang Son under his newly proclaimed independent kingdom of Van Xuan. The independence lasted a brief four years before it was ruthlessly ended by Liang Emperor's army in 548 A.D. The resistance was continued by Bi's brother, Ly Thien Bao in Cuu Chan. He was forced to withdraw into Laos, where he proclaimed himself the independent king of Dao Lang. Another of Ly Bi's associates, Trieu Quang Phuc, meanwhile, called himself king of the Viets in the swampy area of Da Trach. A decade later, both he and Ly Thien Bao's cousin shared authority in most of Nam Viet. The confusing history of that turbulent period brings out the valiant exploits of Trieu Quang Phuc (also called Trieu Viet Vuong, King of Viet), who seems to have successfully eluded the Chinese for three to four decades.

The T'ang dynasty, more powerful and centralizing, was noted for several revolts in Nam Viet and Laos, some of them involving non-Viet minorities. Notable of these was the rebellion of Ly Tu Tien in 687, involving the Di Lao people who succeeded in occupying Tong Binh and killing the Chinese governor. In 722, the Muong people of Ha Tinh led by Mai Thuc Loan revolted against the excessive economic exactions requiring forced delivery of lychee fruit to the T'ang Imperial Court. The rebellion spread to Than Hoa, Nghe An and Ha Tinh, whose people supported Mai Thuc Loan, who secured help from the King of Champa to the South also to overthrow the Chinese governor and occupy the capital of Tong Binh. He was defeated by superior Chinese forces and forced to retreat to his mountain base, Ve Son. A citadel named Van An Thanh (Citadel of Peace) in Nghe An and a temple there remind people to this date of his valiant fight against the Chinese.

Later in the century, two brothers, Phung Hung and Phung Hai led a guerrilla movement in Ha Tay, succeeded in capturing Tong Binh, and proclaiming their independence, which lasted under Phung Hung and his son Phung An until it was terminated by superior Chinese forces in 791 A.D.

In the last decades of the once powerful T'ang dynasty, Nam Viet was attacked and held by the Thais (863–866) from Nan Chao in Yunnan. Although the Chinese rulers of Nam Viet were also able to throw out the Nan Chao forces, the weakness of the T'ang dynasty and its inability to control its distant southern province were bared. When the T'ang dynasty actually fell in 906, the Vietnamese would no longer recognize the suzerainty of the Southern Han dynasty based in Kwantung. At this point, China was undergoing the rule by Five Dynasties (906–960 A.D.). First in 906, a Vietnamese notable, Khuc Thua Du and later his son, Khuc Hao and his son, Khuc Thua My, proclaimed themselves "governor" of An Nam. The Khuc family did not want openly to confront the Chinese rulers with independence for Nam Viet. They had hoped that the disintegration of central Chinese rule would, by itself, in course of time, confirm Vietnamese independence. In 930, however, the last-named Khuc "governor" was replaced by a Chinese governor left behind by the invading forces of the Southern Han dynasty. Less than a decade later, Ngo Quyen (son-in-law of Duong Dinh Nghe, a general of the Khuc family) truly ended the thousand-year Chinese rule in 939 A.D. A brilliant strategist, he is believed to have used underwater iron spikes to wreck the invading Chinese ships. It gave a crucial victory to Ngo Quyen, who proceeded boldly to restore the country's name to Nam Viet with its capital in the ancient city of Co Loa. The independence that he established was conclusive despite the very chaotic state of his country caused by succession dispute after his untimely death in 944 A.D. But for a short period of Chinese rule (1408–1427 A.D.), the Vietnamese enjoyed their virtual independence until the 19th century conquest by the French.

Summarizing the complex Sino-Vietnamese relationship, Professor King Chen notes: "Sino-Vietnamese relations in the past were an enterprise of mutual interest. Politically and militarily China was for Vietnam an administrative tutor as well as an aggressor; economically, China was a promoter and an exploiter; and culturally, China was both teacher and indoctrinator."[5] It is pointed out that the Vietnamese made substantial advances in technology and material life thanks to the Chinese rule: use of the iron plough, art of printing, minting of coins, silkworm breeding, porcelain manufacture and a great involvement in international trade.[6] Keeping in mind, however, the Vietnamese drive and dynamism of the Dong-Son period before the Chinese rule, it is conceivable that the Vietnamese would have progressed in a number of these or other directions, to import technology and knowledge in a variety of fields of human endeavor on their own. The different Chinese roles were imposed on the Vietnamese, who preferred to be left alone to develop themselves as an independent state.

It is difficult, however, to estimate the depth of assimilation of Chinese culture by the Vietnamese. Just like the other Southeast Asian peoples, probably only the court and the elite were able to appreciate and absorb these alien cultural importations. The Chinese mandarin system with its Confucian values helped the elite to erect a wall of authority, which further buttressed their social and economic position vis-a-vis the peasantry.[7] Most of the hierarchical, bureaucratic positions were filled by the elite through a civil service examination, held as in China on the district, provincial and imperial levels. The examinations were rigorous, requiring a very long period of study of Confucian classics, which were highly regarded not only as scholarly works but also as a conceptual aid to find solutions to contemporary problems. Since only the elite could afford the luxury of a long-term education in the Confucian classics, the bulk of the people remained outside the pale of sinicization. The Chinese language written in Chinese characters remained the administrative and literary language of the elite. The masses retained the Vietnamese language, customs and religious beliefs rooted in animism and ancestor-worship. Vietnamese villages with their closely knit families helped preserve their distinct culture and remained firmly resistant to outside influences.

Paradoxically enough, the sinicization of the Vietnamese elite resulted in the latter's desire and ability to acquire and retain their independence of China. As Joseph Buttinger puts it:

> The more they [the Vietnamese] absorbed of the skills, customs, ideas of the Chinese, the smaller grew the likelihood of their ever becoming part of the Chinese people. In fact, it was during the centuries of intensive efforts to turn them into Chinese that the Vietnamese came into their own as a separate people, with political and cultural aspects of their own.[8]

The phenomenon was not unlike the nineteenth and twentieth centuries when Asian nationalism grew in the face of Western powers' efforts to introduce Westernization among the colonial peoples. Chinese rule and intensive efforts to sinicize promoted Vietnamese nationalism. Throughout their history, the Vietnamese culture remained distinct enough for the Vietnamese to resent and revolt against China's political domination.

NOTES

1. Georges Coedes, *The Making of South East Asia*, Berkeley, University of California Press, 1966, p. 79.
2. David Marr, *Vietnamese Anti-Colonialism, 1885-1925*, Berkeley, University of California Press, 1971, p. 9.
3. Le Thanh Khoi, *Le Viet-Nam, Histoire et Civilisation*, Paris, 1955, p. 86, refutes the theory that the Viets are the only ancestors of the Vietnamese.

4. Quoted in Thomas Hodgkin. *Vietnam: The Revolutionary Path*, London, Macmillan, 1981, p. 21.
5. King C. Chen, *Viëtnam and China, 1938-1954*, Princeton, Princeton University Press, 1969, p. 12.
6. Hodgkin, *op. cit.*, p. 29.
7. Jean Chesneaux, *Contribution a l'histoire de la Nation Vietnamienne*, Paris, Editions Sociales, 1962, pp. 26-27.
8. Joseph Buttinger, *Vietnam, A Political History*, New York, Praeger, 1968, p. 29.

2

A Millennium of Freedom

In the tenth century, taking advantage of the fall of the once powerful T'ang dynasty, the Vietnamese declared the establishment of an independent kingdom. Between 939 A.D. and the imposition of French colonial rule in the 19th century, Vietnam enjoyed a thousand years of freedom from alien rule. The only exception was a short period of 28 years from 1407 to 1428, when the Ming rulers of China overran Vietnam and brought it under direct Chinese rule. The millennium of freedom from alien domination followed a millennium of intensely-hated Chinese rule. One would have naturally expected a revulsion for Chinese political and cultural institutions in the new era of freedom. The reaction was, however, mixed not unlike what we witnessed in the post-colonial, independent states of Asia and Africa where a strong revival of indigenous values, traditions and development of political culture has taken place within the general constitutional, administrative, economic, educational and military frameworks inherited from the erstwhile colonial rulers.

As a mark of political expediency, Vietnam maintained formal though nominal links with the Chinese Empire during the period by sending triennial tribute to the Chinese court all the way up to 1885 A.D. The expediency can be explained on several grounds. Firstly, the long Chinese rule, particularly the liberal phase toward its end, had produced a Chinese-Vietnamese aristocracy with intellectual and institutional loyalties to a Confucian court. Such an elite perceived its vested interests to be more secure within the Chinese political system to which they were by then accustomed rather than in a completely independent monarchy without any links whatever with the Chinese Empire. Secondly, the new Vietnamese state had reasons to be concerned about potential attacks from the Thai state of Nan Chao (in Yunnan), which had previously overrun Tongking in the 8th and 9th century A.D. while the latter was still under Chinese rule. Tongking had also suffered from a maritime invasion from the South, from the Sailendra kingdom of Java in the 8th century. And, indeed, there was Champa, the perpetual thorn in the Vietnamese side. It was, therefore, felt by the Vietnamese rulers that a Chinese connection established through the tributary overlord-vassal relationship would serve as a deterrent against any potential aggressive designs of its enemies, particularly the Thais.

The overlord-vassal relationship did not, as in Europe, necessarily obligate the vassal to send troops or funds to help the military adventures of the overlord. It did not really diminish the independence except in a legal, for-malistic sense. On the other hand, the benefits of deterrence were real because a vassal could appeal to his overlord in order to seek assistance in times of need. Thus, as late as 1884, when Annam was threatened by the French, the Annamese Emperor appealed to the Chinese Emperor for protection and the latter did send forces across his Southern border to fight the French at Lang Son.

After the Vietnamese won their independence in 939 A.D., the leader of the independence movement, Ngo Quyen, moved the capital of his new kingdom to the historical site of Co Loa (upstream from Hanoi) from where the ancient kingdom of Au Lac was once governed. The decision to shift the capital reflected the intense nationalist shift of the new leadership of Vietnam. The new kingdom

was, however, plagued by internal conflicts from the very
beginning because of rival claims to the throne made by
ambitious chieftains. The first seventy years of independence saw the rise and fall of three dynasties, each of them
founded by a man of great vigor and dynamism, who was,
however, not followed by equally competent successors.
Thus, Ngo Quyen, who was responsible for pushing out the
Chinese rulers in 939 A.D., lived for only five years thereafter. He had not had much of an opportunity to consolidate his kingdom and establish an institutional structure
which would balance and contain the ambitions of numerous feudal lords. The dynasty established by him lasted
only a quarter century until it was overthrown in 968 A.D.
by Dinh Bo Linh.

Dinh Bo Linh came from a peasant background, by contemporary accounts, a forceful person, who put down the
various ambitious and greedy feudal nobles, consolidated
his kingdom and called it Dai-Co-Viet, Country of the
Great Viet People. He tried everything possible to bring
about unity among his people. Thus it is said that he threw
some of the recalcitrant nobles into cauldrons of boiling oil
or to be devoured by his tigers to end the challenge to the
country's integrity. Unfortunately, Bo Linh too died early.
His family had been butchered by some nobles. In 980, the
only surviving member, a six-year-old boy-king, was overthrown by the army chief, Le Hoan, founder of the early Le
dynasty.

A significant act of Dinh Bo Linh was to send a triennial
tribute to the Sung Emperor of China in return for an assur-
ance that China would not interfere in Vietnam's internal
affairs. Though this made him a vassal, he still wanted to be
designated Emperor (De in Vietnamese; Ti in Chinese).
The Chinese preferred that the Vietnamese monarch be
called "Governor". Realizing that it would be difficult if
not impossible to re-establish control over their southern
province, the Chinese finally agreed to a compromise. The

Vietnamese ruler would be designated a "vassal king" of China. He could style himself "Emperor" in relation to his own subjects and in dealing with his vassals.

Ly and Tran

Both the Ly and the Tran dynasties had excellent rulers at least for the first hundred years of each dynasty, several of the rulers in each dynasty having long periods of reign: the first four Ly kings ruled for a total of 117 years. The Ly rulers moved the capital to Thanh Long (present-day Hanoi), renamed their kingdom Dai Viet and gave it a strong centralized government. In order to facilitate closer administrative ties, a network of roads linking the provincial capitals to the royal capital was built by 1044 A.D. A postal courier service was also established by the middle of the century.

Although Vietnam had become an independent monarchy in the tenth century, it was only in the first half of the following century that major institutional changes came about. The power of the court and the civilization that the Ly dynasty created lasted for four centuries. The Ly rulers created an elaborate apparatus to promote the Confucian cult at the court. Thus, during the last quarter of the 11th century, they established a Confucian Temple of Literature and the Han-Lin Academy for Study in Confucianism at the highest level. In 1076, the National College was founded to train civil service officials. Only scholars well versed in Confucian classics would be able to pass these examinations. Consequently, the principles guiding the government were Confucian while the mandarins who were regarded as social and intellectual leaders would through their personal example propagate Confucian values among the Vietnamese elite. The Chinese model of hierarchical bureaucracy was adopted in 1089 creating nine levels of civil and military officials. Thus, despite strong political hostility toward the Chinese, the Vietnamese rulers deliberately set their nation on a course of voluntary Sinicization.

The Tran dynasty produced a number of great rulers, the most notable being Tran Thai Tong (1225-1258). The many innovative administrative, agrarian and economic measures he introduced were extended more or less along the same continuum by his successors. Thus, he reinforced the Confucian-based civil service examination after the Chinese model, consolidated the hierarchy and glorified it further by creating new, more impressive bureaucratic titles. The kingdom was divided into twelve provinces ably administered by scholar-officials. Tran Thai Tong revamped the taxation system by classifying the rice fields into different categories depending on quality and imposed a land tax. Additionally, he introduced a poll tax payable by landowners. During his reign and almost throughout the Tran dynasty, public works were energetically pursued by construction of embankments all along the Red River right down to where it emptied itself into the sea. Many other irrigation and water control projects were undertaken thus assuring good crops and general prosperity for most of the long period of the Tran dynasty.

A mighty achievement toward the end of Tran Thai Tong's reign was the repulsion of the Mongol invasion in 1257. In a bid to conquer all of China, the Mongols had taken over the southern province of Yunnan in 1253. In order to consolidate their southern flank against the Sung dynasty's armies, the Mongols sent ambassadors to Burma and Dai Viet demanding tribute. Both refused to recognize the rising Mongol political power. Tran Thai Tong imprisoned the ambassadors. In retribution, the Mongol armies swooped down under the leadership of Uriyangadai and reached the Vietnamese capital of Dai-la in 1257. At this point, Tran Thai Tong and his heir-apparent, Tran Thanh Tong, pushed the Mongols across the borders into China.

Mongols Invade Vietnam and Champa

After the conquest of all China in 1279, the Mongol Emperors became heirs to Chinese culture as well as political traditions. They followed the age-old policy of keeping a close watch on neighboring countries to see that they would remain weak and fragmented, never strong enough to attack China. They enforced the tributary system and, at times, insisted on a visit, in person, by the vassal kings at the court in Beijing (which the Mongols established as their capital). Most of the Southeast Asian monarchs lent a grudging cooperation. Champa was the most recalcitrant on mainland Southeast Asia; the Cham king, Indravarman V sent tribute to Beijing but did not comply with the Chinese Emperor's invitation to appear in person. Even the visit of the great Mongol General Sogetu at his court, sent by the Chinese Emperor in 1281, failed to persuade the Cham king to visit Beijing. Thereupon, Kublai Khan sent a punitive expedition under Sogetu by sea because Dai Viet (Vietnam) refused to allow Mongol troops to pass through its territory. Fortunately for the Chams, their relations with the Vietnamese were very cordial during Indravarman V's time. They perceived the common Mongol threat to their independence and decided to act in unison.

In the face of superior forces, the Cham king withdrew from his capital and engaged two separate Mongol expeditions for several years in a guerrilla warfare from his refuge in the mountains, marking a precedent for similar struggles against a militarily superior enemy in recent Vietnamese conflicts against the French and American forces. Indravarman V proferred all kinds of excuses to avoid a personal meeting with Sogetu but showed readiness to send tribute and hold negotiations. In 1285, Kublai Khan sent a third expedition numbering 500,000 men under his own son, Prince Toghani, this time by land through the Dai Viet to help Sogetu's naval expedition which landed directly in Cham ports. The Mongol troops suffered heavy casualties both in the Tongking delta as well as in Cham territory. The guerrillas killed General Sogetu; Prince Toghani suffered an ignoble defeat. Cham guerrilla tactics and sudden ambushes paid off. Kublai's troops finally withdrew without getting the Cham king to appear in person at Beijing. Both Dai Viet and Champa, however, sent embassies to the Mongol Emperor in the same manner that they had done before to previous Chinese Emperors.

During the Mongol attack, like the Champa king, the Vietnamese monarch vacated his own capital and repaired to the countryside to fight the invaders. The hero of the Vietnamese resistance was Prince Tran Quoc Toan, who is deified to this day by the Vietnamese in his posthumous name, Tran Hung Dao. His exploits are still recounted as among the most celebrated in the valiant annals of Vietnamese history of resistance against China. The proud Vietnamese king refused to agree to Mongol demands that he send his sons as hostage to the Mongol court and to supply troops for the Mongol army. Thereafter, the Mongols decided that discretion was the better part of valor and meekly accepted the Vietnamese and Cham triennial tribute in return of peaceful mutual relations.

Fall of Champa

Vietnam's relations with Champa did not always remain cordial. Three provinces, to the north of the Col Des Nuages (between a little north of Hue and south of Vinh), remained a bone of contention for a long time. Even a matrimonial alliance between the two kingdoms (Vietnamese Emperor's sister was given in marriage to the Cham king) in 1306 failed to bring an enduring peace. Finally, in 1312, the Vietnamese Emperor, Tran Anh-tong, was able to inflict a major defeat on Champa retrieving the contested territory and making Champa a vassal state until 1326.

All through the 14th century, Vietnam and Champa were

continually at war with each other. From 1369 when the Vietnamese Emperor, Tran Du-tong, died heirless and until the end of the century, the Vietnamese monarchy was beset with instability and palace intrigues resulting in a series of uncertain successions to the throne. The King of Champa, the famous Che Bong Nga (1360-1390), took sides in these palace plots and attacked Vietnam by sea in 1372, 1377, and 1388, sacking Hanoi on the first two occasions. Champa was able to retrieve the disputed northern provinces and would have brought the Tongking delta under their rule but for a valiant defense organized by Le Quy Ly, an official of Chinese origin who was related to the Vietnamese imperial family. From 1394 to 1400, he served practically as a regent while his infant grandson (daughter's son?) from the Tran family nominally sat on the throne. The Tran dynasty had practically ended in 1394 but nominally lingered until 1400.

A notable feature of the Tran rulers was their very tenuous relationship with China. A proper vassalage relationship was never enthusiastically maintained with the Mongol rulers. In the 14th century, in the declining days of that dynasty and the beginning decades of the Ming dynasty (1368–1644), the Vietnamese sent no tribute to China; on the other hand, Champa improved its relations with China largely to buttress their position vis-a-vis Vietnam. Recognized by the new Ming dynasty as early as 1369, the Cham rulers kept the Ming rulers well posted with the succession disputes and rivalries in Vietnam in the last decades of the 14th century. They openly sided with China in the ensuing Chinese invasion of 1407 because five years before they had lost the northern provinces of Quang Nam again to the Vietnamese under Le Quy Ly.

In 1400, Le Quy Ly himself ascended the Vietnamese throne, in a brand new capital, Tai Do, which he established in Than Hoa province in the southern part of the Tongking delta. He changed his surname and assumed a new name, Ho, presumably his real family name before its migration to Vietnam. The new dynasty called the Ho dynasty became the shortest in the Vietnamese annals (1400–1407).

Chinese Occupation and the Birth of the Le Dynasty

In the 15th century, Vietnam had once again to suffer a Chinese invasion and occupation. The early rulers of the powerful Ming dynasty sought to augment Chinese influence in all of Southeast Asia. In 1407, Ming troops of Emperor Yung-lo entered Vietnam on the pretext of restoring the kingdom from the usurper Ho rulers to the rightful rulers, the Tran dynasty. Instead, the Chinese plainly annexed Vietnam making it a part of the Chinese Empire. Ho Quy Ly (the former Le Quy Ly) and his son were captured and taken to China where they languished and died. Vietnam witnessed the most intensive Sinicization ever. Additionally, every effort was made to demoralize the Vietnamese. Chinese civil service officials were imported and imposed on the Vietnamese. A Chinese style census was undertaken to make it the basis both for conscription to the Chinese army and to levy heavy taxes. The Chinese system of *pan-chia* (collective responsibility) was rigorously enforced. Vietnamese ways of life and religious practices were banned while the people, particularly the higher echelons, were compelled to wear Chinese costumes, women to wear Chinese dress, men to wear long hair. The Vietnamese language was not allowed to be taught in schools. Literature extant in Vietnamese was confiscated and carried to China. Those Vietnamese who resisted, intellectuals as well as artisans, about 100,000, were exiled to Beijing where they were drafted to serve the Empire. A number of Vietnamese were also sent to various parts of Vietnam to procure precious metals, gems, pearls, and ivory for the Ming Emperor. All Vietnamese were treated as suspects and were required to carry an identity card on their person. All such actions naturally provoked the Vietnamese spirit of nationalism and age-old hostility against China.

The Vietnamese reaction was swift and conclusive. By 1418, a leader, Le Loi, an aristocratic landowner from Thanh Hoa province south of the Red River delta, had emerged to lead an armed resistance employing guerrilla tactics that ended a decade later in the capture of Hanoi and expulsion of Chinese troops. He drove out the Chinese officials—civil and military. The proclamation of independence that Le Loi issued on that occasion reflected the Sino-Vietnamese tensions as well as Vietnamese pride and patriotism.

> Our Great Viêt is a country where prosperity abounds,
> Where civilization reigns supreme.
> Its mountains, its rivers, its frontiers are its own;
> Its customs are distinct, in North and South.
> Trieu, Dinh, Ly and Tran
> Created our Nation,
> Whilst Han T'ang, Sung and Yuan
> Ruled over Theirs.
>
> Over the Centuries,
> We have been sometimes strong, and sometimes weak,
> But never yet have we been lacking in heroes.
> Of that let our history be the proof.

Though Le Loi liberated the land of Chinese rule, he could not liberate the peasantry from want of land and pangs of hunger. Le Thanh Ton (1461–1497) solved that problem by conquests to the South at the expense of Champa in 1471. Only a remnant of that once powerful kingdom survived thereafter as a vassal of Vietnam until 1720. The conquest of Champa made possible the Vietnamese expansion first into Central Vietnam and then eventually into the Mekong delta in the eighteenth century. Le Thanh Ton also made Laos (then known as Lan Chang), a vassal of Vietnam. While the Vietnamese thus received tribute from their vassals, they sent in turn tribute to the Chinese Emperors, who recognized them as Kings of Annam, "pacified south."

Le Thanh Ton consciously and deliberately adopted the Chinese system of administration including its recruitment method through the competitive, Confucian-style civil service examination. Whether this mode of cultural accept- ance was simply designed to keep the Chinese out through flattery or whether it was born out of a genuine belief that such Chinese institutions lent social and political stability to a state will never be known. All the traditional Chinese cultural traits like language, art of writing, spatial arts as well as Mahayana Buddhism were adopted. The central administration was patterned on the Chinese model with six ministries: finance, rites, justice, personnel, army and public works. The civilian bureaucracy and military estab- lishment were divided into nine grades each. A Board of Censors carefully watched over the bureaucracy and reported to the Emperor any infractions of rules or pro- cedures. The bureaucracy did not reach the village level. There, the local affairs were managed through a Council of Notables, whose charge was to maintain order, execute of- ficial decrees, collect taxes for the Imperial government and recruit conscripts for the Imperial army.

Recruitment to the civil service was dependent upon suc- cess in the examinations specially conducted for the pur- pose. They were based on the Confucian classics and were held annually at the provincial level, triennially at the regional and national levels. As in China, the candidates successful at the national level were granted an audience by the Emperor himself and were posted to high positions in the administration. Since the social and economic status of the elite was dependent upon their administrative rank, Vietnam became thereafter and until the 19th century a Confucian state dominated by the mandarins. The cultural impact of the system percolated to modern times. Even after the civil service examination was abolished in 1905, the system continued in Vietnam for several years longer. The Vietnamese intellectual elite was drawn from the Confucian-oriented families.

The intense cultural impact of China on Vietnam was a mixed blessing. The civil service examination system produced an educated elite, encouraged a family-oriented hierarchical loyalty, promoted a well-regulated mandarin bureaucracy, resulting into a relatively stable, social, administrative order. On the other hand, the same factors bred an attitude of looking down upon people of other walks of life, looking backward into the past for precedents and for solutions of the present and future problems. The system discounted initiative, originality and creativeness. The doctrine of the Mandate of Heaven underlined the ruler's moral responsibility to the people and allowed the people's right to revolt against an inadequate or oppressive rule. Unquestioned loyalty to the Emperor, father, husband, and older brother were mandatory in "normal times." A way of life and philosophy that regarded non-Confucian outsiders, including Westerners, as barbarians, developed chauvinism, parochialism. An ostrich-like head-in-the-sand attitude could only be suicidal and contribute to stagnation of political and social institutions and inhibit borrowing scientific and technological knowledge from others. Vietnam's relations (like China's) with Western powers in the nineteenth century must be seen against such a backdrop of Confucian legacy.

Notwithstanding such an administrative framework and the civil service examination reflecting immense Chinese influence and impact, Le Thanh Ton sought consciously to move away from Vietnam's intellectual bondage to the Chinese in at least one or two major aspects. The Code of Hong-Duc promulgated in 1483 brought together all the laws, rules and regulations issued from time to time by previous Vietnamese emperors within a single conceptual and legal framework. Another area of Vietnamese assertion was art. The Le dynasty witnessed a large-scale program of construction of temples, tombs, and ceremonial halls all over the kingdom notably in Hanoi, Lamson in Thanh Hoa province and in Hue. These edifices along with steles, balustrades and ornamental gateways still survive, attesting partly to the continuing Chinese Ming influence but also to significant Vietnamese variations of traditional Chinese themes. The best example of such Vietnamese artistic assertion is seen at Hoa-Lu (South of Hanoi), which had been the capital of the Dinh dynasty in the tenth century.

Vietnam's Partition

The inclusion of the former Champa territories made the expanded Vietnamese kingdom an administratively awkward unit. The southern portions of the kingdom hardly felt the impact of the central administration based in Tongking. At the same time, pressures of population in the Tongking delta and an opportunity to fulfill political ambitions encouraged some Vietnamese princes and generals to move to the new territories in the South. The central government's authority weakened progressively. The reign of the last real Le ruler, Le Chieu-tong (1516–1526), was marked by rivalries for power among three families—the Mac, the Nguyen and the Trinh. In 1527, the ruling Le family was deposed by a general, Mac Dang Dung, who seized power in Tongking. The Le family's cause was upheld by a loyal nobleman, Nguyen Kim, who fled to Laos, raised an army there, conquered Hue and in 1533, set up a rival court in the name of the Le kings, with a member of the Le family as a nominal ruler.

This marked the beginning of a protracted civil war, punctuated by periods of truce, which did not really end until the middle of the 18th century. The long periods of relative peace were made possible by China's intervention, which was sought for by rival parties. The first such mediation by China as Vietnam's overlord in 1540 brought about the first "partition" of the country. Mac was recognized by China as the ruler of Tongking, while Le-Nguyen were allowed to make Hue their capital and seek their fortunes in the present Central Vietnam. The settlement was not as significant for its lasting value as it was for setting a precedent for Vietnam's future partition. The Mac rulers were stoutly opposed by Nguyen Kim's son, Nguyen Hoang, as well as by his son-in-law, Trinh Kiem. By 1592, Trinh Kiem's son, Trinh Tung, overthrew the Mac regime in Tongking and restored the throne to the Le dynasty. He brought the nominal Le ruler from Hue to Hanoi thus unifying the divided kingdom of Vietnam. As the suzerain power, China undid the previous "partition," recognizing the Le dynasty as the only legitimate ruler of all of Vietnam (Annam in the Chinese Annals).

In point of fact, however, there were two centers of power as before with the Trinhs ruling in Tongking (with Le as nominal rulers) and the Nguyens in the South also ruling in the name of the Le dynasty. The situation remained very fluid and tenuous for a long time. Technically, the Nguyens were self-appointed governors of the southern province, slowly carving out a kingdom for themselves at the expense of the Khmers. They regarded themselves, however, as loyal appointees of the Le rulers, extending the empire in their name. The Nguyens were generally well regarded by the Le rulers and more importantly by the people under their charge in the South. On the other hand, the Trinhs who had captured all the important posts at the capital, Hanoi (then known as Thanh Long), were regarded as usurpers. By 1620, an open conflict broke out between the Trinh and the Nguyen forces, the latter refusing to pay the Trinh taxes collected in the South in the name of the Le rulers. A military stalemate was eventually reached, broken only by Chinese mediation. In 1673, a durable peace was worked out by China. The territory was partitioned. A wall from the Annam mountains to the sea near Dong Hoi, very close to the seventeenth parallel, which marked the dividing line under the Geneva Agreements of 1954, was erected. The Nguyens were now officially recognized as independent rulers of the territory from Dong Hoi to Cap Varella or Song Cau. Some called it the "Small Wall of Vietnam." The event ushered in an era of peace extending for nearly a century.

Unification of Vietnam — The Tayson "Rebellion"

Once the Trinh threat was removed, the Nguyen power grew rapidly in the South. In the 17th century, they pushed as far as the then Khmer-controlled Mekong delta. In 1720, came the final extinction of the remnant of the Champa kingdom, its last king fleeing with most of his people into the present-day Kampuchea, where their descendants still live. Thereafter, the Vietnamese extended their control in the Mekong delta of Cochin-China, then a part of the Khmer kingdom. No major battles took place for the conquest of these rich and fertile lands. Vietnamese control came about like ink spreading on a blotting paper. The Nguyen rulers encouraged their retired soldiers to establish colonies beyond the Vietnamese frontiers in Khmer areas. Minor skirmishes with Khmer authorities produced prisoners-of-war, who would be used along with other weaker ethnic communities to help the Vietnamese cultivate the lands. By the middle of the eighteenth century, virtually all the Khmer territories of present-day Southern Vietnam had become part of the Nguyen kingdom.

The last quarter of the eighteenth century was a period of great social and political convulsions for Vietnam. The old established regimes were overthrown both in the North and in the South. In 1773, three brothers from the district of Tayson in Central Vietnam—Nguyen Van Nhac, Nguyen Van Lu and Nguyen Van Hue (who adopted the name of the southern ruling family, Nguyen) raised the standard of revolt. They quickly became dominant in the provinces of Qui Nhon, Qhang Ngai and Quang Nam. The Trinh family

ruling in Hanoi (with Le as effete Emperor) took advantage
of the situation, sent troops southward and captured Hue in
1777. A decade later, family feuds developed in the Trinh
family, which gave an opportunity to the Tayson brothers,
who then captured Annam and Tongking, eliminated the
Trinh and deposed the Le dynasty. By 1788, the Taysons
obtained control of all of Vietnam: Nhac was proclaimed
Emperor of Annam, with Van Hue and Van Lu in charge of
Tongking and Mekong basins respectively. In a sense,
Vietnam was unified under the three brothers though the
Vietnamese historians prefer to regard the Tayson revolt as
a catalyst for the real unification brought about by Emperor
Gia Long in 1802.

The Tayson success was helped by the public disgust with
the nepotistic, corrupt Trinh administration in Tongking,
and their belief that the Trinhs had lost the "Mandate of
Heaven." In contrast, the Nguyen family was held in high
regard. While the Taysons were hailed as deliverers in the
North, they were regarded as unscrupulous usurpers in the
South. They were accused of taking advantage of the
tragedy in the Nguyen family where the king had died without leaving an adult heir. The teenage prince, Nguyen Anh,
driven into adversity, received sympathy and secret support
from large numbers of people in the Ca Mau Peninsula
where he had taken refuge. Hardly anyone shed tears for
the debacle of the discredited Trinh family. On the other
hand, Nguyen Anh's adversity lasted slightly over a decade.
His family's numerous supporters and sympathizers enabled him to capture the environs of Saigon from the
Taysons before long. According to a Vietnamese nationalist, Pham Huy Thong, the people regarded the Mandate of
Heaven to have passed from the Le-Trinh not to the
Taysons but to the Nguyens to rule over all of Vietnam.

Unification and Consolidation

Among the supporters of Nguyen Anh was a French missionary, Pigneau de Behaine, who regarded Vietnam as his

second fatherland. In 1787, he went to France carrying Nguyen Anh's son, Canh, to the court of Louis XVI, seeking military assistance for restoring Nguyen Anh to power. Considering the domestic preoccupation and plight of the French monarch, it was a miracle that a Franco-Vietnamese treaty was signed, providing French military aid in exchange for a grant of monopoly of external trade, the cession of Puolo Condore island and the port of Da Nang to the French. The French Government directed its colonial governor of Pondicherry (in South India) to provide the military assistance, an order he failed to carry out. De Behaine, however, raised 300 volunteers and funds in Pondicherry—enough to purchase several shiploads of arms. He arrived in Vietnam on June 19, 1789, barely a month before the fall of Bastille.

The French help was marginal to Nguyen Anh's success. Even before its arrival, he had captured Saigon in 1788; when he conquered Hue in 1801 and Hanoi a year later, there were only four Frenchmen in his army. Bishop Pigneau de Behaine, who himself participated in the military campaigns, died in 1799. The French helped in the construction of Vauban-type forts, casting better and larger cannons and creating a navy. Vietnamese Communist historians have lambasted Nguyen Anh for accepting even this limited foreign assistance comparing him with Ngo Dinh Diem and the French volunteers of the late 18th century to the United States Military Advisory Group of the 1950's and 1960's.

In 1802, Nguyen Anh proclaimed himself Emperor of Annam, with the title of Gia Long, signifying the political unification of the Tongking and Mekong deltas. The title itself was a contraction of Gia Dinh, the name of the region around Saigon and Thanh Long, that of the region around Hanoi. In the following year, he sent tribute to the Chinese Court; for the first time, China recognized the Nguyen dynasty. Emperor Gia Long is recognized as the first unifier of Vietnam.

Gia Long (1802–1820) was as remarkable a leader in peace as he was in war. He reorganized the entire country into three divisions and twenty-six provinces. The traditional center of Nguyen power, Hue, became the capital of the kingdom. Tongking was divided into thirteen provinces, Annam into nine and Cochin-China into four. The provinces were subdivided into districts, subdistricts and villages. Under Gia Long there was considerable autonomy given to the two river basin areas of Tongking and Cochin-China, a policy reversed by his son, Minh Mang.

Gia Long revived the Imperial government as constituted by Le Thanh Ton in the fifteenth century, which was, in turn based on the Chinese model. The Emperor and six ministers in charge of public affairs, finance, rites, armed forces, justice and public works, constituted the Supreme Council. The civil service examination on Confucian lines was reinstituted and a code of laws, based on Chinese principles of jurisprudence, was proclaimed.

Emperor Gia Long also devoted himself to the tasks of reconstruction of the country, ravaged by a three-decade long civil war. The most urgent task was, indeed, to restore the age-old, intricate irrigation system of the Tongking delta. Among his notable public works was the Mandarin Road dubbed Route One by U.S. soldiers from California along the coast linking Saigon, Hue and Hanoi, a distance of 1,300 miles, which could be covered on horseback in eighteen days. Fortifications dotted the strategic points along the entire route built to maintain firm control over most of the country. Such remarkable work has, Communist criticism apart, earned for Gia Long undying gratitude of the Vietnamese people as their country's unifier and greatest monarch ever.

NOTES

1. Quoted in Ralph Smith, *Vietnam and the West*, London, Heinemann, 1968, p. 9.

3

The French Conquest of Vietnam

Despite the long history of French presence in Vietnam, major French territorial conquests had to await the second half of the nineteenth century. The French activity began in the Orient, like that of the Portuguese, under royal patronage and with similar aims: God, Gold and Glory. The first French expedition reached the Orient in 1601. Two years later. an East India Company was formed in Paris. Its trading activities. however. did not flourish at least in the initial decades. thanks to persistently successful Dutch raids against French shipping in the Indonesian waters. There were additional reasons for the French company's failure. Its official sponsorship by the royal court made its fortunes dependent upon the whims of the reigning monarch and subject to court intrigues. Besides, like the Portuguese, the French combined religion and trade. missionaries more often hindering than helping the trade effort. An additional factor that would jeopardize the French future for a considerable period of time was the conspiratorial role of a European adventurer, Constance Phaulkon. at the court of Ayuthaya (Thailand) ostensibly to promote French fortunes.

Vietnam and the French Missionaries

For the first two centuries of their presence in the Orient, the French were far more successful in religious activities than in trade or acquisition of territories. In 1615, some Jesuits opened a mission at Fai Fo, south of Tourane (Da Nang). Its most illustrious member was Alexandre de Rhodes, who beginning from 1627, spent nearly four decades in missionary effort. A great scholar, his most notable contribution to Vietnam was that he devised *Quoc ngu*, a method of writing the Vietnamese language in Roman script instead of the traditional, cumbersome Chinese characters. The *Quoc ngu* is still being used in Vietnam. Rhodes' motivation, like that of many a missionary compiling glossaries, grammars, and dictionaries of different languages and dialects in Asia, Africa and Polynesia, was to use the script to reach the masses easier and convert them to Christianity.

De Rhodes had a chequered career in Vietnam. Born in Avignon, France in 1591, he joined the Order of the Jesuits at the age of twenty and traveled to the East in 1619. All Catholic missionaries going to the East had to land first in Goa under instructions from the Vatican. After a short stay in Goa, Malacca, and Macao, de Rhodes received orders from the Vatican to proceed to Japan. While on way to that country, de Rhodes learned that there was an official ban on missionaries entering the Land of the Rising Sun. He, therefore, stopped in Vietnam. In 1627, he received the Vietnamese Emperor's permission to work in the North but by 1630, he was suspected of political links with Western powers and expelled. A decade later, he returned to South Vietnam and was expelled again for similar reasons in 1649. After three years' stay in Rome, he returned to France and established in Paris the Society of Foreign Missions (Societe des Missions Etrangeres) in 1652. This society sent scores of missionaries to Vietnam and were successful in converting thousands of people to the Catholic faith. By the end of the eighteenth century, French missionaries claimed about 600,000 converts in the South and about 200,000 in the North mostly in the coastal provinces.

Successive French governments had demonstrated a consistent interest in proselytization and missionaries had maintained for most of the time close links with the French court right up to the French Revolution. As a French historian of Vietnam, Charles Maybon notes:

> The History of the new Society [of Foreign Missions is closely associated with the history of French influence in Indochina. One of its founders, Palu, tied the first knot of relations between the French and the Annamese royal courts. The most illustrious of all missionaries was Bishop Adran (Pigneau de Behaine) who officially strengthened these ties: the acts of the Society's members provoked the first French armed intervention in Vietnam.[1]

With the possible exception of Gia Long's personal relationship with Bishop Pigneau de Behaine, the missionaries (even during Gia Long's rule) did not enjoy the trust of the Vietnamese monarchs. Bishop de Behaine was posthumously given the honors due to a duke of the Vietnamese kingdom, but his role in converting the young Prince Canh (Gia Long's son) during his visit to France was neither forgotten nor forgiven. Despite personal courtesies to de Behaine, the Christian converts received harsh treatment even during Gia Long's rule. The numbers of Vietnamese Christians dwindled by sixty percent under Gia Long.

Large-scale persecution of converts and missionaries began in the 1820's under Emperor Minh Mang (1820–1841) and was continued by Thieu Tri (1841–1847) and in the early part of Tu Duc's reign (1847–1883). The Chinese experience with foreigners (during the Opium War and its aftermath) and missionaries (the Taiping Rebellion) had done little to reassure the Vietnamese Court. There was a marked increase in hostility towards the Catholics and, in general, to all foreign influences. Such an attitude was enhanced by continued missionary involvement in Court politics. The close association of the missionaries with the semi-independent, rebellious Governor of Cochin-China,

Le Van Duyet. who attempted to prevent Minh Mang's succession to the throne when Gia Long died in 1820, earned them the extreme wrath of the monarch. The revolt posed a serious threat to Minh Mang because advantage was taken of it by Siam sending its troops to Cochin-China. Recent research indicates that the real reasons for the revolt were not so much religious as political. Contrary to his father's policy of devolution of power, Minh Mang had attempted to control Tongking and Cochin-China from Hue. The Cochin-Chinese rebellion was a protest against Minh Mang's ambitions. The Emperor was, however, a forceful personality in religion and war. He pushed the Siamese troops out of Cochin-China and crushed the rebellion in that region with an iron hand.

Minh Mang was an ardent Confucianist, believing in ancestor-worship. Roman Catholics were encouraged by the missionaries to oppose such practices. In 1833, a French missionary, Father Marchand, was suspected of involvement in a rebellion in Cochin-China led by Le Van Khoi.

It was no surprise, therefore, that Minh Mang's reign witnessed a series of proclamations to eliminate Catholic converts and their institutions. Regarding the missionaries, both to be the auxiliaries of his major political adversary and the agents of an alien power, Minh Mang forbade in 1825 any further entry of missionaries. Eight years later, an extremely severe decree ordered churches to be demolished and made profession of the Catholic faith an offense punishable by death. His edict read: "The wicked religion of the Western people casts its malicious spell on the minds of the people; the Catholic missionaries wrong the people's mind, violate the country's good customs and result in a great harm for the nation." Though the order was not literally applied, many Catholics, including priests, were killed. In 1836, almost coinciding with Chinese strictures against foreign shipping, the Vietnamese monarch closed his ports to European shipping.

If the Chinese experience held lessons for Vietnam, the British success in "opening" China emboldened the French, who employed similar tactics in opening up Vietnam by using the excuse of religious persecution. French missionaries had made it a practice to ignore or violate the laws of some of the Asian states, particularly China and Vietnam, inhibiting travel in the interior and carrying on the work of proselytization. As Cady observes: "In the absence of any French Far Eastern commerce to protect, the missionaries constituted the only tangible aspect of national interest with which [French] naval officers could concern themselves."[2] In the 1840's, French merchant ships and navy, whose presence in the South China Sea had increased following the opening of five Chinese ports, intervened to secure the release of some missionaries awaiting death sentences in Vietnamese prisons. Thus, in 1846, French ships blockaded Tourane (Da Nang) for two weeks and then bombarded the port, demanding the release of Mgr. Dominique Lefevre, who had been condemned to death by the Vietnamese government. Figures of Catholic casualties as well as those of French bombardment of Tourane have been grossly exaggerated. Joseph Buttinger writes: "In seventy minutes, French guns had taken a hundred times more lives than all the Vietnamese Governments in two centuries of religious persecution."[3] The United States *Catholic Digest* says: "In the persecutions of the last century, tiny Vietnam had 100,000 martyrs, far above any single nation's quota since the early Roman persecution."[4] Based on this figure, the seventy-minute French bombardment must have taken ten million lives, a feat beyond the capabilities of any lethal weaponry perhaps until the advent of the nuclear age! Such exaggerated accounts ignore the gap between the letter of the imperial edicts prescribing persecution and their actual implementation. It should be noted that during Tu Duc's reign, when the persecutions had been taken to a higher

level through a decree ordering the subjects to seize missionaries. tie rocks around their necks and dump them into
the sea. a Vietnamese Catholic. Nguyen Trung To (1827–
1871), still served as a high court official. He was able to go
with a missionary to Europe. see the Pope, bring home a
hundred Western books and advise Emperor Tu Duc to
institute reforms in Vietnam. He could not have survived if
the imperial edicts were strictly enforced.

Conquest of Cochin-China

In response to reports of persecution of Catholics, the
French government of Napoleon III wanted to use the
opportunity to compensate for his fiasco in Mexico by success in Cochin-China. The new French imperialism of the
time was widely based on a coalition of diverse interests of
the Church, traders and manufacturers in search of new
markets, and was aided by the egotistic Emperor's lust for
colonies to augment national power and prestige. The business interests were not unaware of the exclusive geographic
advantages their position in Vietnam could give them for
seeking access to the lucrative markets of interior China.
The opening of five Chinese ports in 1842 and eleven more
in 1860 gave equal opportunity to almost all foreigners by
virtue of the most-favored-nation clause in the Treaties of
Nanking and Tientsin. French businessmen interested in
overseas markets were supporting the government of
Cochin-China in the hope of establishing a base in Saigon
rivaling Singapore and Hong Kong for funneling South
China trade.[5]

In 1858, a joint Franco-Spanish expedition proceeded to
Vietnam to save the missionaries. In that year, two
priests—one French and one Spanish—had been killed in
Vietnam. The Spanish quit after the Vietnamese government gave assurances of non-persecution, but the French
continued the fighting for three years until they secured a
treaty from Tu Duc in 1862. The provisions of the treaty

revealed the French intentions clearly: The Vietnamese
Emperor ceded three provinces in Cochin-China, including
Saigon, to France and assured that no part of his kingdom
would ever be alienated to any other power except France,
a clause the latter interpreted to mean that Annam had
agreed to be a potential French protectorate. He further
agreed to pay an indemnity of four million *piasters* in ten
annual instalments and open three ports in Annam to
French trade. Christianity would be tolerated in the future.
Significantly, the treaty gave France the right to navigate
the Mekong. Five years later, the French obtained the
remaining provinces of Cochin-China to enable it to establish full control over the Mekong delta.

How does one explain French success in Cochin-China?
Most historians have based their analyses on French
accounts, blaming the Vietnamese debacle on the inadequate and inefficient administration in the Mekong delta. If
this were so, it is difficult to comprehend how the
Annamese Court directed a war lasting three and one half
years against France, an enemy with far more sophisticated
equipment and economic power than Vietnam. In fact,
what made the Vietnamese Emperor capitulate in 1862 was
the need to divert his forces and attention to putting down a
rebellion which had just broken out in North Vietnam
under the leadership of a descendant of the old Le dynasty.
More accurate explanations are provided by Bernard Fall
and Le Thanh Khoi. Fall attributes the French success to
the alienness of the Vietnamese in Cochin-China, which
they had "colonized" only recently. In his view, they were
"the least secure in their social structure and institutions."
Hence, the comparative lack of resistance among the non-
Vietnamese population in the south to the French colonial
penetration, which became more and more difficult as it
advanced further north.[6] Le Thanh Khoi, an eminent Vietnamese historian, holds that the mandarins hid from the
ruler, "isolated from his people by the high walls of the

Forbidden City national realities as well as the gravity of the crisis in foreign relations." In Le's opinion, it was their "blind pride as well as their narrowness of views which bears a large measure of responsibility for the fall of Vietnam."[7]

There is no doubt that along with Burma and Thailand, Vietnam was the most advanced administrative polity in all of Southeast Asia. The Confucian mandarinate recruited through the civil service examination was still capable of governing the country and conducting a war with the French lasting over three years. It continued to govern Central and North Vietnam for another two decades until the French progressively brought the rest of Vietnam under their control. What was basically wrong was the habit of the mandarins, who continued, like their counterparts in China of the nineteenth century, to look for solutions in Confucian classics of the past to the challenges posed by the scientific and technological innovations brought by the West. Under those circumstances, a national debacle at the hands of an aggressive, Western power was only a matter of time.

De Lagree-Garnier Expedition

Undoubtedly, the most important provision of the 1862 treaty was France's right to navigate the Mekong, which was believed to originate in South-West China. That, and not the protection of Christianity, was the real reason for the occupation of Cochin-China. After all, Vietnamese Christians were not located only in Cochin-China. Within four years of the treaty, the privately-endowed Paris Geographical Society sponsored the exploration of the Mekong under the leadership of two naval officers, Francis Garnier and Doudart de Lagree. It is significant to note that the president of the Society was Chasseloup Lambat, head of the Ministry of the Marine, who was very much interested in securing the interests of the traders. The

Society itself was a front for business interests. In 1873, in cooperation with the Paris Chamber of Commerce, a Society for Commercial Geography was established which sponsored and financed future explorations overseas. Francis Garnier, then a young naval officer, was a scion of a royalist family who, like Dupleix before him in India, held grandiose visions of a French empire rivalling that of the British in the East. Garnier's consuming personal ambition was born of a sense of manifest destiny that he was the divine instrument for elevating France's declining prestige in the world. He had been administrator of Cho-lon near Saigon for four years when he volunteered to join De Lagree on the Mekong expedition.

In their exploration of the Mekong, the De Lagree-Garnier expedition, which left Saigon in June 1866, had soon to pass through Cambodia. Unfortunately, Cambodia had been in grave political trouble for quite some time, and its kings had appealed to France for intervention. With the conquest of Cochin-China in 1862, France claimed to have succeeded Vietnam as overlord of Cambodia. In the following years, the French offered to establish a protectorate over Cambodia, a proposal readily accepted by King Norodom, who had succeeded his father, Ang Duong. A Franco-Khmer treaty was drawn up on August 11, 1863.

There was one major legal hurdle before the treaty could be valid. Norodom had not been formally crowned: the royal insignia was in Bangkok and the Thai monarch insisted on the coronation of his vassal king at his own hands. Norodom's efforts to go to Bangkok were blocked by French gunboats. Thereupon Thailand revealed a previous secret treaty between Bangkok and Phnom Penh confirming Thailand's suzerain rights and acknowledging the Cambodian monarch's status as Thai Viceroy of Cambodia. The ensuing Franco-Thai negotiations finally produced a treaty in 1867 whereby Thailand gave up all claims to suzerainty over Cambodia in return for French recognition of

Thai sovereignty over two Western Cambodian provinces of Battambang and Siem Reap.

Garnier's Tongking Adventure

The De Lagree-Garnier expedition had reported on the unsuitability of the Mekong as a commercial artery into South China. The frequent waterfalls and gorges in North-East Cambodia and Laos impeded navigation on the Mekong. De Lagree lost his life in the upper reaches of the Mekong. Garnier managed to proceed to Yunnan and return to Saigon via Hankow. In a two-volume report of his expedition, Garnier recommended the exploration of the Red River route. He had discovered while in Yunnan that the bulk of the South Chinese trade in silk, tea and textiles passed through Tongking rather than Canton. Garnier argued that the exploration of the Red River route would, in addition to commercial benefits, offer France an opportunity to extend its "mission civilisatrice" to the Tongking delta and beyond.[8]

The serious domestic crisis in which France was engulfed following its disastrous defeat by Prussia arrested all plans for exploration in Indochina for some time. By 1873, however, a chorus of mercantile agitators in Paris and Saigon demanded that France strengthen her hold on Indochina and precipitate access to the markets of interior China before the other Europeans in the region did. Three principal actors of the drama to be enacted momentarily in that year in Tongking were: Admiral Marie-Jules Dupre, Governor of Cochin-China, Francis Garnier and a French adventurer-trader, Jean Dupuis.

Dupuis had been in the East since 1858. An extremely able but unscrupulous man, he had established an official arms procurement agency for the Chinese government to enable the latter to suppress the series of revolts in South and South-West China following the Taiping rebellion there. Dupuis's interests soon extended to trafficking in

minerals and salt between Yunnan and Tongking, violating
the monopoly interest of Vietnamese mandarins in those
items. In 1868, Dupuis discussed with Francis Garnier in
Hankow the possibility of opening the Red River route to
facilitate the flow of trade. Both of them were eager to
"take Tonkin for a French granary and obtain an opportunity to exploit the mines of Southern China."[9] Four years
later, Dupuis was in Paris where he enlisted the support of
the Ministry of the Marine which agreed to have "a naval
vessel to rendezous with him off the Tonkin coast and provide him with information and at least moral support in his
negotiations with the Vietnamese."[10] While in Paris,
Dupuis also met the Governor of Cochin-China, Admiral
Dupre, and apprised him of future plans.

In the decade before Dupuis's incursions in the Tongking
delta, the Vietnamese Emperor's hold over his northern
possessions was at best tenuous. It had taken five years to
suppress the anti-Nguyen revolt of 1862 in the Tongking
delta, but a series of new disturbances had broken out in
the almost inaccessible, mountainous terrain on either side
of the Sino-Vietnamese border. Hordes of fugitive Chinese
bandits and rebels who had participated in the Muslim rebellions of South China for over a decade moved across the
border preying on the produce and property of Vietnam's
Montagnard population. Two of the large, best-organized
bandit armies were the notorious Black Flags and Yellow
Flags, who soon vied with each other for control of the
trade and customs revenue collection of the upper Red
River valley. Such a local context of "rebellion, banditry
and social disorder"[11] was further muddied by the activities
of Jean Dupuis, who was determined to open the Red River
route to Yunnan to facilitate his illicit trade in salt, minerals
and gun-running. In addition to some covert support from
French officials, Dupuis had a well-trained and well-armed
force of 150 men, loaned to him by the Chinese Com-
mander-in-Chief of Yunnan.

Dupuis's force clashed with local Vietnamese elements in Hanoi in May. The mandarins there who were apprehensive of Dupuis's trading activities because they cut into their monopolies refused to allow the Frenchman to proceed upstream on his second attempt with a cargo of salt and arms to China. Dupuis's response was to occupy a section of Hanoi with the help of his Chinese troops and to appeal to Governor Dupre for mediation with Vietnamese authorities. Ironically enough, unaware of the secret ties between Dupuis and Dupre, the Vietnamese Emperor, Tu Duc, also appealed to Dupre to order the French intruder out of Hanoi. This was, indeed, a heaven-sent opportunity for Dupre, who wanted an excuse to fish in Tongking's troubled waters. He decided to send a "mediation force" of two gunboats, two corvettes and a hundred men, including sixty marines, under Francis Garnier, ostensibly to evict Dupuis from Hanoi. Meanwhile, Garnier had resigned from the Navy and, after receiving adequate funds from merchants in France for exploration of new trade routes, had returned to China.[12] He was in Shanghai when Dupre sent for him and entrusted him with the Tongking mission. Ever since he had become Governor of Cochin-China in 1871, Dupre had harbored an ambition to open Tongking to French influence in order not only to be able to reach South China before the British did but also to help Cochin-China's economy, which had been in the red for a long time. He was so keen on achieving these objectives that he even disregarded a dispatch from the new Minister of the Marine and Defense in Paris advising patience toward the Tu Duc government and specifically requesting him to abstain from any military involvement. In the absence of a flat veto from the Minister, Dupre and Garnier decided to go ahead with plans of occupation to Tongking and present Paris with a *fait accompli*.[13]

Once in Hanoi at the head of a picked group of forty men, Garnier threw to the winds the assurances given to

Emperor Tu Duc to evict Dupuis from Tongking. Instead, he joined hands with Dupuis, picked a quarrel with the local mandarins over the quarters provided for his men and initiated other measures which were bound to infuriate the mandarins. On November 16, he unilaterally declared the Red River open to international trade and revised the customs tariffs to make them more advantageous to foreigners. His justification for the action was that it had to be done "in order to safeguard the interests of civilization and France!" Five days later, in a brash and bold action, Garnier stormed the citadel of Hanoi and proceeded to do likewise in all important towns of the Red River valley. Within three weeks, lower Tongking, including Haiphong and Ninh Binh, was under French military control, while Dupuis seemed well entrenched in Hanoi. But the spectacular success was too easy to last long. The mandarins, whose pride, position and profit were hurt by Garnier's actions, used another group to get rid of him. Garnier had already declared himself opposed to Black Flags then roaming and raiding the Tongking countryside. The mandarins instigated them to attack Garnier. On December 21, during a hot chase of the Black Flags, Garnier lost his life.

There is no knowing whether the entire episode stemmed out of the rash initiative of the men-on-the-spot, Garnier and Dupre, acting according to their own whims or whether it was a carefully planned covert maneuver of the French government, which could always denounce the action in the event of failure. The news of Garnier's death shocked Saigon and Paris. France officially disclaimed his actions, ordered Dupuis to leave Tongking and drew up a treaty essentially conciliatory towards Tu Duc. Even so, Garnier's objectives had at least partly been accomplished. The Red River was declared open to foreign commerce, three ports of Tongking were also opened and a French consul and garrison were allowed to be stationed in each of them. The loss of Garnier's life, however, gave a serious setback to further French expansion for at least a decade.

France Completes Conquest of Vietnam

Despite the Garnier episode, France's preoccupation with the critical domestic strife, certain groups continued to press for expansion in Southeast Asia. Those enthusiastic about increasing overseas markets and desirous of a predominant role in the international competition for colonies demanded immediate French initiative in Asia and Africa. Members of the emerging geographical societies were often the most ardent supporters of such an initiative, arguing that colonization projects would afford desirable outlets for surplus population and capital and help the reestablishment of French prestige and power. Such geographical organizations, including the influential Geographical Society of France, were critical of the lack of support for Garnier and Dupre's intervention in Tongking. They insisted that the area would not only be a commercial asset but one where the French could pass on the benefits of their superior culture to the "barbaric" inhabitants.

By 1881, the advocates for imperialism found a most vocal and powerful exponent in the new Premier, Jules Ferry, who was prepared to take risks of pursuing an active and aggressive policy in the Far East. A one-time self-styled economic liberal and free trader, Ferry had changed his views on the value of colonies at the behest of colonial traders and investors interested in opening profitable markets. "There needs to be no hesitation," he wrote, "in affirming that colonies in the present state of the world is the best affair of business in which the capital of an old and wealthy country can engage."[4] He emphasized the importance of colonies to French commerce which was then suffering due to the prevailing depression. He justified his own efforts for the conquest of Tongking delta with yet another reason:

> It is not a question of tomorrow but of the future of fifty or hundred years, of what will be the inheritance of our children, the bread of our workers. It is not a question of conquering

China, but it is necessary to be at the portal of this region to undertake the pacific conquest of it.[15]

The Treaty of 1873 provided France the excuse for the next move. The French alleged that the Vietnamese court had contravened the protectorate clause implicit in that treaty by continuing to send the traditional, quinquennial tribute to China. Besides, the Vietnamese mandarins had severely obstructed a French expedition of 400 men led by Henri Riviere to clear the Red River valley of the piratical Black Flags. In 1883 and 1884, under immense pressure, the Vietnamese Emperor signed further treaties agreeing to become a French protectorate, to surrender administrative responsibility for the Tongking province to France and to accept a French Resident at Hanoi and Hue. At the same time, in utter helplessness, the Emperor appealed to his overlord, the Emperor of China, for assistance in resisting further French encroachments on Vietnamese territory.

As the French approached the Chinese borders, frequent clashes took place between the Chinese and French troops. On March 28, 1885, French forces were badly beaten at the border post of Langson. The incident immediately led to the fall of the Ferry ministry. France, however, retaliated by attacking Keelung in Formosa, occupying the Pescadores Islands, blockading the port of Foochow and destroying the Chinese navy there. Ultimately, the poorly-equipped Chinese forces could not hold ground before the sophisticated French weaponry. The Middle Kingdom signed a treaty at Tientsin on June 9, 1885 recognizing the French Protectorate over Annam and Tongking, permitting French traders in South China, conceding preference to France over all other European powers in Yunnan and granting France the right to construct a railway paralleling the Red River valley from Hanoi to Kunming. The treaty marked the extinction of the nearly two-millennia-old relationship between Vietnam and China and completed the French conquest of Vietnam.

NOTES

1. Charles Maybon, *Histoire Moderne du Pays d'Annam, 1592-1820*, Paris, Typographie Plon-Nourrit, 1919.
2. John F. Cady, *The Roots of French Imperialism in Eastern Asia*, Ithaca, Cornell University Press, 1954, p. 29.
3. Joseph Buttinger, *The Smaller Dragon: A Political History of Vietnam*, New York, Praeger, 1958, p. 133.
4. *Catholic Digest*, February 1962, p. 17.
5. Henri Blet, *France d'Outre-Mer*, Paris, Arthaud, 1950, II, p. 281.
6. Bernard Fall, *The Two Viet-Nams*, New York, Praeger, 1967, p. 16.
7. Le Thanh Khoi, *Viet-Nam*, Paris, Les Editions de Minuit, 1955, p. 365.
8. Francis Garnier, *Voyage d'Exploration en Indo-Chine*, Paris, Librairie Hachette, 1885, 2 vols.
9. H.I. Priestly, *France Overseas, A Study of Modern Imperialism*, New York, Appleton-Century, 1938, p. 217.
10. Ella S. Laffey, "French Adventurers and Chinese Bandits in Tonkin: The Garnier Affair in its Local Context," *Journal of Southeast Asian Studies*, VI (March 1975), p. 41.
11. *Ibid.*, p. 39.
12. Georges Taboulet, *La Geste Francaise en Indochine*, Paris, Adrienne-Maisonneuve, 1956, p. 709.
13. M. Dutreb, *L'Admiral Dupre et la Conquete du Tonkin*, Paris, E. Leroux, 1924, pp. 94-96.
14. Lois E. Bailey, *Jules Ferry and French Indo-China*, Madison, University of Wisconsin Press, 1946. p. 24.
15. Thomas F. Powers, Jr., *Jules Ferry and the Renaissance of French Imperialism*, New York, Octagon Books, p. 191.

4

Dong Minh Hoi—
The Nationalist Movement

The Vietnamese are *par excellence* a freedom-loving, nationalistic people who have had to fight numerous times in their long history to obtain and maintain their freedom. As David Marr observes:

> The continuity in Vietnamese anti-colonialism is a highly-charged, historically self-conscious resistance to oppressive, degrading foreign rule. Possessors of a proud cultural and political heritage, many Vietnamese simply refused to be cowed.

Vietnamese nationalism was nurtured in the cradle of their history of resistance to Chinese domination. The direct Chinese rule from 111 B.C. to 939 A.D. and again from 1407 to 1428 A.D. was punctuated with numerous uprisings and in the final ouster of the northern invaders. As late as the end of the 18th century, the Chinese Emperor, Ch'ien-lung lamented:

> The Vietnamese are, indeed, not a reliable people. An occupation does not last very long before they raise arms against us and expel us from their country. The history of past dynasties has proved this fact.[2]

Despite a policy of Sinicization of Vietnam, whether enforced by the Chinese rulers or voluntarily adopted by the Vietnamese Emperors, the Chinese culture had failed to obliterate the Vietnamese social traditions particularly in the countryside where the bulk of the people lived. Sinicization affected mainly the upper classes while the villagers were left to themselves. Thus, the peasants clung to the Vietnamese habits of chewing betel-nut, worshipping hosts of village genii and spirits of their ancestors, mountains and rivers. They rejoiced in the ceremonies and festivals that predated the advent of Chinese culture. In that sense, the Chinese domination had never posed much of a threat to the traditional modes of Vietnamese social behavior as the French administration did particularly toward the end of the nineteenth century.

The French administration in Vietnam destroyed the peasants' traditional civilization, which had persisted with nominal external interference for two thousand years. Each Vietnamese village was a bamboo-fenced, practically autonomous social entity, governed by a council of village notables, who collected taxes on behalf of the central government, determined the agrarian chores and distributed the rice product among the peasants. They also dispensed justice. The Imperial government interfered only for purposes of census or recruitment of soldiers in times of war. As the folk-saying had it, "The laws of the emperor are less significant than the customs of the villages." The French broke the village autonomy, instituted regular registration of births and deaths resulting in more accurate tax polls and more efficient tax collection than before and a generally tighter control over fiscal matters. Later, they substituted elections for cooperation of council members. The elections progressively returned Western-educated individuals who lacked the traditional following or influence among the peasants. The traditional notables joined the ranks of the opposition.

Early Resistance Against French Rule

Opposition to French rule began almost as soon as it was

introduced in Cochin-China in 1862. It v/as led by all types
of people, including peasants and fishermen, who were not
prepared to abandon their time-honored culture for that of
people separated from them "by thousands of mountains
and seas." The resistance movement grew to revolutionary
proportions after the French conquest of Annam in 1885.
The so-called "pacification" program, like its British
counterpart in Burma, was most intense until 1895 but
extended in Vietnam to 1913. In a particularly vicious
campaign from 1909 to 1913, the French hounded the resistance leaders including De Tham, "the tiger of Yen Tre"
and murdered them one by one. The peasantry harbored
and supported the leaders of the resistance movement,
which included the scholar-gentry or the Vietnamese
mandarin class. In the decades before 1900, the mandarins
appeared to believe that the French occupation of their
lands might spell loss of political control but not a cultural
or spiritual loss. By 1900, however, a new generation of
maturing mandarins grew apprehensive that the educational and cultural impact of French culture had become
pervasive. They were "haunted" by the image of *mat nuoc*,
of "losing one's country" not merely in political terms but
more seriously in the sense of their future survival as Vietnamese. They were mortally wounded by the attitude of
collaborator mandarins and of the royal family who had
fallen prey to French temptations and imitated their ways.
Mandarins thus fell into three groups: those who had col-
laborated with the colonial masters, those who withdrew to
the villages in a sort of passive non-cooperation and those
that struggled desperately through participation in the
resistance movement to bring new meaning and ethnic salvation, *cuu quoc*, to their countrymen.[3]

Two major events in Asia changed the direction of the
Vietnamese opposition to French rule from their urge to
restore monarchy and *status quo ante* to a demand for popular democracy whether through a constitutional monarchy
or republicanism. One was Japan's spectacular rise as an

industrially and militarily strong nation. The other was the Boxer Uprising in 1899 against Western presence and domination of China followed by China's reform movement and overthrow of the decadent Ch'ing monarchy. The reform movement in China was led by K'ang Yu-wei and Liang Ch'i-ch'ao. The latter's writings inspired the Vietnamese and led them to read and absorb Chinese translations of great Western political philosophers notably Locke, Rousseau and Montesquieu. Numerous Vietnamese intellectuals were also influenced by Sun Yat-sen and his revolutionary leadership in overthrowing an autocratic, decadent monarchy in China and introducing a republican government with individual rights to freedom.

Phan Boi Chau and Phan Chau Trinh

Two Vietnamese anti-colonialist leaders, Phan Boi Chau (1867–1940) and Phan Chau Trinh (1871–1926) were directly influenced by these happenings in East Asia. Born into a mandarin, scholar-gentry family, Phan Boi Chau, passed the regional examination in 1900 and had by 1902 acquainted himself with Liang Ch'i-ch'ao's writings. In that year, he published a book, *Ryukyu's Bitter Tears*, superficially dealing with the loss of sovereignty of the Ryukyu Islands to the Japanese but, in reality, alluding to the Vietnamese loss of freedom at the hands of the French. Two years later, Phan Boi Chau and a number of his pupils and associates launched the *Duy Tan Hoi* (Reformation Society). This organization, standing for revolutionary monarchism, secured the support of Prince Cuong De and decided to obtain outside assistance to achieve their nationalistic ends. The monarchy they supported would not be an old Chinese or Vietnamese model but rather on that of Japan, whose emperor had allowed the development of a constitutional government in response to the challenges of the West. In 1905, Phan Boi Chau secretly went to Japan where he met Liang Ch'i-ch'ao, and through him Sun Yat-

sen and other Chinese revolutionaries from whom he learnt
the techniques of starting a revolution. Phan Boi Chau was
introduced by Liang also to the Japanese leaders, who
promised liberal scholarships to Vietnamese students but
no millitary assistance to overthrow the French rule.
Shortly thereafter, Phan published the *History of the Loss
of Vietnam*, which quickly went into five editions in China
and which clandestinely circulated all over Vietnam. The
book had tremendous impact both among the scholars and
the common people in Vietnam because of its non-tradi-
tional style and translation into *quoc ngu*, Romanized
Vietnamese. Soon, there were scores of Vietnamese
students enrolled in Japanese institutions including the
military academy.

Meanwhile, Phan Boi Chau had made Canton his base
for revolutionary activity in Vietnam, establishing for the
purpose *Vietnam Quang Phuc Hoi* (Association for the
Restoration of Vietnam). In 1914, a resolution to organize
a "Restoration Army" was passed. Phan Boi Chau was
thereupon put behind bars by the Governor-General of
Canton at the instigation of the French colonial government. In 1917, the " Restoration Army" attempted an uprising on the Vietnam border but failed miserably. Later in
the same year, Sun Yat-sen's exertions resulted into setting
Phan Boi Chau free.

Phan Boi Chau spent the next few years in Canton and
Shanghai. He was responsible for getting forty Vietnamese
admitted to the Whampoa Military Academy where
Chinese Nationalists and Communists worked together.
Despite the Nationalist-Communist honeymoon phase
(1924-1927) of politics, Phan Boi Chau got into trouble
with the Communists. In 1925, he was seized in Shanghai at
the instance of Ho Chi Minh and "sold" to the French
concession there for 100,000 piasters.[4] Phan Boi Chau was
brought to Hanoi, sentenced to death though later, because
of widespread public protests and the somewhat liberal
policy of the new Socialist Governor-General, Alexandre

Varenne, the sentence was commuted to life.The great patriot languished and died in 1940.

For Phan Chau Trinh, however, monarchy as an institution had become outdated. He was a firm believer in democracy and an advocate of a Western-style republican constitution. He led a tax-resistance movement in 1908, was arrested and later deported to French prisons until 1925. A few months after his release, he managed to reach Saigon, where he perceived that politics had changed so much during his long absence that he could not take part in the nationalist movement even if he wanted to. His death on March 24, 1926, however, unwittingly fueled the nationalist movement. Nguyen An Ninh, a reformer and editor of *La Cloche Felee*, wrote a eulogistic obituary for which he was arrested and his paper censored. The arrest provoked strikes among students, bank and postal employees. Several hundred students were expelled from colleges and universities for defying the ban on wearing bands mourning the passing away of a great patriot.

Beginnings of Modern Nationalist Movement

In the second decade of the present century, the purpose and leadership of the nationalist movement underwent gradual changes. The effects of French education began to show . Many young individuals from well-to-do families with benefit of higher education in Vietnam and France became nationalist leaders. A large group of Vietnamese youth crossed over to China after the Chinese Revolution of 1911. In 1913, they established the Association for the Restoration of Vietnam and instigated a number of small uprisings in Tongking and Cochin-China. They had a short-lived success despite the assistance of the Emperor, Duy Tan (1907–1916). In 1916, a somewhat serious uprising was severely suppressed by the French authorities sending Duy Tan and his father, the former Emperor, Than Thai, into exile. That, in a sense, marked an end to the old, conservative, restorative, monarchical phase of the nationalist movement. After the exile of Duy Tan, no Vietnamese nationalist seriously presented restoration of the Nguyen monarchy as an alternative to French rule. After 1916, the alternatives were clearly populist, republican or revolutionary. The immediate inspiration was provided by the Chinese Republic established after the overthrow of the Ching dynasty in 1911.

Such a change favoring a wider, popular base for the nationalist movement was also helped by the events of World War I. Many of the more than 100,000 Vietnamese soldiers and workers who saw wartime service in France returned home full of new aspirations for freedom which were, in French view, subversive ideas. Some of them joined the nationalists in making modest demands for participation in the councils and for greater accommodation in civil service positions. Such were the moderates in politics who were further inspired by pronouncements of Western leaders, including President Wilson of the United States, whose Fourteen Points included the right of self-determination of nations. Even a would-be radical revolutionary like Ho Chi Minh was apparently so impressed by the promise of self-determination of nations that he attempted to seek a meeting with the Western leaders gathered at the Versailles Conference. In the aftermath of the war, frustrated nationalists like Ho Chi Minh and many others, who were fascinated with the success of the Russian Revolution, turned to Marxism as a means of liberating their motherland from colonial rule.

Many Communist and non-Communist youths received their initial, intellectual, organizational and revolutionary training across the frontier in China. While a good number of non-Communist leaders had been educated in French schools in Vietnam and France, almost all the Communist leaders (with the major exception of Ho Chi Minh) were trained in China. The exploits of the Kuomintang (KMT) as well as of Communist leaders in China inspired the Vietnamese nationalists. A distant but nevertheless potent source of inspiration was India, where a virulent and popular mass movement had been launched by Mahatma Gandhi challenging the continuation of British rule on the sub-continent. A Vietnamese nationalist, Duong Van Gieu, met Jawaharlal Nehru at the Brussels meeting of the League Against Imperialism and for National Independence in 1927 and attended the meeting of the Indian National Congress the following year.

The twenties proved to be a decade of tremendous political, intellectual and ideological ferment over most of Southeast Asia. In Vietnam, a new class of educated young people had come up replacing the old mandarin class. The French themselves sought to create a new type of Vietnamese, yellow gentlemen, who would accept French beliefs, standards of deportment and values. The colonial educational system mirrored metropolitan models for reasons both of pride and pragmatism. The needs of colonial administration as well as those of the new economy, particularly of the French enterprises, required large numbers of French-speaking indigenous subordinate staff. The Vietnamese did not, however, limit themselves to such a rudimentary level of education. Being one of the most intelligent people in the world, the newly-educated Vietnamese mastered the French writings included in the political and economic fields.

The new Vietnamese elite consisted of government employees, professionals, France-returned college and university students, educated landowners and businessmen. They were articulate enough to inspire the support of non-commissioned army officers and skilled workers. Vietnamese intellectuals quickly and clearly saw the contradiction in the French profession of the hallowed principles of equality, liberty and fraternity and their practice of denial of fundamental freedoms in an atmosphere of official repression. They would soon demand important positions in high administration as well as legislation equating the

Vietnamese status with that of French settlers. Above all, they demanded freedoms of speech, association and press.

The educated Vietnamese, particularly those educated in France, perceived the difference between the freedom in metropolitan France, where even the colonials could enjoy the democratic freedoms and Vietnam, where they were denied such rights. They also noted that the colonial civil service, which was much inferior to that in France, was marked by unequal pay and unequal standards of eligibility for the Vietnamese, who were discriminated against irrespective of their competence. Vietnamese businessmen rankled against the government regulations that favored the French-owned enterprises vis-a-vis indigenous ones. The lack of representative institutions inhibited the efforts of the intelligentsia and business class to voice their grievances or make suggestions for improvement. The new elite produced a leadership which would articulate the problems of the semi-literates and skilled workers and organize the economically dissatisfied peasantry, and, in so doing, promote nationalism among the masses.

The VNQDD

The most prominent of the non-Marxist organizations of the twenties was the VNQDD (Viet Nam Quoc Dan Dang-Vietnamese Nationalist Party) founded in Hanoi in 1927. Organizationally modeled on the Chinese Kuomintang (KMT), it adopted Sun Yat-sen's principles of Nationalism, Democracy and People's Livelihood and committed itself to overthrow the French colonial rule with the KMT's help. A preparatory conference of the VNQDD had invited Phan Boi Chau to lead the new party. His arrest and absence put Nguyen Thai Hoc, a twenty-three year old teacher and revolutionary, at the head of the party.

The VNQDD was dominated by its leftist wing using terrorism as a political weapon. A number of such "terrorists" infiltrated the Vietnamese units in the army, inspiring and provoking them to rise against their French commanders. Contemporaneous with the VNQDD was the growth of a number of Marxist groups — Communists and Trotskyites. They would be brought together in 1930 by the most dynamic of their leaders, Ho Chi Minh, who was still abroad. Even so, in 1930, the VNQDD held far greater appeal among the masses than the Communists.

The Uprisings of 1930-1931

In 1930, the VNQDD decided that it was time for a nationwide revolt. The timing of the revolt was perhaps forced by the Communists. On February 9, 1929, Rene Bazin, director of employee recruitment for rubber plantations, was killed by a Vietnamese youth, possibly at Communist instigation. The French authorities suspected the VNQDD's hand and reacted quickly by imprisoning several VNQDD supporters and ordering a thorough, secret investigation of the VNQDD's underground activities. Afraid of French retaliatory action that could destroy the VNQDD, its leader Nguyen Thai Hoc, ordered preparations for nationwide insurrection on February 10, 1930. When, at the last minute, the date was changed to February 15, chaos broke out. The military garrison at Yen Bay were not aware of the change in date and consequently led their own uprising on February 10 by killing their French officers. The VNQDD expected the Yen Bay uprising to spark a general revolution. There were sporadic peasant uprisings in some provinces, but hardly a nationwide movement. Besides, unfortunately for the nationalists, the French police had been alerted. They easily suppressed the disturbances and conclusively destroyed the effectiveness of the VNQDD, many of whose members fled northward to China. Many others were arrested and executed. The VNQDD underwent gradual attrition in Yunnan where for some time, it faced competition from another non-Marxist Vietnamese organization, namely, Phan Boi Chau's Association for the Restoration of Vietnam. At the end of World War II, a remnant of the VNQDD would be brought by Chiang Kai-shek's troops to Vietnam to fish in the troubled waters of Vietnamese politics. The French destruction of the VNQDD accounted for the lack of strong and effective non-Communist leadership among the Vietnamese nationalist ranks in the post-1930 period, opening immediate opportunity for the Communists and virtually guaranteeing their ultimate control of the movement. The leader of the Vietnamese Communist movement was Ho Chi Minh.

Ho Chi Minh

Ho Chi Minh was born in 1890 in Kim-Lien village in Nghe-An province in a modest mandarin family. His original name was Nguyen Sinh Cung, which he changed several times both out of fancy as well as to conceal his real identity.[5] Such aliases included Nguyen Tan Tranh (Nguyen Who Will Succeed), Nguyen Ai Quoc and Ho Chi Minh (He Who Is Enlightened). His father, Nguyen Sinh Huy, was a scholar and a revolutionary who had passed the civil service examination and held a mandarin's title of Pho Bang. His schooling was very sporadic though records indicate his enrollment at Quoc Hoc (National Studies) College in Hue.

Ho Chi Minh left Vietnam as a cabin boy on a merchant vessel, *Admiral LaTouche Treville* in 1913. After many odd jobs in England and France as a kitchen aide, photographic retoucher, painter of French-made "Chinese antiquities," Ho established his reputation as a good pamphleteer in leftist circles in Paris. He utilized his stay in London (1913–1917), most of it at the Carleton Hotel as a helper to the famous French chef, Escoffier, studying English but also learning his activist ropes as a member of the Overseas Workers' Union, a secret anti-colonial body, mostly under Chinese leadership.

Ho Chi Minh.

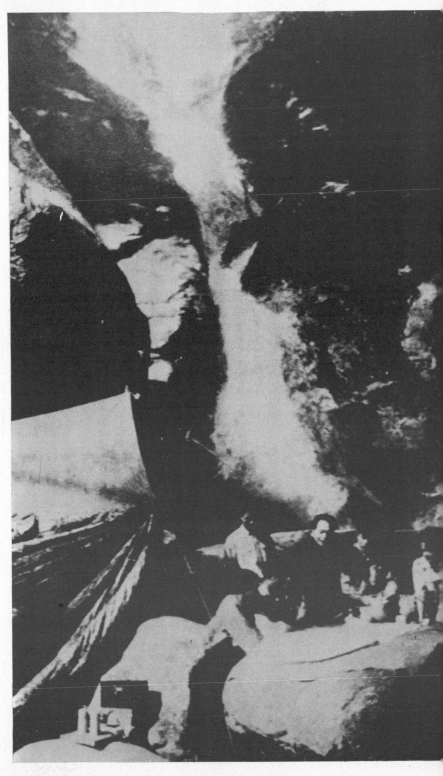

General Giap, the hero of Dien Bien Phu, at his Command Post.

National Liberation Army on the march.

Vietnam army's bicycle transport!

Vietnam People's Army militia girls.

Women workers' political education at Viet-Tri electrochemical complex.

"Before, our life was good. There was peace. We had to work very hard, but we were not afraid of anything."

Rural Vietnam: ricefields, buffaloes ..

Buddhist monks in procession.

Nguyen Trai (1380-1442).

In 1919, Ho Chi Minh appeared outside the Versailles Peace Conference intending to present to the statesmen assembled there his eight-point program potentially leading to the right of self-determination for his country. His demands were: a general amnesty for Vietnamese political prisoners; equal rights to French and Vietnamese, abolition of the criminal court misused as an instrument for persecution of Vietnamese patriots; freedom of the press and of thought; freedom of association and of assembly; freedom of movement and of travel abroad; freedom to go to school and to open technical and vocational schools for the Vietnamese; substitution of the system of law for that of decrees; and appointment of a Vietnamese representative in Paris to settle questions concerning Vietnamese people's interests.[6]

The realization that the doctrine of self-determination propounded by President Wilson was to be applied only to East European nations created by the break-up of the Austro-Hungarian Empire and not to non-European countries brought disillusionment to Ho Chi Minh. It led him directly to the Marxist fold. As Ho himself has averred, until then, he did not understand "neither what was a party, a trade union, nor what was Socialism nor Communism." Thereafter, he became very active in the French Socialist Party, attending its Congress in 1920 and voting with the majority for the Third International and for Communism. It was after reading Lenin's "Theses on the National and Colonial Questions" that Ho felt drawn to Communism. To quote Ho: "At first, patriotism, not yet Communism, led me to have confidence in Lenin and in the Third International."[7] One can reasonably assume that it was the French intrasigence that pushed many Vietnamese frustrated nationalists into the Communist fold and that most of them like Ho Chi Minh remained nationalist first and Communist second.

In 1923, Ho Chi Minh was sent by the French Communist Party to Russia for further training. There, he was enrolled in the newly-opened University for the Toilers of the East. Ho also represented the French Communist Party at the Peasants' International or Krestintern meeting in October 1923. He was elected a member of the Executive Committee of the Peasants International for the next 18 months. In June-July 1924, Ho attended the Fifth Congress of the Communist International as a delegate. It was his performance there that caught the attention of the Soviet hierarchy and, later in the year, he was sent to Canton ostensibly as a translator to assist Mikhael Borodin, adviser to the KMT, but really to organize the Communist movement in Vietnam.

A year later, Ho Chi Minh formed the Association of Vietnamese Revolutionary Youth or the Thanh Nien, in Canton, which had attracted numerous fugitive revolutionaries from Vietnam. Many of them already belonged to other existing nationalist associations or groups but Ho managed to wean away some of the younger activists to his organization. Many members of the Hanoi Students' Movement joined the Thanh Nien. For six months, Ho trained his followers teaching them Marxist revolutionary techniques. The movement was progressing slowly, the major problem being paucity of funds. In order to further finance the movement, some Thanh Nien members resorted to robberies and violence to secure the necessary capital. At this point, Ho Chi Minh himself betrayed his early youth idol, the great nationalist, Phan Boi Chau, to the French for a reward of 100,000 piasters, a sum he used for developing the Thanh Nien organization. Many years later, Ho's action was explained away by his associates on grounds that Phan Boi Chau was a spent force, that he was too old to lead the movement, that his arrest could only help the nationalist movement better through the wave of protest and hostility against the French that his arrest would surely arouse in Vietnam. All these were, indeed, unacceptable rationalizations of a dastardly and unpardonable act on Ho Chi Minh's part. Cooperation between the Nationalist groups and the

Thanh Nien ceased thereafter.

Over the period of the next two years, Ho Chi Minh trained about 250 men in Marxist techniques, got some of them enrolled in Whampoa Military Academy and sent some others to the Soviet Union for studies in Marxism. Most of these young men later comprised the leadership of the Indochina Communist Party and of the Democratic Republic of Vietnam. One of the trainees he sent to Whampoa was Pham Van Dong, who had been expelled by the French from Vietnam and who was later to rise to be Ho's right-hand man and Prime Minister of Vietnam. In 1927, due to conflicts between the Chinese KMT and the Russians, many Comintern members in China were obliged to leave for Moscow, among them Ho Chi Minh. Because of these developments the Communist movement among the Vietnamese was driven off the course charted for them by the Comintern.

Two years later, the Comintern sent Ho Chi Minh to Bangkok where the Comintern South Seas Bureau had been established. Ho worked there among the Vietnamese immigrants for a while trying to win converts to Communism. By that time, the Thanh Nien and the small number of Communists in Vietnam itself were badly divided into several groups. In 1930, Ho fused the three prominent Vietnamese Communist factions in Hong Kong into a single Vietnamese Communist Party. The name was quickly and significantly changed to the Indochina Communist Party (ICP), although there were hardly any Communists then in Laos and Cambodia. Since he was so successful, Ho was appointed Head of the Far Eastern Bureau of the Comintern. By 1931, the ICP claimed 1,500 members besides 100,000 peasants affiliated in peasant organizations.

Undeterred by the VNQDD failure and, in fact, to offset the VNQDD's relative popularity among the masses, the ICP decided to exploit the prevalent peasant unrest brought on by successive crop failures and the economic depression.

Strikes in plantations and factories were organized beginning May Day, 1930 and "Soviets" were established in the
provinces of Nghe An and Ha Tinh. Ho Chi Minh did not
favor an immediate major uprising, which was advocated by
the majority of the hot-heads in his party. He relented. The
ICP met the same fate as the VNQDD at the hands of the
French police. Hundreds were killed, many more arrested.
Ho fled to Hong Kong where he was arrested by the British
police on June 30 of the following year. He was later admitted to a Hong Kong hospital for tuberculosis. In 1933, Ho
suddenly disappeared from there and for the next eight
years remained practically incommunicado. Except perhaps
for a few senior members of the Comintern, no one knew
Ho's whereabouts in those days. During Ho's absence, the
French Communist Party acted as the intermediary between Moscow and the Vietnamese Communists.

The two uprisings — the VNQDD's and the ICP's — had
a tremendous impact on the Vietnamese masses, whose
resentment against the French rule multiplied manifold.
According to Vietnamese nationalists, more than 10,000 of
their countrymen had been executed, tortured to death or
killed with bombs or bayonets, grenades or guns during the
two violent uprisings. The bombing of unarmed marchers at
Vinh taking several hundred lives was most unpardonable
as also the several hundred guillotined without a trial. Some
French Legionnaires were known to round up suspected
villagers and shoot nine out of ten before interrogating the
sole survivor. Prisoners were brutalized in the worst imagi-
nable manner, cutting off parts of their body and leaving
them with their festering sores. Many of the Communist
detenus were interned in the crowded dungeon cells on the
Puolo Condore island off the coast of South Vietnam.
where their ideological beliefs and the zest for independence hardened further as a reaction to the brutal treatment
there.

The two uprisings also affected public opinion in France
leading some liberal colonialists to advocate reforms in

Indochina. In September 1932, Prince Bao Dai was brought back at the age of eighteen from France to head a reformed monarchy with a moderate nationalist, Pham Quynh, as his Chief of Cabinet. That was an opportunity for nationalists like Ngo Dinh Diem, Bao Dai's new Minister of the Interior and Chief of the Reform Commissions to push the reformist movement ahead. Diem came from an illustrious Catholic family with excellent connections. He was given to understand by the Governor-General Pierre Pasquier that the newly-constituted Emperor's Council would have genuine authority to carry out reforms. In a few months, he was to realize that the French colonials, not for the first nor for the last time, could not be trusted. The disillusioned Diem left Bao Dai's Cabinet and went into virtual political retirement while the frustrated young Emperor sought solace in the life of a playboy monarch spending more time on the beaches of Southern France and in vice haunts than in Vietnam, something for which Diem never forgave him.

The VNQDD apparatus had been crushed by the French repression but the ICP was soon able to reassemble its party machinery thanks to its superior organization and party discipline. Its greater fortune lay also in the politics of the period of *detente* (1936–1939) in France when the Popular Front recognized the Communist Party of Indochina and in the early months of 1936, released all political prisoners including Communists. While the other Vietnamese parties remained without a coherent program or organization, the ICP took advantage of the political situation to organize a broad Democratic National Front under the leadership of Pham Van Dong and Vo Nguyen Giap aimed at uniting all social classes and political groups, indeed, with the exception of their staunch enemies, the Trotskyites. With the outbreak of war, the Popular Front Government fell in France, the honeymoon with Communists ended and the ICP was banned. Most of its cadres went underground while some fled to China.

Birth of the Viet Minh

In August 1940, following the lead of the collaborationist
Vichy Government in France, the Governor-General of
Indochina signed a general accord with Japan, which allowed the French administration to continue in Indochina
in return for placing the military facilities and economic
resources like rice, coal, rubber and other raw materials at
Japan's disposal. Toward the end of 1941, the Japanese
used Indochina for consolidating their land and sea forces
to launch massive attacks against Malaya, Hong Kong, the
Philippines and Indonesia. Just before the war ended, the
Japanese interned the French in March 1945. The subservience of the French and their humiliation at the hands of an
Asian nation completely obliterated the image of European
colonial invincibility. Never again were the Vietnamese to
regard the French with awe. When the French returned in
September 1945 at the behest of the Allies, many Frenchmen, particularly those who had spent a lifetime in
Vietnam, were shocked at the new attitude of insouciance,
self-confidence and challenge among their Vietnamese
subjects.

During the war, the Soviet Union and Nationalist China
joined the Anglo-American forces in a common struggle
against the Japanese, a situation making for strange political bedfellows. Ho Chi Minh was released from a Chinese
prison at Chiang Kai-shek's orders to enable him to lead a
resistance movement in Vietnam against the Japanese-
dominated Vichy Government and military and other supplies were made available to him among others by the Office of Strategic Services of the United States Government.
The French power had suffered a mortal blow, however, in
the eyes of the Vietnamese, who saw the defeat of the white
man at the hands of the yellow Japanese and realized that
the former were no more invincible.

Meanwhile, the ICP's Central Committee met in Southern China in May 1941 and decided to subordinate its plans

for agrarian reform and class revolution to the immediate goal of independence and freedom for all Vietnamese. A new organization, the Viet Minh or the *Viet Nam Doc Lap Dong Minh Hoi*, the Vietnam Independence League, was launched to "unite all patriots without distinction of wealth, age, sex, religion or political outlook so that they may work together for the liberation of our people and the salvation of our nation." Salvation Associations called *Cuu Quoc* were to be organized throughout the country for popular participation in politics. The Viet Minh, though led by Communists, chose to seek a broader political base of patriotism and nationalism. They had a two-stage plan that called for a nationalist revolution first to be followed by a Communist revolution.

It was easier for the Vietnamese Communists to play down their doctrinaire loyalties during World War II and make it appear to the nationalists that they placed the nationalist and democratic interests above those of Communism. This was because of an alliance between the Soviet Union and Western powers. Parenthetically, it may be observed that to the Vietnamese, the doctrine of capitalism had manifested itself as the control of the economy by white foreigners. Democracy had represented to them a vague idea which looked attractive but which, whenever it was tried, had been easily suppressed by the French. Thus, capitalism had come to be equated with French interest while the democratic forces had shown themselves too weak to stand up to French repressive policies. Therefore, a nationalist movement led by anti-capitalist Communists who could harass the French through their underground, terrorist, revolutionary techniques won favor with a large number of people yearning for the country's liberation. Further, despite the early intervention on the part of the Soviet Union in the twenties and the thirties through Ho Chi Minh, the Communists escaped the foreign label during World War II because of the peculiar international situation of the Soviet Union being one of the Allies. The Viet

Minh led by Communists thus gained acceptance of the Vietnamese people as the viable representatives of nationalism.

The Viet Minh employed guerrilla strategy from the very beginning. In December 1944, with 34 men, Vo Nguyen Giap formed the first platoon of a guerrilla force. Its weaponry was limited to one light machine gun, seventeen rifles, fourteen flintstock rifles, two revolvers and some modest amount of ammunition. This would grow into a well-trained and well-equipped army of six divisions in a decade by the time of the Battle of Dien Bien Phu in 1954.

The guerrilla strategy, psychological and military, used in this early period was similar to that used later to defeat the Americans. The Viet Minh would select for attack small isolated outposts of the French, keeping in mind exactly how many men and weapons awaited them. They would make surprise attacks always with superior numbers and in places where they were sure of success. They were eventually able to arm their increasingly growing army with weapons captured from the enemy. Such a strategy wore out the French and later on, the Americans, who were unfamiliar with the Vietnamese mountainous areas and marshy terrains and who were untrained and incapable of dealing successfully with guerrilla warfare.

By September 1944, the Viet Minh had an army of 5,000 men and the three mountainous provinces of Cao Bang, Lang Son and Bac Kan under their control. Ho Chi Minh could clearly see that the day of his country's independence was not too far. From the jungles of Northern Vietnam, he wrote in the same month:

Zero hour is near. Germany is almost beaten, and her defeat will lead to Japan's. Then the Americans and the Chinese will move into Indochina while the Gaullists rise against the Japanese. The latter may well topple the French Fascists prior to this and set up a military government ... Indochina will reduce to anarchy. We shall not need even to seize power, for there will be no power... Our impending uprising will be carried out in highly favourable conditions, without parallel in the history of our country.[8]

Ho's crystal-gazing powers were later proved substantially right. In March 1945, the Japanese took over the direct control of administration, interning French officials. During those critical months, the Viet Minh received tremendous public support, the situation ironically helped by a gross human tragedy. A terrible famine stalked North Vietnam killing two million out of an estimated population of eight million. Neither the Japanese administration nor the restored French officials in South Vietnam took steps to rush rice to Tongking. Much of the relief was organized instead by the Viet Minh. Taking advantage of the situation, the Viet Minh quickly established guerrilla bases and administration over three more provinces.

In the meantime, the Japanese had asked the Emperor Bao Dai to abrogate the 1884 Protectorate Treaty with France and declare Vietnam independent. A puppet cabinet was appointed under Tran Truong Kim, a respected old scholar, as Prime Minister. The Japanese promised to transfer all general government services to the Bao Dai Government by August 15. The Japanese also asked the Kings of Laos and Cambodia to declare their independence.

Establishment of the DRV

When Japan surrendered to the Allies on August 7, 1945, the Viet Minh emerged from the sidelines to the center of politics. A National Congress of the Viet Minh met at once and elected a National Liberation Committee, which was like a provisional government headed by Ho Chi Minh. A ten-point plan approved by the Congress was to seize power, to gain independence for the Democratic Republic of Vietnam (DRV), develop the army, abolish inequitable taxes, promulgate democratic rights, redistribute communal lands and maintain good relations with the Allies.

There was no mention of any major agrarian reform or nationalization of any kind of property. It was a nationalist, not a Communist, program. On August 26, after the Viet Minh took over Hanoi, Bao Dai abdicated handing over the sword and seal as signs of sovereignty in favor of the provisional government thus providing the new administration with legitimacy. He was made Supreme Councillor of State. A week later, on September 2, 1945, an enthusiastic crowd of half-a-million in Hanoi heard Ho Chi Minh proclaim the birth of the Democratic Republic of Vietnam. On that occasion, Ho Chi Minh read out his Declaration of Independence, which contained passages lifted directly out of the American Declaration. It was a nationalist victory but with a strong base of power for the Communists inasmuch as ten members out of the fifteen in the new cabinet were Communists, though they did not openly admit their ideological affiliation. Ho Chi Minh himself successfully strove to project an image of a nationalist leader. In order to give his government a nationalist appearance, Ho invited among others the Catholic Ngo Dinh Diem from his hideout in Tongking. Diem was not the only one to refuse to join a Communist-dominated government. The nationalist ranks were thus divided soon after the birth of the DRV.

The new Republic was not recognized by any country. The Allies, meeting at Potsdam, had decided to establish the *status quo ante* and to that end asked Nationalist China to occupy Vietnam north of the sixteenth parallel and Britain south of it. France maintained that the future of Indochina was an exclusively French concern. The Chinese forces arrived in North Vietnam in early September while the British troops under General Gracey arrived in Saigon on September 12. Gracey immediately released the French from prison and put them in charge of administration of South Vietnam. Liberated France was, ironically enough, planning to reassert its colonial rights in Indochina despite an impassioned appeal to General de Gaulle from Emperor Bao Dai:

You would understand better if you could see what is happening here, if you could feel the desire for independence which is in everyone's heart and which no human force can any longer restrain. Even if you come to re-establish a French administration here, it will no longer be obeyed: each village will be a nest of resistance, each former collaborator an enemy, and your officials and colonists will themselves ask to leave this atmosphere which they will be unable to breathe.[9]

The Viet Minh would have easily established themselves in the North but for the presence of the Chinese troops and the members of the VNQDD and the Dong Minh Hoi, who had accompanied them to Tongking. By September 16, Hanoi was divided, the Central and Southeast suburbs under Viet Minh control while the pro-Chinese nationalists held the Northeastern parts. Besides, the pro-Chinese nationalists held several provinces. In South Vietnam, the Viet Minh acted as the Committee of the South acting swiftly against Trotskyites, Cao Dai and Hoa Hao. The French treated South Vietnam as a separate unit much to the consternation of the DRV leaders who maintained that Vietnam was a single unit. After the French took over the South, the Viet Minh continued the pressure on the government through guerrilla warfare but their advances were not spectacular until at least a year later.

Ho Chi Minh, therefore, took several measures. First, on November 11, 1945, to the surprise of the non-Communists, he announced the dissolution of the Indochina Communist Party! Secondly, he offered the VNQDD 70 seats in the upcoming free (!) elections to the National Assembly in January 1946. Power was ostensibly shared in a new cabinet composed of Viet Minh, Dong Minh Hoi, VNQDD and others. On March 6, along with the Vice-President (a Dong Minh Hoi representative) and Minister of Foreign Affairs (a VNQDD member), Ho Chi Minh signed an agreement with the French allowing a limited number of French troops to enter North Vietnam to replace the Chinese in exchange for French recognition of the DRV as a "free state having its own government, its own parliament and its own finances, and forming part of the Indo-chinese Federation and the French Union." France also agreed to sponsor a referendum to determine whether Cochin-China should join the Union and to withdraw its troops gradually from all of Vietnam. The agreement was to be followed by negotiations for the resolution of other outstanding issues.

Why did Ho Chi Minh agree to the return of the French to Hanoi? It was principally to get rid of the Chinese troops, which had rampaged the countryside in a campaign of loot, plunder and rape. Secondly, with their withdrawal, the power of the VNQDD and the Dong Minh Hoi could be easily broken. Thirdly, he felt that it would be easier to oust a distant power like France than the closer, traditionally dominant China. On this matter, Ho is reported to have remarked to a friend, in his customary earthy fashion: "It is better to sniff the French dung for a while than to eat China's all our lives."[10] Besides, he knew he could always blame the agreement itself on his VNQDD and Dong Minh Hoi colleagues and he did!

The First Indochina War

Meanwhile, the French attempted to strengthen their military and political position. Having no desire to give up its sovereignty, France hesitated, hedged and finally reneged on most of the assurances. It is possible that the French were reluctant to share power and eventually to relinquish it because the Viet Minh was led by the Communists. Ho Chi Minh tried to convince them that he and his associates were primarily nationalist but to no avail. He also pointed out that the Americans were about to grant independence to the Philippines and that the British were planning to transfer power in India but the French were hardly ready to give up their empire in any part of the world.

Negotiations between the French and the DRV continued through most of that year, neither side yielding
ground and both sides preparing themselves for what
seemed like an inevitable open warfare. In November, a
French attempt to take over control of the Customs in
Haiphong met with Vietnamese resistance. The French
demanded that the Vietnamese lay down their arms. When
the Vietnamese refused, the French used their cruiser,
Suffren, to bomb the Vietnamese quarter of Haiphong on
November 23, 1946, killing over 6,000 civilians in a matter
of hours. Negotiations failed and the Viet Minh attacked
the French troops stationed in Hanoi on December 19,
1946. That became a signal for the outbreak of general
hostilities between the Viet Minh and France. The DRV
leadership and its army of 40,000 trained troops withdrew
confidently to the same limestone caves in Northwest Tongking from which they had descended only seventeen
months earlier. The First Indochina War (1946–1954) had
broken all over Vietnam, North and South, and the French
had to face the Viet Minh at once on scores of fronts.

The French intrasigence had led to the popularity of the
Viet Minh although its Communist nature was known to
many Vietnamese nationalists. Having officially dissolved
the party in November 1945, the Communists maintained
that they were first and last nationalists. The devotion and
dedication of the Viet Minh cadres to the cause of independence and their ascetic way of life had won over large
segments of the population, whose only other alternative
was the French-backed, largely self-serving and servile
nationalist coalition. Besides, time seemed to be on the side
of the Viet Minh. As Milton Osborne observes, after decades of disorientation, the people were pre-disposed to
change. The old feudal values of the mandarinate had been
shattered; so was the impression of invincibility of the
French. The new leaders had demonstrated their willing-
ness and ability to work with the peasants to alleviate the
problems which had been pressing upon the rural popula-

tion for generations. During its brief tenure in office, the DRV had grappled with the famine in the North mobilizing the people to cultivate quick-growing crops on every spare inch of space available. The Viet Minh had also held relatively fair and free elections in Annam and Tongking and won handsomely. On the other hand, it was true that the Communists among the Viet Minh had employed terror tactics against non-Communists within the Viet Minh and even murdered most of the prominent opponents. Quite a few people were turned away from the Viet Minh because of such excesses. Yet, the vast majority, at least in Tongking, seemed to approve of the DRV Government's actions and, indeed, they resented the restoration of French rule at any cost.

On March 8, 1949, France announced the Elysee Agreements between the French President and Emperor Bao Dai under which the State of Vietnam would, along with Laos and Cambodia, be an associate state within the French Union. It made very little difference in practice because the major instruments of power were still under French control. Even nationalists like Ngo Dinh Diem refused to cooperate with the government of the Republic of Vietnam. France had shown some softness in policy because of the tremendous losses in men, money and materiel caused by the "dirty war" as it was called in France. The war annually killed as many officers as were produced by St. Cyr, France's Military Academy. Their reluctance to transfer real power was partly because of their lingering concept of national glory, partly because it would set a chain of events in their other colonies and importantly because of the substantial economic interests, particularly in rubber and rice. But as long as the French showed no genuine desire to part with power, their political moves were not going to gain any appreciable measure of endorsement from the Vietnamese masses.

The year 1949 must be considered crucial to the Vietnamese freedom struggle. The establishment of the

Communist regime in China in October 1949 altered the complexion of the Vietnamese movement. Almost immediately, the Communist elements in the Viet Minh asserted themselves openly admitting their affilliation with international Communism. In August 1949, when the Communist victory in China appeared imminent, Ho Chi Minh told an American journalist that "it changed the centre of gravity of power in Asia," but that "Vietnam is relying as always, on its own strength to win its independence." Similar discretion was not demonstrated by his colleagues some of whom took measures to strengthen control over the non-Communist elements within the Viet Minh. In November 1949, some of them attended the famous Beijing meeting of the World Federation of Trade Unions of Asia and Australia at which China's Liu Shao-chi exhorted the colonial countries to adopt the Chinese path in their "struggle for national independence and people's democracy." The Vietnamese Communists returned from China with directives from their Chinese counterparts as to how to conduct their fight for freedom from French rule. In December, the moment of gloating glory came for these extreme elements in the Viet Minh when the Chinese Communists reached the Vietnamese frontier and unfurled the red flag at the international bridge linking Mon Kay and Tunghing.

From that point on, despite Ho Chi Minh's protestations and even genuine reservations, the Viet Minh subordinated nationalism to international Communism. The shift did not necessarily benefit Ho Chi Minh's movement; if in the earlier years the French had played into his hands and helped him secure sympathy from former colonial peoples, the Viet Minh now played into French hands. At a time when the French were stalemated in Indochina, weakened militarily and economically, with little prospect of extensive foreign support, the Viet Minh made them a present of large-scale American aid against the Vietnamese nationalist movement, not to maintain French colonial rule, which the United States had no particular reason to uphold but to fight Communism. The Indochina War thereafter became part of the worldwide struggle between Communist and the "free world" forces.

In January 1950, with the recognition of the DRV by the Soviet Union and China, the cold war lines were clearly drawn. Bao Dai's Vietnam became an outpost of the Western bloc, protecting all of Southeast Asia against eventual expansion by China. United States Secretary of State, Dean Acheson, declared that Russian recognition should remove "any illusions as to the 'nationalist' nature of Ho Chi Minh's aims and reveals Ho in his true colors as the mortal enemy of native independence in Indochina." The United States recognized the Bao Dai regime in the hope that the Elysee Agreement would form the "basis for the progressive realization of the legitimate aspirations of the Vietnamese people." France was already receiving American help indirectly under the Marshall Plan thus allowing her to release francs for military expenses in Indochina. But from early 1950, with the signing of a Mutual Assistance Program, United States aid to the French effort in Indochina was to be direct. It amounted to three billion dollars by 1954. The Indochina situation was becoming internationalized and the cold war seemed to extend from Eastern Europe to Indochina, for the first time in Asia.

It is difficult to clear the maze of propaganda and identify the real reasons for the Viet Minh's military success and successive French defeats. Both sides made blunders costing heavy casualties, the French generals hardly knowing how to fight a non-conventional guerrilla war and the Viet Minh forces lacking experience of pitched battles. After the cease-fire in Korea in 1953, the Communist countries concentrated on Indochina. Large amounts of Russian and Chinese ammunition and weapons came across the Northern borders to strengthen the Viet Minh supply position. By early 1954, the French forces were thoroughly demoralized, particularly by the public opinion at home, which overwhelmingly pressed for ending the "dirty war". Cabinets fell rapidly until the Prime Minister of the twentieth government to hold office since the end of World War II, Pierre Mendes-France, who became Premier on June 17, 1954, vowed to resign his office if a settlement in Indochina were not reached by July 20, 1954.[12]

Dien Bien Phu

The last French commander, Henri Navarre, the fifth commander in as many years, pledged "to break up and destroy regular enemy forces in Indochina." For years, French military officials had consoled themselves that the ill-clad, "cowardly" Viet Minh succeeded because of their hit-and-run tactics and that in a pitched battle of the conventional type, which the French armies were trained to fight, the Viet Minh would be crushed. The battle of Dien Bien Phu was contrived not so much by General Giap as by General Navarre. His plan was to lure the core of the Viet Minh forces into a set-piece battle in the remote valley of Dien Bien Phu close to the Laotian border, deemed strategically very important. He expected the Viet Minh to pass through the valley in early 1954 for a second attack on Laos. With their air superiority and better fire-power, the French expected an easy victory and large-scale destruction of Vietnamese forces, which had no aircraft, no tanks and hardly any means of transport fit for mountain warfare. A major defeat of Giap's forces there would be crippling to the Viet Minh's military effort. The French General had, however, underestimated the Viet Minh's ability to transport large cannon on human backs and ordinary bicycles and positioning them in the surrounding hills besieging the French troops. Logistically, the valley of Dien Bien Phu was the most indefensible site since the French troops became "sitting ducks" directly within the long range of artillery fire of the Viet Minh, who occupied the surrounding hills. The only way to supply the French troops was by air, which was also made extremely hazardous by the Viet Minh guns directed at the airplanes.

In April and early May 1954, the use of nuclear weapons seemed to the U.S. Secretary of State, John Foster Dulles, the only way to save the beleaguered French garrison from total extermination by the Viet Minh. But the United States would act only jointly with Great Britain and the latter firmly refused to go along and thereby open the prospect of a third world war as the action would have probably brought in massive Soviet retaliation. The situation enabled General Giap to register his greatest triumph at Dien Bien Phu on May 7, the eve of the Geneva Conference on Indochina. The losses on both sides were colossal. Of the 15,000 French troops, 1,500 were killed and 4,000 wounded while of the 51,000 Viet Minh troops, 8,000 died and 15,000 wounded. The Viet Minh's victory completely demoralized the French troops in Vietnam and the French politicians and diplomats at Geneva.

The Geneva Settlement of 1954

The Geneva Agreements of July 21, 1954 temporarily divided Vietnam along the seventeenth parallel into two zones, the question of reunification to be decided by a Vietnam-wide election in 1956. The Viet Minh accepted the settlement most reluctantly under pressure from their Communist allies, the Soviet Union and China, who were at the time espousing a global policy of peaceful co-existence with capitalist powers. China would have a special reason of its own, its historical policy being not to encourage a political consolidation among its neighboring countries. The Soviet Union was possibly concerned that in the event that an agreement was not reached by the deadline set by Premier Mendes-France, fighting would be resumed by the French and United States might enter the fray directly on the French side. To the United States, it appeared like the Viet Minh would soon take over the southern part of Vietnam. It refused to sign the declaration of the Geneva Conference and proceeded to support the Government of South Vietnam of which Ngo Dinh Diem was the newly-appointed Premier.

The Viet Minh or Communist leaders had urged a division of Vietnam at least along the fourteenth parallel and that the proposed elections for the reunification of the country take place no later than six months from the signing of the Geneva Agreements. If negotiations are to some a continuation of war by other means, to the Vietnamese Communists they represented a big power game which had snatched away a sure political victory from their hands. The Geneva Conference sounded the death-knell of French colonialism in Southeast Asia without, however, assuring freedom to Vietnam as one nation and without guaranteeing continued peace to an already war-weary land.

NOTES

1. David Marr, *Vietnamese Anti-Colonialism, 1885-1925*, Berkeley, University of California Press, 1971, p. 4.
2. Truong Buu Lam, *Patterns of Vietnamese Response to Foreign Intervention, 1858-1900*, New Haven, Yale University, Southeast Asia Studies, 1967, p. 3.
3. For a detailed analysis along these lines, see Marr, *op. cit.*, pp. 95-97.
4. Hoang Van Chi, *Colonialism to Communism*, New York, Praeger, 1964, p. 18.
5. King Chen has compiled a list of Ho's aliases, numbering 19, some repeated at different times in his life. King Chen, *Vietnam and China, 1938-1954*, Princeton, Princeton University Press, 1969, pp. 37 and 40 footnotes.
6. Pham Van Dong, *President Ho Chi Minh*, Hanoi, Foreign Languages Publishing House, 1960, pp. 41-42.
7. M.E. Gettleman, ed., *Vietnam*, New York, Penguin, 1965, pp. 37-39.
8. Quoted from a Viet Minh pamphlet by Jean Lacouture, *Ho Chi Minh, A Political Biography*, New York, Vintage Books, 1968, p. 88.
9. Quoted in Ellen Hammer, *The Struggle for Indochina*, Stanford, Stanford University Press, 1954, p. 102.
10. Quoted in David Halberstam, *Ho*, New York, Vintage Books, 1971, pp. 84-85.
11. Milton E. Osborne, *Region of Revolt, Focus on Southeast Asia*, Ruschutters Bay, Australia, Pergamon Press, 1970, p. 100.
12. The Geneva Agreements were signed in the early hours of July 21. The French Premier's plane engines were buzzing at that time ready to take him from Geneva to Paris to submit his resignation in case the talks failed!

5

The Second Indochina War—
The Roots

The International Context

The Geneva Conference which ended the First Indo-china War (1946–1954) divided Vietnam at the seventeenth parallel. It created two zones for the rival military forces to regroup and withdraw to the respective zones. The partition of the country was to be temporary, for two years, at the end of which elections were to be held to reunify the country. The implementation of the Geneva Agreements, including the elections, was to be supervised by an International Control Commission under Indian chairmanship, with pro-West Canada and Communist Poland as members. The success of the Commission's[1] work depended, indeed, on the cooperation of the governments of North and South Vietnam. Great Britain and the Soviet Union acted as Co-chairmen of the Geneva Conference to whom the International Control Commission reported periodically. The United States and the new Government of South Vietnam had refused to sign the Geneva Agreements, though the United States assured at Geneva that it would "not use force to disturb the Geneva settlement"; that instead it would seek "to achieve unity through free elections, supervised by the United Nations to ensure that they are conducted freely." United States' actions in the next two years completely contradicted these statements and were primarily responsible for the unfortunate events of the next two decades in Vietnam. The United States, in effect, encouraged the Diem Government to turn the Southern Zone into an independent state and convert the provisional demarcation line at the seventeenth parallel into an international border. Further, Saigon refused to cooperate with the International Control Commission in the planning of the elections scheduled for 1956. Those elections were never held.

The American policy toward Vietnam was principally governed by the doctrine of containment of Communism almost consistently all the way from the early fifties to at least the end of the following decade. Within days of the Geneva settlement the U.S. Secretary of State, John Foster Dulles, pursued the "united action" strategy in a new fashion by getting Britain and France, among others, to sign a pact, which would, in essence, counter the Geneva spirit. Dulles's efforts resulted in the Manila Pact on September 8, 1954, creating the South-East Asia Treaty Organization (SEATO). Its name belied its membership; it included only three Asian members—Pakistan, Thailand, and the Philippines—to complement the United States, the United Kingdom, France, Australia and New Zealand. The major non-aligned powers of South and Southeast Asia— India, Burma, Cambodia, and Indonesia—opposed the Pact. The SEATO did not include Laos, Cambodia and South Vietnam as this would have directly violated the Geneva Agreements; however SEATO's Article V included these areas as "protocol" countries to be defended by SEATO powers, thereby legitimizing later American involvement in the Vietnam conflict.

SEATO represented a resumption of the cold war in Southeast Asia. It conflicted with the purposes and goals of the Geneva Accords which, in turn, reflected the principles of peaceful co-existence contained in the Sino-Indian agreement of April 1954 on Tibet. It was no surprise that the SEATO could enlist only three Asian members while others followed India's lead in staunchly opposing any military pacts that were likely to perpetuate Western military or "neo-colonial" presence in Southeast Asia on the pretext of containing China. The Manila Pact and, specifically, the U.S. policy in Vietnam in the years following Geneva aggravated tensions and frustrated the Vietnamese people's yearning for a peaceful reunification of their country. Writing a decade later, a critic of U.S. policy observed:

> In these two years can be found the roots of the critical political military situation as it has existed in Vietnam since 1960. In 1954 and 1955 the United States could still have charted a different course. But once it chose the direction it did in 1954 and proceeded in that direction through 1956, it became a captive of its policy and committed to its continuation.[2]

The "Two Vietnams" : Internal Conditions

Diem Family Rules South Vietnam

While the Geneva Conference was in session, on June 16, the French Government, along with Emperor Bao Dai, announced appointment of Ngo Dinh Diem as Premier of the "State of Vietnam." Diem was a "mixture of monk and mandarin" hailing from a prestigious Catholic yet Confucian family from Phu Cam in Central Vietnam converted to Christianity in the 17th century. His family had successively served as mandarins. Diem's father, Ngo Dinh Kha, was counsellor to the Emperor Than Thai, deposed by the French in 1907. Extremely bright in his studies, Diem, like his older brother, Khoi, had been promoted by the French in the 1920's to the high office of provincial governor. An anti-Communist but also a nationalist, Diem was by no means a collaborator with the colonial regime. In 1933, the French showed readiness to restore some of the long-lost authority of the Imperial council and advised the 18-year-old Emperor Bao Dai to appoint Ngo Dinh Diem his Minister of the Interior. Diem sought and received assurances from the French that the council would have genuine authority to institute administrative reforms. He was disillusioned and quickly resigned his post within three months, much to the consternation of the French, who took reprisals against his family and threatened to arrest him. Bao Dai quickly lost, if he ever had any, interest in administration. He spent the next two decades as a "playboy emperor" largely in the gambling houses and high class brothels in distant pleasure spots in Southern France or in nearby Hong Kong.

Diem remained in contact with the other non-Communist nationalists over the next decade but not very actively in the movement. There was no love lost between him and the Viet Minh who killed his brother Khoi and Khoi's son and at one point attempted to kill Diem. His reputation as a nationalist and a good administrator was regarded important enough for Ho Chi Minh to invite him to join his government in 1945, which Diem refused to do because of the Viet Minh's heinous acts towards his family and hundreds of other innocent people. In August 1950, Diem left Vietnam for the United States where until 1953, he lived mostly at Maryknoll Seminaries in Lakewood, New Jersey and Ossining (New York). During that period he became a spokesman of Vietnamese nationalist movement in the United States, lecturing and also meeting a number of prominent politicians including the then Senators John F. Kennedy and Mike Mansfield and Justice William O. Douglas. In May 1953, he left for Europe spending some time in the Benedictine monastery of St. Andre les Druges in Belgium. Around the time of the Geneva Conference on Indochina, he was in Paris along with his brother, Luyen, hobnobbing with French politicians. At that point the French Government and Bao Dai, independently of the United States, chose Diem to head the government of the "State of Vietnam."

With the partition of the country in July 1954, Diem faced numerous challenges to his authority. For the most part, South Vietnam was under the irregular control of three religio-military sects: Cao Dai, Hoa Hao, with private armies estimated at fifty thousand men each and the Binh Xuyen, which held vice concessions in gambling houses, narcotic dens, night clubs and brothels and virtually controlled Saigon's police force. With admirable ability, Diem succeeded in the first six months of his administration in crushing the sects and eliminating all extra-legal challenges to his government. His handling of the problem of rehabilitation of nearly a million refugees, mostly Catholics from North Vietnam, won Diem international acclaim, notably in the United States. In order to secure his position, Diem held a referendum on October 23, 1955, in which he received an embarrassing 99 percent vote resulting in the removal of Bao Dai and making Diem the President of the newly-proclaimed Republic of Vietnam. Diem then announced his plans for election of a "national" assembly on March 4, 1956 which would draw up a constitution for the new republic. He repeatedly repudiated any obligations arising out of the Geneva Agreements including the crucial provision for Vietnam-wide elections for reunification of the country. Recognized by the United States and thirty-five other countries of the Western bloc, the "Republic of Vietnam" became by late 1955, for all purposes, an independent member of the international community. From a situation of a total collapse of governmental authority at the time of the country's partition in mid-1954, Diem had miraculously emerged as the central authority in South Vietnam.

In all these moves, the United States supported Diem to the hilt, parading him as an intense anti-French, anti-Communist, nationalist leader with a legendary record of honesty and integrity. The Americans held Diem as a "nationalist alternative" to Communist Ho Chi Minh. But Diem had been out of Vietnam for too long before 1954 to be in touch with people's aspirations in a period of fast-paced political upheaval. Further his style of government

was paternalistic and aloof like that of the outdated mandarins, withdrawing himself increasingly within the walls of
the "Forbidden Palace" and depending for information and
guidance on a close coterie of "court" sycophants and even
more so on members of his extended family. Diem's popular base was slim, mostly the Catholics, constituting a 10
percent minority, largely refugees. They were hated by
most of the Southern Buddhist population both because of
their religion and Northern origin.

With the advantage of historical hindsight, one can blame
all the future problems of South Vietnam on the unfortunate choice by the United States of the person it decided
totally to support. In 1954, despite misgivings of Diem's
popularity the influential United States Senator, Mike
Mansfield, had recommended that if the Diem Government
collapsed, "the United States should consider an immediate
suspension of all aid to Vietnam ... except that of a
humanitarian nature."[3] The U.S. State Department interpreted this to mean that all aid should be given to the Diem
government to avoid its fall. On November 3, 1954, President Eisenhower's special representative, General J.
Lawton Collins, announced in Saigon that the U.S. would
give "every possible aid to the Government of Diem and to
his government only ..." On February 19, 1955, President
Eisenhower formally offered the Diem Government un-
conditional support against its Communist as well as non-
Communist foes.

Diem did not have the aura of prestige, sacrifice and
struggle against colonialism to match Ho Chi Minh's reputation. In contrast to the gentle-looking (despite his ruth-
lessness), ascetic (though atheist), simply-clad (fatigues
and rubber sandals) Ho Chi Minh, Diem always dressed
nattily in shark-skin and Irish linen suits and, as a fervent
Catholic with a monastic background, appeared more a
sectarian than a national leader. Both were bachelors. That
is where the comparison ended. Lack of family ties was an
asset to the avuncular Ho Chi Minh (he was called Uncle

Ho); the nation became his family. Having no family ties whatsoever, Ho Chi Minh stood above suspicion of nepotism. He had gained a reputation for honesty and sincerity and the trust of the masses. Instead of living in the former Governor-General's palace in Hanoi, Ho preferred to live in the guest house with the same old simple habits.

Diem's strong ties with his extended family became his greatest liability; he almost equated his family with the state. He distributed powerful positions among his family: his brother, Nhu, and his vitriolic-tongued wife, Madame Nhu, became the President's closest advisers. The megalomaniac Nhu kept himself intoxicated, perhaps without Diem's knowledge, on drugs and shared with his President-brother an abstract philosophy of "personalism," which was unintelligible to everyone, perhaps including themselves. Madame Nhu, a recent convert from Buddhism to the Catholic religion, became an ardent champion of her new faith and of puritanism in public life. Having a magnetic hold on the President, she was singly responsible for alienating large sections of the predominantly Buddhist population through her ill-advised pronouncements on religious as well as secular matters. Diem's elder brother, Thuc, was, in his capacity of Archbishop of Hue, the highest Catholic official in the land; another brother virtually ruled Annam as a personal fiefdom while yet another brother served the Government as ambassador to Great Britain. The increasing involvement of all these members of the President's family in Governmental affairs was in direct proportion to the growing isolation of the President from his people. Diem's life in the Presidential Palace was more akin to the former Emperor's in the Forbidden Palace, increasingly aloof and alienated from his people. Consequently, he became a prisoner of his family with access only to such information as would be made available by them, notably the Nhus. Under their influence, Diem suppressed newspapers, clamped strict censorship, exiled men by administrative fiat, suspended court judgements. A Western commentator lamented that instead of confronting the totalitarian North with the evidences of freedom, the South Vietnamese Government "slipped into an inefficient dictatorship."[5]

Communist Rule in North Vietnam

Initially, Hanoi also had to grapple with a host of problems that engendered considerable discontent among the people of North Vietnam. The Democratic Republic of Vietnam (DRV) embarked upon its promised agrarian reform of redistribution of land in the already congested and overfragmented Red River delta, where agriculture had suffered dismally in the final phase of the fighting immediately before the Geneva settlement. Imminent famine conditions could not be relieved by imports of grain because of lack of foreign exchange. At the instance of the United States Government, the French managers had removed the American-made installations from the coal mines which had been North Vietnam's principal earners of foreign exchange. Furthermore, the DRV launched a crash program of building roads and railroads leading to China by using forced labor on a massive scale. All these factors combined with the most potent of them, the religious factor, helped to swell the flood of refugees from the North to the South. The DRV's efforts to stem the migration had very little effect, particularly upon the Catholics, who had been told in their parishes that God had moved South, where the Government was headed by one of their Catholic brethren. At least one million people, mostly Catholics, migrated from the North to the South during 1954-55. There still remained over 800,000 Catholics in North Vietnam.

In 1956, the land reform campaign, which had been given up in 1955, was resumed, with results not edifying in the least. Many Party cadres exploited the new land laws as weapons to settle scores with their old enemies or to secure material advantages for themselves. Land reform became a major terror campaign according to the critics of the DRV, taking toll of hundreds of thousands, perhaps as many as half a million lives. The figures may have been exaggerated though the fact of large-scale peasant discontent and repression is incontestable.

The DRV quickly adopted a socialist system on the Russian model. In 1955, the State Planning Committee was established but it was not before 1961 that the First Five Year Development Plan was launched. The escalation of the war in the South and American bombing of the North beginning February 1965 compelled the DRV to scrap the planning process until 1976 when after the reunification of Vietnam, the Second Five Year Plan was launched.

The core of the new economic system in the DRV was to be the agrarian cooperative. The basic philosophy seemed to be that the society could move directly to socialism without any transitional capitalist stage. This was because there were few, if any, major Vietnamese-owned capitalist enterprises to be nationalized. Collectivization of agriculture proceeded by definite stages. By the early 1960's, thousands of cooperatives consolidating the traditionally fragmented, small units of land, were created. Most of the cooperatives were, however, small and, therefore, not able to generate adequate money or manpower for large-scale irrigation projects. In fact, each cooperative had to be helped out by the government in the initial years to the extent of about 135,000 dongs per annum. By the late sixties, the small cooperatives were consolidated into "high level" collectives, providing for common ownership of all means of production and distribution of the net revenues to farmers in proportion to their contribution. The high level collectives controlled more land, money and manpower enabling substantial improvement in the irrigational infrastructure. The government established production targets as well as prices for purchase and sale of agricultural products.

Despite such far-reaching, intensive measures, the internal saving capacity of each collective remained very low. In 1975, the government estimated such re-investment funds to be capable of expanding the cultivable area in each collective by no more than one hectare. Nor were they enough to buy some basic machinery to improve farming in each collective. There is no doubt that some considerable portion of the surplus generated in the North was used for financing the war effort in the South. In the absence of any reliable documentation it is not possible to estimate the costs of the assistance provided by the DRV to the NLF in the South. Such documentation, except for whatever was seized from prisoners of war, is most unlikely to be ever available because of the official denial on the DRV's part of its participation in the struggle in the South. Except for the half decade in the fifties, the extraordinary political and military situation in which the DRV was involved until 1975 inhibited any sustained effort to implement the agricultural reforms in North Vietnam.

Paralleling the creation of agrarian collectives, the DRV also reorganized business enterprises, be they large, medium or small, in different areas of human activity—industries, forestry, fisheries, transport and communications. Some private enterprises were converted into State-private partnerships, though they were virtually controlled by the Government, which gave very low priority to consumer goods limiting them to "basic necessities and subsistence." During the decade of the Second Indochina War, 1964–75, consumerism in North Vietnam declined to among the lowest levels in the world, diplomatic staff in Hanoi reporting mostly empty shelves in the capital's consumer stores. A whole generation thus grew up in North Vietnam, political and military leaders included, who had learnt to live on bare basic necessities. No wonder when the North

Vietnamese troops and cadres marched into Saigon in April 1975, they went on a mad spree of acquisition of American-made consumer goods.

In terms of political stability, however, North Vietnam contrasted sharply with South Vietnam. The state was headed by a legendary hero, Ho Chi Minh, who was known for his qualities of determination, sacrifice, austerity and whole-hearted devotion to the cause of his country's liberation, reconstruction and reunification. He had endeared himself to the masses through his simple habits. As an old Bolshevik, Ho also commanded respect in the Communist world. Ho's cabinet comrades followed his example, inspiring the common cadres to dedicate themselves to the achievement of socio-economic goals. Their firm commitment to the reunification of the country further endeared them to the majority of the people, both in the North and in the South. As President Eisenhower observed in his memoirs: "I have never talked or corresponded with a person knowledgeable in Indochinese affairs who did not agree that had elections been held at the time of fighting, 80 percent of the population would have voted for the communist Ho Chi Minh as their leader rather than Chief of State Bao Dai."[6] That was in 1954.

The Second Indochina War, 1964-1975

Diem's Oppressive Policies

The problem of "subversion" in South Vietnam was principally of Diem's making. After the suppression of Cao Dai, Hoa Hao and Binh Xuyen sects, Diem could have liberalized politics and turned to the much-needed alleviation of social and economic problems. Instead, he unleashed, in 1957, a "denounce Communists" and "mopping up" campaign using emergency powers and vague definitions of espionage and treason to carry out arbitrary arrests of- Communists and non-Communists alike. His brother Nhu's security apparatus included a secret police force trained by experts from the Michigan State University. It terrorized all opponents and herded them into prison camps, several thousand "Reds" being placed in concentration camps like Phu Loi, where among other atrocities massive poisoning was reported. Diem's base of power was very narrow, members of his own extended family and Catholics who constituted a ten percent minority, largely refugees from the North who were hated by most of the Southern Buddhist population because of their religion and northern origin. Dissident nationalists whose numbers increased rapidly were soon branded Communist traitors and a censorship was clamped down on the press, more severe than at the worst time of the French colonial rule. The repressive policies were based from May 1959 on the infamous 10–59 law creating special military tribunals, which delivered summary judgments within three days after the accused were cited for "provoking economic disturbances" or "disrupting the security of the state" awarding death sentences with no appeal.

As for the rural areas, Diem did introduce some land reform. But his policies were ill-conceived and ill-implemented and, therefore, disastrous in their effect. Thus, he sought to rehabilitate refugees and the landless poor by expropriating and redistributing land holdings beyond the high ceiling of 247 acres, which made very little land available for redistribution. Diem also abrogated a major land distribution program that had been undertaken during the First Indochina War, when over half-a-million hectares of rice land had been re-distributed to the peasants. Only about 15 percent of such distribution was confirmed by the Diem Government. Such a measure alienated the peasantry. Since most of the requisitioned land, primarily in the Mekong delta, was now given to "foreign" landlords, supporters of Diem from Central Vietnam and prominent Catholic refugees from North Vietnam, large numbers of "established " peasants in the Mekong delta became hostile to the Government.

Diem's land reform program envisaged only 20 percent of the rice land to pass from large to small farmers; in reality, only ten percent of all tenant farmers benefited. As much as 47 percent of the land remained concentrated in the hands of 2 percent of the landowners; fifteen percent of the land-lords owned 75 percent of all land. The peasant discontent was further fueled by increased land rents, which according to the pro-Diem paper, *Tu Do*, in actuality, allowing for extortionist officials, amounted often to 45 to 50 percent of the crop. The few farmers who benefited from Diem's pro-gram were more often than not northern Catholic refugees, inviting the charge of favoritism, and thereby further deepening peasant alienation in Cochin-China. There were even widespread allegations that the Diem family had enriched itself by manipulating land transfers.

To add insult to injury, in June 1956, the Diem Government replaced village notables with its own appointees, again northern Catholic "outsiders," summarily terminat-ing the 2000-year-old Vietnamese tradition of village auto-nomy. They were unable to contain or resolve the dis-content much less inspire confidence and trust among the peasantry.

By 1960, Diem, the "all-knowing Mandarin," had alien-ated all major sections of South Vietnamese population. The intellectual elite was rendered "politically mute," labor unions "impotent," Buddhists distrustful, Montagnards suspicious, while loyal opposition in the form of organized parties was stifled out of existence. Diem's policies virtually assured that political challenges to him would have to be extra-legal and violent. Ultimately, these emerged from diverse sources in South Vietnam: the armed forces, the religious sects, intellectuals, Communists and indeed, the peasantry.

The National Liberation Front

It is against such a backdrop of large-scale urban and rural discontent caused by the Government's policies of alienation and repression, nepotism and corruption, family rule and religious insensitiveness that the birth of the National Liberation Front in late 1960 must be viewed. The NLF was a grass roots organization, which consisted of various elements within the South Vietnamese society. For most of its 15-year existence, the common factor binding them all was not Communism but nationalism, a determination to overthrow the regime in Saigon and to set up one which would end foreign intervention and guarantee a minimum of democratic liberties. On the other hand, despite its considerable non-Communist membership and a non–Communist Saigon lawyer, Nguyen Huu Tho, as Chairman, the real authority and leadership increasingly lay in its Communist constituents—the People's Revolutionary Party and the Liberation Army—both taking their direction if not direct orders from the Politburo in North Vietnam. The NLF's objectives did include reunification of the country but not necessarily under the hegemony of the North.

The origin of the *Mat Tran Dan Toc Giai Phong*—the National Liberation Front lay in the Saigon Cholon Peace Committee formed in August 1954 to protest Diem Government's shooting at a rally of peaceful demonstrators asking for immediate release of political prisoners in terms of the Geneva Agreements. It consisted of Saigon intellectuals and left-wing progressives (but not Communists). Its ranks swelled as Diem refused to implement the provisions of the Geneva Agreements in regard to the reunification of the country. Their protests were peaceful following the proper legal channels. They suffered, however, more than any others after 1957 when under Nhu's security setup, South Vietnam became a quasi-police state. As the governmental repression particularly after the passing of the 10-59 law became unbearably severe, the dissidents adopted violence to fight back. The Communist (former Viet Minh) cadres left behind in 1954 in the South took advantage of the situation wanting to engage themselves in armed attacks but were discouraged by their comrades in the North on the grounds that the conditions were not yet conducive or ripe for such a stage of the struggle. Hanoi warned the southern cadres: "To ignore the balance of forces and rashly call for a general uprising is to commit the error of speculative adventurism, leading to premature violence and driving us into a very dangerous position."

Despite such inhibiting instructions, the Southern Communists joined the militants in a number of attacks against government officials in the countryside. A number of events during 1959-60 culminated in the establishment of the NLF. Thus, in 1959, two significant revolts among tribesmen—the Kar in January and the Hre in July—took place. In March 1960, Nguyen Huu Tho, President of the Saigon-Cholon Committee for Peace urged his fellow compatriots in Eastern Cochin-China to resist. In May, some army units in coastal Quang Nai province revolted and in November, a coup was attempted by three crack paratrooper battalions and a marine unit under Lieutenant Colonel Vuong Van Dong. It was against such a background that various movements and political parties— Armed Propaganda Groups of the People's Self-Defense Forces, the Associates of Ex-Resistance Members, the Saigon-Cholon Committee, the Democratic Party and others—coalesced into a national movement creating the NLF as an organizational framework within which a general political military struggle could take place.

For quite some time, Hanoi had been under pressure from the Southern Communist militants to support their movement. They criticized the North's weak protest of the non-observance of the 1956 general elections and Hanoi's relative passivity to Diem's repression during 1957–59. In early 1959, Le Duan, Secretary-General of the Lao Dong

Party, who had led the independence struggle in South Vietnam traveled to the South to ascertain the situation and reported to the party that if the Southern Communists did not join the other militants they would lose credibility with the people.

Despite misgivings on the correct timing of the insurrection, the Northern leadership finally conceded. On May 13, 1959, the fifteenth plenum of the Lao Dong Party's central committee meeting in Hanoi declared that "the time has come to struggle heroically and perseveringly to smash" the government of South Vietnam. The Party leaders resolved to create a unified Vietnam through all "appropriate means." The following year, in September, the Third Congress of the Party authorized the support for a "genuine revolutionary organization in the Southern Zone." In December, the NLF was established in South Vietnam. The creation of the People's Revolutionary Party (PRP) on January 1, 1962, within the Front represented Hanoi's attempt to direct the Southern insurgency, via Northern Communists, such as Nguyen Don, the director of Military Region Five (the northernmost third of South Vietnam) and alternate members of the Lao Dong Central Committee. The PRP had only the appearance of an independent existence; actually it was nothing but an extension of the Lao Dong Party.

Opposition to Diem's Rule

How far was the opposition in South Vietnam to Diem's rule an indigenously inspired movement and what was the degree of Hanoi's involvement in it? A few dates are significant though not conclusive in this respect. Until July 1956, Hanoi had hoped that the reunification of the country would be accomplished through elections. Thereafter, until early 1959, North Vietnam was compelled by considerations of Sino-Soviet global policies of peaceful co-existence to refrain from resorting to a violent alternative for achieving the country's reunification. During this period, the North Vietnamese hoped that the Diem regime would disintegrate in the South because of its own weakness. The first rumblings of the Sino-Soviet dispute leading to China's decision to oust Soviet technicians and rejection of Soviet aid in 1959 may have led to alterations in Hanoi's posture in regard to the South. Throughout the Second Indochina War, the Communists claimed that the war in the South was entirely a Southern affair, the assistance from the North being no more than moral, ideological and diplomatic. On the other hand, the official view of South Vietnamese government and the United States of the "insurgency" is summarized by Douglas Pike:

> The National Liberation Front was not simply another indigenous covert group, or even a coalition of such groups. It was an organized effort, endowed with ample cadres and funds, crashing out of the jungle to flatten the GVN ... (Government of South Vietnam) ... A revolutionary organization must build; it begins with persons suffering genuine grievances, who are slowly organized and whose militancy gradually increases until a critical mass is reached and the revolution explodes. Exactly the reverse was the case with the NLF. It sprang full-blown into existence and then was fleshed out. The grievances were developed or manufactured almost as a necessary afterthought. The creation of the NLF was an accomplishment of such skill, precision, and refinement that when one thinks of who the master planner must have been, only one name comes: Vietnam's organizational genuis, Ho Chi Minh.[7]

Even if the Southern movement received organizational and material assistance from the North, its initial stimulus was undoubtedly Southern. It is true that there was a core of Communist cadres at its center. When the Viet Minh regroupment was carried out in terms of the Geneva Accords during 1954-55, a network of five to ten thousand cadres was left in the South, with instructions to blend into the new environment and agitate for elections. The Viet Minh also left behind large caches of weapons. But of these, ninety percent had been liquidated by the "extreme manhunt" carried out by Diem's Government between 1955 and 1957. The Southern movement undoubtedly began as a response to Diem's "mopping-up campaign" of 1957 and was basically manned by Southerners. As George McTurnan Kahin and John Lewis observed:

> The insurrection is Southern rooted; it arose at Southern initiative in response to Southern demands. The Liberation Front gave political articulation and leadership to the widespread reaction against the harshness and heavy-handedness of Diem's government. It gained drive under the stimulus of Southern Vietminh veterans who felt betrayed by the Geneva conference and abandoned by Hanoi ... Contrary to U.S. policy assumptions, all available evidence shows that the revival of the civil war in the South in 1958 was undertaken by Southerners at their own—not Hanoi's—initiative.[8]

According to a Rand Corporation study, between 1956 and the launching of the NLF, approximately 30,000 Northern agents, regroupees, were sent South. While the regroupees did have an influence on the Front, particularly in terms of military strategy and political goals, they could not have dictated their demands due to the local conditions and the NLF's heavy reliance on the grass roots structure. Geographically, the resistance forces were isolated from the North, making communication and transportation extremely difficult. In fact, the early NLF successes were without aid from the North. From the very beginning, the main military activity occurred in the deep South; the first "liberated" area was the Ca Mau peninsula. Most weapons used by the NLF were those captured from their enemy; approximately 80 percent of their weapons were of American manufacture. It was only after the massive infusion of American manpower and weaponry in South Vietnam from the mid-sixties that North Vietnam used the Ho Chi Minh Trail through Laos and Cambodia to supply the South with North Vietnamese manpower and materiel manufactured in Communist countries.

The NLF was originally intended to be a political rather than a military movement. Its initial doctrine was 'Khoi Nghia or the General Uprising. It would inspire the Vietnamese in the nation's 2,500 villages to such a pitch that at some precise moment there would come a spontaneous uprising, and the people would seize power, led of course by the NLF. This was constantly drummed into the minds of the peasants by NLF cadres working in villages. Therefore, the NLF's organizational structure relied heavily on the participation of individuals, associations and, in the countryside, entire villages. By 1963, the NLF became a gigantic organization composed of various departments such as the Farmers' Liberation Association, the Women's Liberation Association and the Youth Liberation Association. The Front's Central Committee in charge of political and military strategy consisted of representatives of such diverse elements including also the political parties of South Vietnam like the Democratic Party, the Radical Socialist Party and, indeed, the People's Revolutionary Party.

As noted before, the NLF had given primacy to the political struggle, armed resistance being secondary. However, after mid-1963, the armed struggle gained precedence over the political aspect of the movement. Several factors were responsible for the shift in policy. Firstly, the increasing use of sophisticated combat weaponry by the ARVN (Army of South Vietnam) against the NLF. The latter, therefore, augmented its guerrilla units and military capabilities. Their success against the ARVN supported the argument for larger, more numerous and better-equipped guerrilla units which would bring a quicker ultimate victory. Secondly, the Northern cadres reinterpreted the revolutionary doctrine placing greater stress on the armed struggle. Therefore, politically as well as militarily, the management of the NLF after 1963 passed on increasingly to the Hanoi-trained Communists of the People's Revolutionary Party, the aim of the Lao Dong Party in South Vietnam. The DRV's assistance to the NLF in the form of military training, arms supplies and manpower stepped up phenomenally after 1964 in direct correlation to American commitment of men, money and materiel. Equally, the Americans claimed that their increased involvement was a direct response to the level of insurgency in the South, which they alleged was entirely inspired, directed, manned and supported by the North. Beyond this, as Henry Kissinger points out, there was a mistaken belief in the mind of successive American administrations all the way from Kennedy to Nixon that the Vietnam conflict was "a test case of a theory of revolutionary warfare centrally directed from Moscow and Peking." It was an attitude consistent with the U.S. policy of containment followed in Indochina for a quarter of a century.

The Buddhist Crisis

Ironically, Diem's downfall was brought about by non-Communist elements in South Vietnam. Two military coup attempts in November 1960 and February 1962 had failed. The most serious challenge was posed in the Spring and Summer of 1963 by religious malcontents. The movement, led by Buddhist monks and nuns, drew its strength not from the abstractions of Communist ideology, which could only be antithetical to Buddhism, but from the wave of social discontent silently sweeping the population.

Traditionally, the Vietnamese had not perceived religion and politics as separate entities. Their religion was a blend of Confucianism, Taoism, Buddhism as well as animism. As in most of Asia, religion provided "the authority for and the confirmation of, an entire way of life—agriculture, social structure, and a political system."[9] It is well said that the "Vietnamese are Confucians in peacetime, Buddhists in times of trouble."[10] Buddhism had always stressed a morality that lay "beyond loyalty to existing authorities" and the Buddhist bonzes had provided in the past an intellectual and moral leadership to oppose an oppressive regime.

During French rule, the Buddhist monks had remained, by and large, apolitical. They had been allowed internal autonomy in the running of the monasteries and freedom to celebrate the numerous Buddhist holidays. Unlike the Catholics, the Buddhists did not have a well-organized "church" hierarchy; each pagoda was, for most purposes, an independent entity. With Diem's overtly pro-Catholic policies, however, the Buddhists felt threatened enough to organize themselves and form the General Buddhist Association in 1955. In 1963, in direct response to the religious crisis, the Unified Buddhist Church was born. Its political arm, styled the Buddhist Institute for Secular Affairs, continued to operate even after Diem's downfall until April 1966 when it was replaced by the Vietnam Buddhist Force. The position of the Buddhist associations vis-a-vis Communism and Communist regimes was one of absolute neutrality, neither praise nor condemnation. In fact, they did not take sides in the ongoing conflict in South Vietnam until the Government blatantly acted against the Buddhists in 1963.

Even more than President Diem, one of his brothers, the Catholic Archbishop Ngo Dinh Thuc, deliberately antagonized the Buddhists. Since the exodus of nearly a million Catholics from the North to the South in 1954, the Government had favored the Christian minority, not only through programs of rehabilitation of refugees but by giving preferred positions in government to them. They certainly held more positions in civil as well as military services than their numbers, estimated at 2,200,000 (10% of the population), warranted. During the French rule, the Catholics had got used to receiving a preferential treatment. Percentage-wise, more of them spoke and read French than any other community; they were more sophisticated and better organized through their churches. They had shown inveterate hostility toward the Communists and the Viet Minh before 1954 and the Viet Cong after 1960. As such, they were the natural allies of the pro-West, anti-Communist Diem regime. Being co-religionists of the Diem family in power, there flowed even greater advantages to them. A French Catholic publication, *Informations Catholique Internationales,* averred in March 1963, that it was because of Archbishop Ngo Dinh Thuc's efforts that the missionaries had found it easy to baptize entire villages collectively. With official help the Archbishop built a spectacular center, "our Lady of La Vang," thirty kilometers south of the seventeenth parallel. Government officials irrespective of their faith were compelled to donate funds to the center. For example, lottery tickets in support of the center were sold by policemen, who made drivers of public and private vehicles to buy them in lieu of payment for traffic offenses.

If the people in South Vietnam were looking for some divine indication that Diem had forfeited his mandate to rule the country, a clear sign appeared in Spring 1963. On May 7, Archbishop Ngo Dinh Thuc forbade the display of Buddhist flags in Hue to commemorate the birth of the Buddha and banned the general festivities as well. As a result, 3,000 would-be celebrants stormed a radio station and demanded that they be allowed to broadcast a program in honor of the Buddha. What the crowd received in response was tear gas and shooting in which nine persons lost their lives

To protest the Government's action, the Buddhists launched a series of self-immolations, beginning with Thich Quang Duc, a venerable monk, who poured gasoline over himself and set fire in the full view of the public. A few weeks later, the celebrated Vietnamese novelist, Nhat Linh, who was to be tried for opposition to the Diem Government, committed suicide by taking poison. Such acts of supreme sacrifice symbolized the general frustration among the people, bringing masses of people closer as equals against a common tyranny. The self-immolations persevered as the Government refused to negotiate.

Madame Nhu publicly ridiculed the sacrifices as a "barbecue of bonzes" while her husband, Ngo Dinh Nhu, ordered the police to raid the pagodas. The press and television coverage brought the magnitude of the Government's injustice and callousness as well as the sacrifices of the Buddhist bonzes to an international audience. While the Confucianists had theorized on a possible rebellion against those who had lost the mandate of heaven, the Buddhists now provided an emotional and spiritual platform to bring down an oppressive government.

United States' Policy and Diem's Assassination

The Buddhist crisis exposed the excesses of Diem's rule to the world. It also changed official American views of the merits of his administration. So far, the U.S. had been totally impervious to Vietnamese opposition to Diem, viewing the conflict exclusively as an extension of the clash between the forces of freedom and Communist totalitarianism. The U.S. had perceived the problem as being more military than political. In the Diem era, seventy-five percent of U.S. economic aid provided to South Vietnam was used to bolster the country's military budget. Not until 1961 was U.S. influence brought to bear on the Diem Government to redress socio-economic imbalances which would improve the hopes of the masses for a better future. Such a belated change in policy yielded no positive results; it only helped to estrange the relationship between the U.S. and the Diem Administration. The misplaced emphasis on military outlay is best indicated by the fact that a twenty-mile highway between Bien Hoa to Saigon, used mostly for military purposes, absorbed more American funds than all the aid provided for social welfare and education programs in South Vietnam during 1954–1961. Even in late 1961, despite the evidence generated by its own agencies to the contrary, the U.S. perceived the conflict in South Vietnam mainly in terms of aggression by North Vietnam. A White

Paper entitled *A Threat to the Peace* blandly stated:

> The determined and ruthless campaign of propaganda, infiltration, and subversion by the Communist regime in North Viet-Nam to destroy the Republic of Viet-Nam and subjugate its people is a threat to the peace. The independence and territorial integrity of that free country is of major and serious concern not only to the people of Viet-Nam and their immediate neighbors but also to all other free nations.[11]

This was despite the fact that only a month before the publication of that document, a National Intelligence Agency Report of October 5, 1961, had placed the Viet Cong strength at less than 17,000 men, adding that eighty to ninety percent of them were Southerners. It had added that the Viet Cong were hardly dependent upon outside assistance.[12]

U.S. military commitment to Vietnam was raised sharply thereafter. During the Kennedy administration itself the number of American military "advisers" went up from several hundred to 16,500 men. Socio-economic reforms and nation-building were, indeed, considered important objectives but were subordinated to the immediate task of liquidating the "subversion." From mid-1963, however, American support of Diem rapidly declined because of the latter's intrasigence toward the Buddhist majority. The Ngo brothers wanted American aid, equipment and troops but no American advice on how to handle the Buddhist question, which they regarded as a purely domestic matter.[13] Consequently, the U.S. did not discourage the generals who decided to overthrow the Government and assassinate President Diem and his brother, Nhu, on November 1, 1963.

The liquidation of the Diem regime did not solve any of South Vietnam's basic problems. The political instability worsened with several generals playing musical chairs for power. All of them were pro-U.S. and dependent upon the U.S. to keep them in power. With the exception of General

Duong Van (Big) Minh, who was inclined to establish a "neutral" government with NLF participation, they were all thoroughly anti-Communist, believing that the conflict was first and last a Communist conspiracy hatched in Hanoi. Throughout the decade from Diem's assassination to the withdrawal of American forces from Vietnam in 1973, the U.S. continued to give priority to the pursuit of the war effort, only half-heartedly insisting, after 1966, on democratic trappings like elections, believing that major socio-economic reforms would have to await a successful conclusion of the war.

NOTES

1. For the most elaborate study of the Commission's work, see D. R. SarDesai, *Indian Foreign Policy in Cambodia, Laos and Vietnam, 1947-1964*, Berkeley, University of California Press, 1968.
2. Victor Bator, *Vietnam: A Diplomatic Tragedy*, New York, Oceana Publications, 1965, p. 172.
3. U.S. Senate Committee on Foreign Relations, *Report on Indochina by Senator Mike Mansfield, October 15, 1954*, 82nd Congress, 2nd Session, Washington, D.C., Government Printing Office, 1954, p. 14.
4. President Eisenhower to Bao Dai, February 19, 1955, in *Department of State Bulletin*, XXXII (March 14, 1955), p. 423.
5. Graham Greene in *The New Republic*, May 9, 1955.
6. Dwight D. Eisenhower, *Mandate for Change, 1953-56*, New York, Signet Books, 1965.
7. Douglas Pike, *Viet Cong*, Cambridge, Mass., M.I.T. Press, 1965, p. 76.
8. George M. Kahin and John W. Lewis, *The United States in Vietnam*, New York, Dial Press, 1967, p. 119.
9. Frances Fitzgerald, *Fire in the Lake*, New York, Vintage Books, 1972, p. 18.
10. *Ibid.*
11. U.S. Department of State, *A Threat to the Peace*, Washington, Government Printing and Stationery, 1961, p. iii.
12. *Pentagon Papers*, II, p. 75.
13. David Halberstam, *The Making of a Quagmire*, New York, Random House, 1965, p. 68.

6
The Indochina Imbroglio

The coups and counter-coups producing "revolving door" governments in South Vietnam resulted in further alienation of the government from the people. That was part of the reason the war was going badly for South Vietnam. In April 1964 the U.S. Department of Defense estimated that the South Vietnamese Government controlled 34 percent of the villages as against the NLF's control of 42 percent, with the loyalties of the remaining villages still being contested. The Strategic Hamlet Program had collapsed. The Northern Communists were not far behind in taking advantage of the deteriorating situation in the South. In order to step up the level of guerrilla warfare to the stage of attacking towns and larger army units, Hanoi began to infiltrate large tactical units along the Ho Chi Minh Trail through Laos and Kampuchea into South Vietnam. The United States felt frustrated that its plans to withdraw troops from South Vietnam had to be abandoned in a year when the Presidential elections were due. The U.S. was looking for a pretext to invade the North so as to halt the deteriorating situation in the South. The excuse was provided by the Gulf of Tongking Incident.

In a dramatic nationwide television broadcast on August 2, 1964, at eleven-thirty P.M., President Johnson charged that the U.S.S. Maddox and Turner Joy had been wantonly attacked by North Vietnamese torpedo boats and that the U.S. aircraft had retaliated by bombing North Vietnamese

strategic targets. Three days later, an emotionally-charged
U.S. Congress passed the much-heralded Gulf of Tongking
Resolution authorizing the President to take "all necessary
measures to repel any armed attacks against the forces of
the United States and to prevent further aggression,"[1] a
blanket authority that was in the ensuing years to involve
the U.S. far more deeply than the legislators had envisaged
into the quagmire of the worst war in U.S. history. Armed
with the authority, Johnson sent a force of ultimately half-
a-million to Vietnam to fight in an "undeclared war" without further reference to the Congress. The resolution
remained in force for six years until its repeal in the face of
the mounting anti-war sentiment in the country. As the
Pentagon Papers revealed later in 1968, Captain Herrick,
the local U.S. Commander in the South China Sea, had
informed Washington that there was no direct, visual evidence of any North Vietnamese torpedo attack and that the
Sonar operators may have mistaken "freek atmospheric
conditions" for torpedoes.

Nonetheless, with such a sweeping Congressional authority and a national consensus behind him, Johnson exercised
no restraint in escalating the war. After the NLF's attacks
on the U.S. air base at Pleiku on February 7, 1965, the U.S.
bombing of North Vietnamese military installations and
"staging areas" was undertaken on a regular basis as part of
Operation Rolling Thunder. The Operation's objectives
were to cripple the DRV's economy, reduce the flow of
men and supplies to the South and to force the North
Vietnamese to agree to a negotiated settlement. Such
bombing, however, had very little effect on the progress of
the war and soon became almost an end in itself. North
Vietnam offered very few bombing targets of real strategic
value since its economy was largely agrarian, most of its
sophisticated military equipment coming from Soviet and
Chinese sources. For one-third of the year, during the monsoon season, poor weather conditions obscured the land-
scape and inhibited the efficacy of strategic bombing.

Moreover, the NLF's dependence on North Vietnamese supplies was not absolute; most of the NLF's ammunition was, in fact, obtained by capturing South Vietnamese and American arms depots. The effect of bombing the North was to unite the people there and make them ever more determined to fight "the enemy."

Amazingly enough, by 1965-66, the South Vietnamese government became relatively stable. The premiership of Nguyen Kao Ky, the flamboyant Air Marshal and the presidency of General Nguyen Van Thieu lent an outward semblance of stability. Ky remained in the Government as Vice–President and a real power at least until the Communist offensive of 1968, when a number of his powerful allies in the armed forces were killed. Thereafter, until 1975, the U.S. Government's policy was to strengthen the Thieu Government. During the Ky-Thieu and later Thieu regimes, the people continued to be alienated; the Government never enjoyed the trust and confidence of the people who criticized it in private for its acts of crass corruption and nepotism.

By Spring 1965, U.S. forces in South Vietnam mumbered 45,500; in the next twenty-four months the numbers would rise to a staggering half a million.[2] Corresponding U.S. estimates of "V–C" were 160,000 in Spring 1965 and 250,000 two years later. The U.S. military strategy was to "search and destroy" the enemy in the South through a variety of means, including bombing, chemical defoliation, psychological warfare, and counter-insurgency operations. The criterion of success was not how much territory was conquered or brought under control but how many Viet Cong were killed. Consequently unit commanders were compelled to justify previous requests for aerial support by manipulating figures of enemy casualties even if the latter were not matched by actual counts of dead bodies or captured weapons. Discrepancies in the body count were explained by the Viet Cong "practice" of not leaving dead bodies behind. Accounting for weapons was manipulated

by counting caches previously captured but not reported.
At the same time, the U.S. gave massive economic and
military aid to the Saigon government, whose armed forces
numbered nearly one million by the end of the sixties. The
economic aid did not help the countryside. The combined
effect of the military operations in the South was to produce
millions of desperate refugees who flocked to the cities
beyond what their infrastructure would bear.

The inevitable consequence of such a policy coupled with
growing American military presence was the militarization
of South Vietnamese society. The dominance of the armed
forces was evident everywhere. The opportunities available
to military officials for graft and corruption in a U.S.-
funded war were unlimited and had debilitating effects on
the larger society. Black marketing of necessities of life,
smuggling of foreign goods, pilferage from U.S. and South
Vietnamese military bases, foreign exchange racketeering,
substandard performance in military construction jobs
became rampant. A class of *nouveau riche* emerged that
completely undermined the old social system in which
bureaucrat-intellectuals and monks had commanded
general respect.

The effects of the war on the common people were disastrous. In the countryside, many youths either volunteered
or were forced by the NLF to join its military forces. Others
were drafted by the ARVN (Army of the Republic of Vietnam). Still others escaped NLF recruitment or deserted the
ARVN by "dissolving" themselves in the burgeoning population of Saigon-Cholon. American aid to South Vietnam
did not improve the lot of the people there. A substantial
proportion of the American funds went not into agricultural
or industrial development but into the creation of services
for the Americans. Some proportion of the aid, indeed,
went to improving the fighting efficiency of the South
Vietnamese troops but a substantial proportion of it was
used to line the pockets of the generals. A large part of the

economy consisted of a "support" population of secretaries, translators, interpreters, maids, shoeshine boys and
prostitutes, none of whom contributed to economic production of goods. Agriculture suffered because of the paucity
of manpower, bombing raids, defoliation and the general
lack of incentive. Many of the unfortunate migrants in cities
remained unemployed or found themselves in the army or
became beggars or pimps, or mafia underlings or joined
street gangs. A large segment of the population came to
depend on the continued influx of the U.S. aid. Tempted by
the lures of city life and fast money or simply due to
economic necessity, young girls migrated to Saigon or to
the periphery of American military bases to become prostitutes. According to a 1975 World Health Organization estimate Saigon alone had about 400,000 prostitutes, making
the city, in the words of Senator William Fulbright, a huge
brothel. Small boys, in thousands, touted as pimps or
homosexual objects. The city's population expanded from
the pre-war two million to over seven million, placing an
unbearable strain on the city's infrastructure.

In terms of human costs the figures up to August 1971
were: 335,000 civilian dead, 740,000 wounded; five million
refugees in Vietnam besides one million in Laos. By 1975,
there were an additional four to five million (two-thirds of
the country's total population) refugees in Kampuchea
alone. As of December 31, 1971, the U.S. armed forces had
lost 45,627, besides 302,896 wounded; the South Vietnamese army lost 137,000 with three times that number of
casualties. According to the U.S. estimates, the NLF lost
788,000 which, in the words of McNamara, included "unarmed parties and bystanders."[3] By 1971, the U.S. had
spent over 150 million dollars, averaging more than 300,000
dollars per NLF member killed. An MIT study pointed out
that the costs of the war, including future payments to vete-
rans, equalled the entire gross national product of the
U.S. —over 750 billion dollars in 1971.

United States Disengagement

The realization of the futility of the war in Vietnam came to a number of high Government officials as early as 1967, though such were then in a minority. The American mentality refused to accept defeat or acknowledge that their tremendous superiority on land, water and sky in sophisticated weaponry was ineffective in the face of a poorly-clad, poorly-fed and poorly-equipped "Viet Cong," who were determined to sweep their land clean of foreign intruders once and for all regardless of the sacrificial costs. It took a long time for the United States generals trained in conventional warfare to realize the socio-political implications of a guerrilla warfare and the frustrating inability to crush a "people's war."

Among the high U.S. officials who began questioning the purposes of the war and America's role in it was the Defense Secretary, Robert McNamara. In a memorandum dated May 19, 1967, McNamara stated:

> The picture of the world's greatest superpower killing or seriously injuring 1,000 noncombatants a week while trying to pound a tiny backward nation into submission on an issue whose merits are hotly disputed is not a pretty one.

McNamara resigned in March 1968. His successor, Clark Clifford, soon came to a similar conclusion:

> I was convinced that the military course we were pursuing was not only endless, but hopeless. A further substantial increase in American forces would only increase the devastation and the Americanization of the war and thus leave us even further from our goal of peace that would permit the people of South Vietnam to fashion their own political and economic institutions.[4]

Such discordant voices in the American administration had been preceded by a nationwide student concern. By 1968, an election year, the anti-Vietnam war protest movement had widened to include most of the intellectuals, and created a severe rift in the Democratic Party's ranks. After the war's initial benefits to the U.S. economy, deterioration in economic conditions had set in. Recession, growing unemployment and a declining dollar boosted public clamor to end the "dirty war." Both sides in the Vietnamese war kept an eye on the U.S. political situation. North Vietnam and the NLF's decision to launch a major offensive on all the main cities and towns of South Vietnam around the time of the Tet festival (January 1968) must have been taken with a view to exploit the American electoral politics. The attack would be followed by negotiations in which the Americans would be at a distinct disadvantage.

The Tet Offensive produced a military stalemate, though it did have a tremendous impact on American politics. The NLF was not successful in holding any of the cities and towns except Hue and that too only for a short period. The NLF's expectation that the Tet Offensive would inspire major popular risings in its favor all over urban Vietnam did not materialize. Its losses were heavy, about 40,000 killed, with many more casualties. The impact of the offensive on U.S. and South Vietnamese forces was disastrous. In Washington, a major debate on the potential costs of continuing the war took place based on the assumption that only a quarter of North Vietnam's forces were involved in the Tet Offensive. From that point on, the U.S. seemed resolved to disengage from Vietnam "with honor." Bombing and other forms of warfare would be continued to secure the best terms in the ensuing negotiations. An immediate result of all this was President Johnson's decision not to seek office again. By the end of the year, the former "Cold War" hero, Richard Nixon, was elected to the presidency on a platform of "end the war and win the peace" in Vietnam.

From 1969 to the signing of the Paris Accords in January 1978, the U.S. followed, albeit with some modifications, the "Two Tracks Plan"[5] of Henry Kissinger, Nixon's

National Security Advisor and later, U.S. Secretary of State. While the U.S. and the DRV would negotiate a military settlement of the war, the Saigon Government would seek a political accommodation with the NLF. While American forces would be gradually withdrawn, a greatly expanded ARVN armed and supplied by the United States would bear the brunt of the fighting. This was dubbed "Vietnamization." The ARVN soon attained a strength of over one million men, including eighteen- and nineteen-year-old draftees, making the Government even more unpopular among the poor peasant population while the large numbers of city-bred people managed to escape the draft through bribery or influence. The greater flow of American monetary aid only helped to further worsen the social situation.

On the larger plane, Nixon promulgated a new Doctrine in May 1969 to limit America's role in future Vietnam-type situations. The U.S. response to aggression which did not involve one of the nuclear powers would thereafter be "to provide elements of military strength and economic resources approximate to our size and our interests," and to regard the "defense and progress of other countries" as "first their responsibility and second, a regional responsibility."[6] The new policy was also based on rapprochement with China, which seemed eager to grasp the American hand of friendship progressively in the hope of using it against the Soviet Union. A Chinese undertaking not to attack Taiwan precipitately and to tolerate an American presence in Vietnam on the same reduced level as in South Korea were allegedly agreed upon during Nixon's visit to Beijing in February 1972. Beijing's own interest in leaving Vietnam divided fitted into traditional Chinese policy of weakening its neighbors, whether Communist or not.

The Plan for "gradual" withdrawal of U.S. troops was not achieved without further bloodshed. Efforts to make the operation compatible with the achievement of "peace with honor" involved resumption of more saturation bombing of

North Vietnam (which had been halted by President Johnson) and of South Vietnam and mining of Haiphong harbor
to stop Soviet supplies reaching North Vietnam. From 1970
to 1973, the Vietnamese conflict became truly an Indochina
war. Its implications were grave. The bombing of Laos and
Kampuchea was undertaken to strike at Communist bases
and supply routes from North to South Vietnam passing
through those countries. The large-scale invasion of
Kampuchea in 1970 was aimed at capturing the alleged
underground headquarters of the Central Office of South
Vietnam (COSVN). It was not found. A large number of
peasants were killed in these operations, causing millions of
refugees from the countryside to flock into Kampuchea's
capital of Phnom Penh, contributing to the swelling of its
population from half a million to four million equal to half
the country's entire population. The bombing during
Nixon's first two years, aimed at securing peace, surpassed
the total tonnage dropped by the U.S. in Europe and the
Pacific during World War II. In May 1972, the daily costs of
bombing were estimated at twenty million dollars.

Kampuchea Since Geneva

Sihanouk's Leadership

Kampuchea (formerly Cambodia) was the most successful of the three Indochinese states in achieving a national
integration and preserving its independence despite the
fires of war raging around it. The success could, in a large
measure, be attributed to the magnetic, complex personality of Norodom Sihanouk who was the country's king at
the time of French withdrawal in July 1954. He abdicated
the throne in favor of his father in March 1955 but led the
country's Government until his sudden overthrow in 1970.
Wielding untrammeled power and unparalleled popularity
in his kingdom, the cherubic-faced, dynamic prince amazed

foreign observers by his flamboyant style of diplomacy that saved his small country from serious entanglement in the nearby holocaust. His domestic success in the fifties and sixties was due at least partly to the traditional Khmer reverence for their divine monarchs and Sihanouk's track record of intense patriotism.

Kampuchean foreign policy during the Sihanouk Era could be summarized in one phrase: the struggle for survival as an independent state. Wedged between traditional foes on either side—Vietnam and Thailand—independent Kampuchea was fearful and apprehensive of aggressive intentions on the part of its neighbors. In April 1955, at the Afro-Asian Conference at Bandung, thanks to Nehru's mediation, Sihanouk received from China and the DRV adequate assurances of non-interference in the affairs of his country. Thereafter, Sihanouk adopted neutrality in foreign affairs as a "dictate of necessity."[7] Until the early 1960's, he alternated between pro-West and pro-Communist policies. By the mid-sixties, however, he became convinced that the future lay with China as the regional power while the United States' interest in the region and ability to control it were limited and transient; secondly, that the North Vietnamese and NLF represented the winning side in the Vietnam conflict and, therefore, potential neighbors of Kampuchea. Consequently, friendship with Chinese and the Vietnamese Communists became the anchors of Kampuchea's foreign policy, though the Kampuchean leadership trusted neither of them. Sihanouk was additionally suspicious of the Vietnamese for their traditional expansionism at Kampuchea's expense. Further, he was apprehensive of Communists, in general, be they Chinese or Vietnamese, in whose eyes a feudal prince would be a logical candidate for political liquidation. Yet, Sihanouk knew that friendship with China could be used as a lever against the Vietnamese, who were historically suspicious of their northern neighbors. Sihanouk thus followed the Kautilyan foreign policy dictate of befriending one's enemy's enemy.

Vietnam Conflict and Kampuchean Neutrality

Since Kampuchea's principal concern was to safeguard her national integrity, she trowned upon violations of her frontiers by Communists and non-Communists alike. In 1964-65, exasperated by frequent frontier incursions by American and South Vietnamese forces in pursuit of guerrillas, Sihanouk severed diplomatic relations with the United States. In the following years, however, the Communist use of Kampuchean territory increased. The American bombing of North Vietnam and of the Ho Chi Minh Trail passing through Southeast Laos had made it necessary for North Vietnam to seek alternate routes of supply. The Ho Chi Minh Trail was extended to Northeast Kampuchea, which lay beyond the American bombing zone. More significantly, the Communists used the facilities of the new port of Sihanoukville to bring in supplies and materiel from North Vietnam and China. These would be transported by profit-seeking Chinese entrepreneurs in Phnom Penh to the eastern provinces, where the Communists had built underground storage facilities. As the war expanded, the Communists occupied larger chunks of Kampuchean territory, using them as sanctuaries allegedly for about twenty percent of their forces.

There is no doubt that the Communists badly needed the sanctuaries and would hold them with or without Sihanouk's consent. Recognizing the "inevitable," the Kampuchean Prince strove to keep Communist occupation to a limited area by obtaining their promises of self-restraint. To maintain some degree of control over the Vietnamese Communists, Sihanouk recognized the NLF, allowing it to maintain a legation in Phnom Penh.

The Communists abandoned such restraints towards the end of 1968. The area of the sanctuaries under Communist use and control increased. Well-staffed hospitals, extensive training camps and ammunition manufacturing facilities replaced the rudimentary structures of earlier days. The Communists established an almost complete administration in the area even collecting taxes and growing crops. By the beginning of 1969, varied accounts, Kampuchean and American, placed the estimates of Communist troops in the sanctuaries at 40,000 to 50,000. The American intelligence further claimed that the headquarters of the guerrilla movement, COSVN, was itself based in the sanctuaries well within Kampuchea's borders.

The Khmer Rouge

Of immediate concern for Sihanouk's government was the increase in the activities of the *Khmer Rouge*, the Kampuchean Communists. In 1954, because of Sino-Soviet pressures at Geneva, the Viet Minh had abandoned the cause of the *Khmer Rouge*, agreeing that it be disbanded and that its cadres retreat to Hanoi. Consequently, about 5,000 *Khmer Rouge*, later labeled "Hanoi Khmers," withdrew to North Vietnam. A few radicals, styled the "Khmer Viet Minh," were decimated by Sihanouk's government. The radical ranks were later reinforced by younger and newer leaders like Ieng Sary, Khieu Samphan, Hou Yuon and Saloth Sar (later known as Pol Pot),[8] mostly trained in law or economics. In contrast with the Hanoi based *Khmer Rouge*, many of whom were married to Vietnamese women, the new breed of Kampuchean Communists (also known as *Khmer Rouge*) were nationalist Communists, fiercely anti-Hanoi, and independent of the ICP (Indochina Communist Party). They claimed that the Kampuchean Communist Party was born in 1960 instead of 1951 when the ICP was split and separate national parties of Vietnam, Laos and Kampuchea were created. This was to show their resentment of the ICP. The new *Khmer Rouge* never forgot nor forgave the Vietnamese Communists for their "betrayal" in 1954.[9] In the late sixties, contrary to Hanoi's wishes, the new *Khmer Rouge* conducted *maquis*-type operations against Sihanouk's government.

Sihanouk was not privy to the internal dispute between the *Khmer Rouge* and the Vietnamese Communists. In

January 1970, he went abroad, ostensibly for medical treatment of chronic obesity but really to try to bring diplomatic pressure on Hanoi to restrain the *Khmer Rouge*. During his absence in March 1970, his Prime Minister, General Lon Nol, staged a coup deposing him. While Sihanouk was on his way home via Moscow, he learnt of the coup. He proceeded to Beijing, accepted asylum in China, heading the Government-in-exile. In a book written from exile, he blamed the CIA for his ouster.[10] The *coup* delivered the Prince, who was still immensely popular in Kampuchea, to the Communists who made him the nominal head of the *Khmer Rouge* drive to capture power in the country.

Meanwhile, the U.S. withheld support from the Lon Nol regime for a "respectable" period of five weeks. Thereafter the Nixon administration stood stolidly behind the Lon Nol government with plenty of military assistance to fight the *Khmer Rouge*, who had, by April 27, 1970 blocked five out of the seven approach roads to the capital. Washington used its new leverage with Phnom Penh for enlarging the Vietnam conflict. In a gross reversal of his policy of withdrawal from Vietnam, Nixon decided on April 30 to invade Kampuchea and capture the COSVN, which he described as "the headquarters for the entire Communist military operation in South Vietnam." The official explanation was that one such decisive victory would tilt the balance and compel Hanoi and the NLF to agree to a political settlement at the Paris talks.

The United States' action, indeed, fueled a civil war in Kampuchea, a "gentle land" which had so far been an oasis of peace in the midst of the holocaust in neighboring Laos and Vietnam. As for the military value of the adventure, it was very limited; large caches of ammunition were found but not the COSVN itself.

The Paris Accords, 1973

The Paris Accords finally signed by the four parties concerned — the DRV, the Provisional Revolutionary Government (PRG), the Governments of South Vietnam and the United States — on January 27, 1973 brought about a cease-fire in Vietnam, Kampuchea and Laos. The Accords provided for withdrawal of all American troops, the return of prisoners of war, a cease-fire in place without demarcation lines. A democratic solution for the South was envisaged. The PRG and the Thieu Government were to resolve their conflicts through mutual consultation. A Council of Reconciliation and Concord was to be established for organizing elections in the South. Thereafter, a tripartite coalition government of Thieu, the PRG, and neutralists would be established. Reunification of Vietnam could be considered through subsequent consultations between the North and the South. As for Laos and Kampuchea, the Paris Accords confirmed the provisions of the Geneva Agreements of 1954 and 1962. An unwritten clause of the Accords was an alleged U.S. undertaking to pay 3.2 billion dollars toward the reconstruction of North Vietnam ravaged by U.S. bombing. The sum was never paid. Hanoi's march into Saigon in April 1975 had, in Washington's view, absolved the U.S. of that promise.

The Accords brought a Nobel Peace Prize jointly to Le Duc Tho, chief North Vietnamese negotiator (who did not accept it) and Henry Kissinger but no real peace to the states of Indochina. The three Vietnamese parties to the Accords viewed the agreement as a temporary truce, giving all of them time to prepare for the final phase of the conflict. The Accords had implicitly allowed the DRV to station about 140,000 troops in the South until a political solution was reached. The cease-fire left South Vietnam with pockets of territory under PRG rule. The withdrawal of U.S. forces left the South exposed to an eventual invasion by the North.

Communist Victory in Vietnam and Kampuchea

Following the Peace Accords, all three Vietnamese

parties—the PRG, DRV, and Thieu — broke faith. Thieu asked for immediate withdrawal of DRV troops as a prerequisite to elections. Neither the DRV nor the PRG had ever acknowledged the presence of North Vietnamese troops in the South. Thieu would not allow the PRG candidates freedom of movement for campaigning. War was resumed by the end of the year as Thieu mounted a new offensive against the PRG-held areas. The level of military operations was, on the whole, low-keyed on all sides, however, because of the reduced levels of external support from the U.S., China and the Soviet Union. The sudden decision of the DRV to launch a major offensive in March 1975 was not expected to yield quick results judging from the surprise expressed after the "fall" of Saigon on April 30. The DRV's gamble was perhaps predicated on the military weakness of the Thieu Government caused by reduced U.S. aid and the perception that the Ford administration would be incapable of any retaliation because of the post-Watergate American political environment and the lack of will to fight in Vietnam. The gamble paid off. Thieu's order to his army in the Central Highlands to make a "tactical retreat" ended up in a disastrous disarray and defeat. Thieu resigned on April 21 and left the country. A government established under the neutralist General Duong Van Minh, surrendered to the Communist forces on April 30. It was a victory for the bulk of the Vietnamese people, who had fought long for this moment. In recognition of Ho Chi Minh's contribution to the movement, Saigon was renamed Ho Chi Minh City.

Meanwhile, in Kampuchea, the *Khmer Rouge* had continued its guerrilla operations against the Lon Nol regime. The *Khmer Rouge* ranks were not, however, united. In the early 1970's, Hanoi had sent to Kampuchea about 5,000 *Khmer Rouge* who had lived in North Vietnam since 1954. These "Hanoi Khmers," as they were disparagingly called by the indigenous *Khmer Rouge* under Pol Pot's leadership, were expected to control the latter and inhibit their love of independence and desire to frustrate the long-term North

Vietnamese ambitions to dominate all Indochina. After the Paris Accords of January 1973, conflict developed between the "Hanoi Khmers" and the home-grown *Khmer Rouge* in which large numbers of the former were purged or killed by the Pol Pot group. The *Khmer Rouge* did not comply with Hanoi's urging to lay down arms as stipulated in the Paris Peace Accords. Even though Hanoi cut off all further military assistance, the *Khmer Rouge* continued with the offensive, bringing down the Lon Nol regime, a fortnight before Hanoi's victorious march into Saigon. The new government formally named the country Kampuchea.

Reasons for the American Failure in Vietnam

The U.S. debacle in Vietnam can be attributed primarily to the incorrect diagnosis of the reasons for the insurrection. The conflict was not as much pro-Communist as it was anti-Diem and later anti-Ky and anti-Thieu because of their failure to initiate and implement the much-needed political and socio-economic reforms. The movement began with southern initiative and was primarily manned and supported by Southerners and not by Hanoi, as Washington wrongly perceived. The conflict had to have a political, not a military, solution, possibly satisfying a widespread urge to reunify the country.

The infusion of massive American military aid had the effect of fueling the inflation. The economic aid was not substantial. Moreover, as much as forty percent of the economic aid, according to the *New York Times* estimate, was swallowed by corrupt contractors, high administrators, generals, business intermediaries and government officials. American supplies meant for the war effort were pilfered on a gigantic scale. As a former Premier, Nguyen Cao Ky, wrote in 1976: "In Qui Nhon market, you could buy anything from army rations and clothing to washing machines and grenades ... and if you wanted to buy a tank or a helicopter it would be arranged."[11]

The infusion of American military manpower had an even worse effect—the specter of alien forces on Vietnamese soil revived anti-colonial, nationalist sentiment. The Second Indochina War was as much directed against the American presence as was the first against the French colonial rule. The Vietnamese rightly perceived that it was because of U.S. support that several corrupt, self-serving discredited military dictatorships had survived in Saigon for a decade and in Kampuchea for half a decade, contributing to social and moral decay, spiralling inflation and devastation of the countryside. The NLF's ranks swelled after 1964 to include large numbers of non-Communist university students and faculty and professionals who seemed, like their forefathers at the turn of the previous century, to be gripped by the fear of "losing their country". The U.S. failed in the early years to insist on socio-economic reforms or liberalization of the political process. Its policies failed to create among the South Vietnamese people a stake in the country's independence and a desire to support the central government. The failures of the Diem regime were basic; the momentum lost during that time was never regained. The postponement of socio-political reforms until the end of the military conflict and the characterization of that conflict itself in Communist-anti-Communist terms was fatal.

NOTES

1. John Galloway, *The Gulf of Tongking Resolution*, New Jersey, Associated University Press, 1970, pp. 36-37.
2. The U.S. was helped by token forces from its allies: New Zealand (500), Australia (7,000), the Philippines (no combat troops, only a hospital corps and an engineer battalion), South Korea (10,000), and Thailand (2,500).
3. *Pentagon Papers*, New York, Bantam Books, 1971.
4. Clark Clifford, "A Vietnam Reappraisal," *Foreign Affairs* (July 1969), p. 612.
5. John S. Stoessinger, *Henry Kissinger: The Anguish of Power*, New York, W.W. Norton, 1976, pp. 51-52.
6. For an analysis of the U.S. policy of the time, see Stephen P. Gilbert, "Implications of the Nixon Doctrine for Military Aid Policy," *Orbis*, *XVI*, 3

(Fall, 1972), pp. 660-681. Also, *U.S. Foreign Policy for the 1970's: A New Strategy for Peace, A Report to the Congress by Richard Nixon, February 18, 1970*, Washington, D.C., Government Printing Office, pp. 55-56.

7. Norodom Sihanouk, "Cambodia Neutral: The Dictate of Necessity," *Foreign Affairs*, XXXVI (July 1958), pp. 582-586.

8. For short biographies of the eight most prominent members of the *Khmer Rouge* High Command, see John Barron and Anthony Paul, *Murder of a Gentle Land: The Untold Story of Communist Genocide in Cambodia*, New York, Reader's Digest Press, 1977, pp. 43-45.

9. Pol Pot's speech, September 28, 1977, *BBC Summary of World Broadcasts*, October 3, 1977.

10. Norodom Sihanouk, *My War With The CIA*, Harmondsworth (England), Penguin Press, 1973.

11. Ky, 1976, p. 108.

7

The New Vietnam

Legacy of the War

Few countries in the world can claim to have suffered as much as Vietnam did since the end of the World War II period. Continual conflict from 1940 to 1975 with only a brief period of peace following the Geneva Settlement of 1954 has marked its recent history. Millions of Vietnamese children grew up to adulthood in that period carrying memories of bloodshed, terror, bombing, dislocation— man's inhumanity to man. Vietnam occupied the front page of newspapers and figured prominently in other media consistently for years, more than any other single country or event. The Vietnamese conflict divided public opinion all over the globe more particularly in the United States whose social, political and economic fabric was rudely shattered by the long "undeclared" war. The spectacle of a small, wiry people with far less sophisticated weaponry than their opponents and with hardly any use of air power, immobilizing the most advanced, militarily best-equipped nation in human history questioned the very basis of strategic defense in the modern world.

The loss in human lives was staggering. Eight million tons of bombs, four times the tonnage used in World War II, had been rained on a tiny country. Ten million gallons of a chemical, Agent Orange, had been sprayed in order to destroy the green canopy of a lush green country. The U.S.

spent nearly 150 billion dollars, lost 57,000 lives with several times that number maimed or disabled for life; the figures for the Vietnamese on both sides of the conflict are unavailable but are roughly estimated at over two million casualties. The disruption of normal life was spread over decades for some, but at least for a decade for the nearly five million refugees from the countryside who flocked to major cities for protection. Saigon became a cesspool of vices where a large segment of the non-combatant population busied itself in corruption of diverse sorts. Human morality and values seemed to lay in irreparable ruins all over South Vietnam. It was, therefore, a great relief for millions of people to see the end of the long drawn out Vietnamese conflict in 1975. The end of the war and the reunification of Vietnam a year later were hoped to usher in an era of peace and reconstruction to a war-ravaged country.

The Communist leadership in Vietnam has not shown itself as adept in peace and reconstruction activities as in war and revolution. The dismal economic situation in Vietnam since the end of the war in 1975 may, in some substantial measure, be attributable to the particular conditions in the previous decade. The socio-economic legacy of a long, brutal war, the special character of U.S.-subsidized, capitalistic-oriented economy of South Vietnam, a succession of natural calamities like drought and floods from 1976 to 1978, wars with China and occupation of Kampuchea, non-realization of anticipated foreign assistance may all be advanced as factors responsible for lack of success in plans to stabilize the economy and fulfill the expectations of a people, whose primary needs had been denied for decades. The leadership appeared divided between those who stood for ideological purity and would brook no delay in the transformation of South Vietnamese economy to socialism and the pragmatists and moderates who saw no alternative to making concessions, offering capitalistic incentives particularly to boost agricultural production in the South. Consequently, the economic policies vascillated from liberalism in 1975-76 to rigidity during 1976–79, to make way again for limited private trade and manufacturing and practical incentives to farmers. The implications of such a policy of postponing the creation of a Communist society to the morale of revolutionary cadres must, indeed, be staggering.

The adverse impact of the long war on the economy of North Vietnam and on the society and economy of South Vietnam had been incalculable. The war in the countryside had turned South Vietnam, formerly a leading exporter of rice, into an importer of grain to feed a large population that could not attend to agriculture, had been conscripted in the army or had simply fled to urban centers. On the other hand, the war created a false sense of prosperous economy particularly in Saigon and around the American military bases. The vast array of imported consumer goods including shiny automobiles, stereo systems and electrical appliances was subsidized by the United States. The large amounts of external funds pumped into the economy resulted in a galloping inflation, impoverishing the middle class and people with fixed incomes. The only people who seemed to prosper in the U.S.-sponsored "free enterprise" system were smugglers, black marketeers, building contractors, middlemen of all sorts not to mention pimps and prostitutes.

During the Second Indochina War (1964–75), the Southern economy had thus become almost parasitical, dependent on external financing and on purchases by the U.S. armed forces of South Vietnamese goods and services. It became an economy in which more than fifty percent of the gross national product was generated by a service sector almost completely dependent upon a U.S.-funded war and in which imports (equal to 25 percent of the GNP in 1971) were 12 times the exports. The industry accounting for the 8 percent of the GNP was 85 percent dependent upon foreign countries for raw materials and one hundred percent dependent on foreign machines and fuel. Consequently, with the beginning of the withdrawal of American forces from 1971, the service sector suffered grievously, bringing the rate of growth of the GNP in the following four years to about one percent per annum while the population increased by about 3 percent. The subsequent debacle of the Saigon Government burst the economic bubble completely with devastating results for a large number of South Vietnam's population.

The economic situation in North Vietnam too was critical. The losses there due to U.S. "strategic" bombing from 1965 to 1972 were staggering. A United Nations Mission visiting Vietnam in 1976 reported that the entire North Vietnamese economic infrastructure had been blasted out of existence during those seven years. Rail-roads had been thrown out of commission for long stretches of several miles on various lines as most of the bridges on the Hanoi-Lang Son and Hanoi–Vinh lines had been blown up. Tongking's dyke system, built over two millennia, suffered grievously as 183 dams and canals and 884 water installations needed major repairs. Twenty-nine of thirty provincial capitals and thousands of villages were damaged, some of them completely destroyed.

Hanoi had, however, taken advantage of the time — about 28 months—that elapsed between the cessation of U.S. bombing of North Vietnam and the Communist victory in the South to restore its infrastructure, including Tongking's intricate and vital dyke system. By mid-1975, the government had repaired or rebuilt the numerous cement and glass enterprises as well as dockyards in the Haiphong industrial sector, the chemical enterprises in Viet-Tri and the steel complex in the Thai Nguyen industrial center. Roads and bridges had also become serviceable again.

The greatest damage in the South had been caused due to its ecological balance. The Report of the U.N. Commission to Vietnam pointed out that chemical warfare had created a large number of "blank zones" in the countryside. The U.S. armed forces had engaged in large-scale defoliation because the thick foliage helped the guerrillas to hide and also obstructed the U.S. aircraft landing. The defoliation operations were undertaken, however, in the name of a "food denial program" to the guerrillas. By 1969, more than 5 million acres of forests and fields had been spread with herbicides, mostly Agent Orange, against forest vegetation and Agent Blue (which had arsenic in its composition) against rice and other food crops. The ruinous impact of these chemicals on the productive abilities of the soil was incalculable. The removal of the jungle canopy increased the exposure of the soil to sunlight which altered the properties of the soil. The rate of soil erosion increased with rapid exhaustion of humus. It was estimated that an equivalent of three decades of South Vietnam's timber supply had been destroyed, and that it would take "anywhere from five years for the fruit trees to a century or so for the rare timber trees to become productive again."[1]

New Economic Measures

After the Communist victory in 1975 the new Government took up the task of reconstruction at all levels: economic, social, political, ideological. The problems it found were truly stupendous. Professor Huynh Kim Khanh summarized the gamut of socio-economic woes of the new Vietnam thus:

> The legacy of the U.S.-Thieu regime was an economic and social *malaise* of unknown proportion: an economy that was on the verge of bankruptcy; a threatening famine in the northern provinces of Central Vietnam; more than three million unemployed people, excluding an army of a half-million prostitutes about to be out of work; six to seven million refugees who had been forced by wartime activities to flee their native villages into cities, etc.[2]

Moreover, fleeing officials and bankers had stolen most of the country's foreign exchange reserves. The new government also had to do something about the former employees of the deposed pro-U.S. Government of South Vietnam. Such included: 1.1 million regular troops in addition to a half-million para-military forces, 125,000 police and 350,000 civil service officials, very few of whom could be relied upon for their loyalties to the Communist regime. Given the ideological context, reconstruction in the South meant not only rehabilitation of urban refugees but relocation and "re-education" of several million individuals, practically one-third to one-half the population of South Vietnam. Another important aspect of the relocation was the large number of handicapped persons from out of an estimated 2.2 million war casualties, some of whom could not be expected to contribute to the rebuilding of the economy at full strength and who, in fact, might need state assistance of some kind or the other for periods of time.

The new government's short-term strategy was twofold: to convert the economy from "free enterprise" to socialist and to integrate the South Vietnamese economy with its Northern counterpart. Its immediate tasks included efforts to restore the industrial capacity of the Saigon-Cholon area and to relocate a large number of its population to the countryside for resumption of agricultural activity. The Government planned an immediate additional employment for over one million people in agriculture and allied occupations by bringing more than half a million hectares of fallow land in the Mekong delta under cultivation. The new slogan in mid-1975 was: "Break with the past, return to the countryside to work for production." As in post-revolutionary China, the new program had its sadistic overtones in compelling the city-bred, soft-lived intellectuals, civil service officials and vast numbers of army officials of the former government "to work with their hands like the rest of the proletariat" in a "re-education" program. Whereas the early Maoists distrusted technology claiming it would be deleterious to socialist values, the Vietnamese had only financial constraints in the use of technology. They perceived no contradiction between the building of a modern economy and of a socialist society, not unlike the thinking of the present-day post-Maoist leaderhip in China itself.

Other short-term measures announced by the government were largely in the area of banking and currency reform. Thus, private banks and other financial and lending institutions were abolished in August 1975. A month later, all individuals and organizations were required to exchange old dong notes at the rate of 500 to 1 for new notes issued by the National Bank of Vietnam. Limits were announced for categories of individuals and organizations in terms of how much of the old notes could be exchanged; the surplus funds were to be deposited in savings accounts. Any large withdrawals had to be sanctioned by the government. The new government thus created at one stroke a large amount of surplus capital for re-investment. The sectors of the society most affected by the new measures were the so-called "comprador-bourgeois" class, mostly merchants, importers and middlemen who had become wealthy by dealing solely with the U.S. and South Vietnamese governments.

Since the new government was socialist and revolutionary, it predictably announced a number of anti-capitalist, anti-West measures. Thus, immediately after the take over of Saigon, the government declared a policy of nationalization of foreign enterprises. It also refused to honor the fallen South Vietnamese Government's debt obligations. Domestically, the government nationalized all manufacturing and industrial activity even though the prospects of success were not very bright because of the lack of raw materials, fuel and above all, American-made spare parts. Only retail trading remained in private hands.

After the initial demonstration of revolutionary zeal, the

Government bowed to the tactical needs of foreign exchange and capital. In 1977, the government announced a number of measures calculated to woo foreign capital. In a reversal of its previous policy, it accepted responsibility for the South Vietnamese Government's debt obligations to Japan and France. Ideological purity was clearly abandoned in favor of pragmatism. The government welcomed outside investment of finance and technology on a joint-venture or production-sharing basis, Vietnam supplying the labor, allowing remission of profits and assuring that the new joint enterprises would not be expropriated. A little earlier Vietnam had joined the International Monetary Fund, unlike most Communist countries (with the significant exceptions of Yugoslavia and Rumania) which had either refused to join the international body or withdrawn from it. Vietnam also joined the World Bank and the Asian Development Bank while remaining only an observer of the Moscow-dominated Comecon International Investment Bank. All these steps softened the attitude of some countries, most particularly, the European Economic Community, Sweden and Japan, who signed economic assistance agreements with Vietnam. Vietnam also made specific efforts to attract capital from non-Communist countries for oil exploration, mining of tin, tungsten, apatite, phosphate and anthracite coal. However, the foreign investment, including that of India, has so far been mostly limited to oil exploration.

Five Year Plans

Despite such handicaps, Vietnam (formally reunited on January 2, 1976) adopted an ambitious "Second" Five Year Plan (1976-80) at the Fourth Congress of the Communist Party. It should be noted that because of the war, the DRV's economic planning had practically been in abeyance since 1965. The Second Plan constituted a hurried revision of a plan originally formulated only for North Vietnam in 1974 and now expanded to include projects for South Vietnam. The process of formulation of an integrated plan for all of Vietnam took some time. Hence the late announcement of the plan in December 1976, allowing only four instead of five years to meet its targets.

Of the projected outlay of 7.5 billion U.S. dollars, at least half the sum was expected to come from outside donors. The Soviet Union promised 2.7 billion and East European countries 700 million. China was expected to contribute 600 million. Vietnam also expected aid from friendly Western countries. More importantly, Hanoi expected the United States to fulfill a "promise" made at the time of Paris Peace Accords to give Vietnam 3.2 billion dollars in reconstruction aid. By the forcible capture of South Vietnam in April 1975, the North Vietnamese had, in American official view, violated those Accords and absolved the United States of that "promise." Vietnam, however, continued to hope that some U.S. assistance would be forthcoming, particularly after the advent of the Carter administration and as a reward for Hanoi's efforts in investigating the whereabouts of U.S. fighting men Missing in Action (MIA's). The U.S. aid never materialized. Assistance from Socialist countries also dropped below expectations or as in China's case, altogether dried up, making Vietnam's foreign exchange problems acute and the prospects of the Plan's implementation bleak.

The Second Five Year Plan's objectives were twofold: to build a material and technological base for the new socialist state and to raise the standard of living of the population. To this end, the Plan proposed a threefold program: reorganization of production in the South along the lines of collectives in North Vietnam, reallocation of labor and implementation of a "correct investment" policy through better economic management.

The Plan combined major agricultural and industrial projects involving large-scale demographic changes. Out of the total planned expenditure of 30 billion dongs, 9 billion were marked for agriculture, 10.5 billion for industry and an equal amount for transportation and services. In the first year of the Plan, 1976, only 3.6 billion would be spent, the subsequent years' allocation being double that amount. The Plan stressed the primary sector of the economy though it aimed also at laying the groundwork for heavy industry. Thus, 30 percent of the total outlay was earmarked for agriculture in the expectation by 1980 of a food production of 21 million tons not including meat and saltwater fish (one million tons each) and other fish and fishmeal (about 450,000 tons). Accordingly, the country was expected, after feeding its population, to have a surplus of three million tons of rice for export.

Most of this agricultural development was to be achieved in the South by reclaiming 2.6 million hectares of land mostly in the Mekong delta. Large-scale collectivization of agriculture was envisaged through the creation of some 250 giant agro-farm collectives, one in each district of South Vietnam, each employing about 100,000 persons in South Vietnam alone. By 1978, before the march into Kampuchea, the Hanoi Government claimed to have established 137 such collectives in South Vietnam. The establishment of such collectives reportedly released some four million people who were then settled in the New Economic Zones (NEZs) in both parts of the country. Additionally, half of the population of Saigon-Cholon Gia-Dinh area as well as from the densely populated Red River delta were relocated in the NEZs particularly on the country's border with hostile Kampuchea. The Economic Plan thus involved demographic relocation on a gigantic scale, not unlike what the Soviet Union and China did after their respective revolutions. The Vietnamese Government also announced plans to remove in the following two decades about ten million people from the country's overcrowded areas to the mountainous zones in the north and west bordering all three of the country's neighbors. From the Red River delta and the central coast alone, about 4 million would be re-settled in the mountainous zone, Mekong delta, eastern coast and offshore islands, particularly the Spratlys.

The concept of organizing the territory into New Economic Zones (NEZs) was not new; it had been earlier adopted in North Vietnam in 1970 creating 23 NEZs in 14 provinces. In the South, however, the motives for the establishment of the NEZs were not purely socio-economic. In the view of a critic, they were primarily aimed at population control thereby facilitating the work of the internal security police and the strategic purpose of peopling the under-populated regions along the country's borders. As economic units, the NEZs would develop centers of light industry, helping to produce articles of consumption not only for the domestic population but also to help exports. In previously sparsely-populated regions, the NEZs would be used for bringing new areas under cultivation.

The plans for industry and commerce matched the pattern earlier implemented in North Vietnam during the First Five Year Plan. Thus, all private enterprises, small and large, in such diverse fields as industry, transport and communications, forestry and construction, fishing and the service sector were newly designated as state-private partnerships. The previous owners were compensated with government bonds and were re-employed by the Government for the management of state-private partnerships. Later, in March 1978, the government took over the retail trade partly by compensating the owners and rehiring many of them as managers of what became now government-owned stores. Another major economic measure was the integration of the currencies of North and South Vietnam in May 1978 by issuing a new currency which became a legal tender throughout the country.

Transport and communications were allocated the same high priority investment as industry. This was, indeed, necessary because the transportation systems had been severely damaged by American and South Vietnamese army's bombing both in the North and the South. The

Second Five Year Plan envisaged repairs to all arterial highways, bridges and ports, particularly Haiphong, which had been the North's principal port for international trade and had been badly damaged by U.S. bombing and mining in late 1972. The wartime road network was to be adapted to peacetime activities; additionally, new major roads would be built connecting the North and South to supplement the old coastal highway.

Failure of the Second Five Year Plan

Vietnam's wars with Kampuchea and China in 1978-79 (see the following chapter) cost Vietnam dearly. The continued occupation of Kampuchea by Vietnamese forces and the state of preparedness on the Sino-Vietnamese border limited the funds that could be more fruitfully spent on developmental programs. These factors adversely influenced the implementation of the Second Five Year Plan. The Central Committee of the Party decided at its Sixth Plenum in 1979 to decentralize the industries as part of the national defense strategy and in the folllowing year, the government formally stepped up the defense expenditure to absorb almost half of the nation's budget. A number of major policy decisions in planning were made altering the government's priorities adversely affecting, for example, the plans for further development of the NEZs and population resettlement schemes.

Vietnam's conflicts with Kampuchea and China were not the only reasons for the failure of the Second Five Year Plan. The Plan had run into major problems almost from the very start. It stands to the credit of the Vietnamese leadership that it openly admitted the gross failure of the Plan and assessed the reasons for the poor performance. The Party's Central Committee's Sixth Plenum in September 1979 and the Ninth Plenum in December 1980 provided a thorough critique. Everything seems to have militated against the successful implementation of the Plan.

Paucity of funds, internal and external (particularly caused by American and Chinese boycotts), was one factor. The Hanoi-based government's lack of appreciation of the socio-economic structure of pre-1975 South Vietnam and the forced pace of changes was cited as another. Many loyalists of the former anti-Communist regimes were actively "sabotaging" the state plans. Thirdly, the Party cadre and officials, who had served the country efficiently and selflessly during the critical war years, were now accused of maldistribution of goods, bureaucratic bottlenecks and widespread corruption. Lastly, three successive years of bad weather, floods and drought had severely affected agricultural output.

In terms of funds, no more than two-thirds of the total planned investment became actually available; loans and grants from abroad fell far below expectations. China granted only loans from 1976 and even those were completely cut off in 1978. The U.S. would not accept responsibility for the alleged promise to grant 3.2 billion dollars in reconstruction aid; the U.S. embargo on trade with Vietnam continued. Even the Soviet economic aid was reduced presumably because the Soviet Union was paying heavily on defense expenditures, an estimated 3 million dollars a day towards Vietnam's military commitments in Kampuchea. As for aid from Western countries, three-fourths of the promised amount was held back after early 1979 because of resentment over Vietnam's march into Kampuchea.

Economic assistance from the Soviet Union has nevertheless played a major role in Vietnamese planned expenditure. Soviet technical assistance has been forthcoming in agriculture, public health, transport and communications, geological explorations and energy. There are nearly 80 Soviet-aided projects in diverse fields like coal mining, electricity, cement, textiles, garments and even planting and processing of tropical medicinal herbs. The Treaty of Friendship and Cooperation signed in November 1978 provided for economic cooperation between the Soviet Union and Vietnam for ten years. A special agreement was signed in July 1980 for offshore drilling for oil. Because of Vietnam's food scarcity problem caused by successive crop failures, some of the Soviet economic aid had to be diverted to supply about 10 to 15 percent of Vietnam's foodgrains requirements. Throughout the Second Five Year Plan and thereafter, Vietnam depended on the Soviet Union heavily for machinery and petroleum requirements. On the fifth anniversary of the Soviet-Vietnamese Friendship Treaty in November 1983, Tran Quynh, Vice-Chairman of the Vietnamese Council of State, wrote in *Nhan Dan* that Soviet aid had been further stepped up "to counter attempts by Vietnam's enemies to paralyze the nation's economy." He indicated that the Soviet Union was supplying 100 percent of Vietnam's fuel and lubricant imports, more than 90 percent of fertilizers and metallurgical products and large quantities of other materials. It is clear that unless Vietnam's foreign policy changes, its economic and military dependence on the Soviet Union will remain precarious.

Vietnam's foreign exchange predicament was further compounded by its export trade lagging far behind the plan's projections of an annual increase of 10 percent. Vietnam's exports in 1980 were only about 15 percent of its imports. Most of its trade has been with Socialist countries, the Soviet Union and Rumania leading the list. Of the non-Communist countries, France and Japan have been the greatest trading partners. Vietnam's principal export is coal, responsible for 95 percent of the total while major imports have included wheat, wheat flour, fertilizers, machinery and oil.

The State Planning Committee's report submitted by Vice-Premier Nguyen Lam in December 1980 revealed that the food production had not kept pace with the increase in population, that severe shortage of raw materials and energy had crippled the industry to about half its capacity and that the per capita income had actually declined during

the Plan period. National income had increased by 9 percent in 1976, by only 2 percent in 1977. In the remaining
years of the Plan, national income actually declined
because of inclement weather conditions affecting agricultural output and the costly wars with Kampuchea and
China during 1978-79. The report stated that during the
Plan period, agricultural output increased only by 18.7 percent and industrial production by 17.3 percent against a
projected *annual* growth of 10 percent. Total area under
agriculture increased by 1.8 million hectares, that under
irrigation by 600,000 hectares. Mechanized ploughing
through use of tractors increased 37 percent. There was an
all-round progress in the production of coal, construction
materials and industries. In no area, however, the planned
targets had been reached. Thus, in 1980 the agricultural
crop was about 12 million tons against a target of 21 million.
Part of the reason for low agricultural production was, indeed, a succession of natural disasters. Droughts, floods,
typhoons (the worst in 35 years in 1978) and harsh winter
had a devastating impact on crops every year of the Plan.
There were, therefore, severe shortages of food. From June
1977, rice was rationed to a level matching the lowest point
of supply in North Vietnam during the war. About 3 million
tons of rice had to be imported annually between 1977-80.
A population growth rate of 2.5 percent and the meager
increases in national income since the reunification of
Vietnam actually lowered the standard of living of the
people.

Part of the reason for the Plan's failure was the inordi-
nate hurry on the government's part to unite the two halves
of the country and transform it into a socialist state. North
Vietnam, which did not have enough qualified management
personnel and technicians, took upon itself to administer a
country suddenly doubled in size, refusing to put trained
South Vietnamese into administrative positions of trust,
technical know-how, and responsibility. The short-sighted-
ness of not fully integrating the South was the key to the

failure of the Five Year Plan. The strategies and plans, originally devised for North Vietnam, were merely extended to the South. The distinct character of the South and its special problems of transition from a U.S.-subsidized capitalistic economy were not adequately taken into consideration.

Economic Liberalization

Realizing the reasons for the failure of the Plan, the Central Committee's Sixth Plenum decided in September 1979 to decelerate the collectivization and cooperativization of agriculture in South Vietnam both because of social resistance to such a process and, more importantly, because it had failed to yield results. After 1979, the government instructed that family farms which were run efficiently should be left alone. Others which had been converted into cooperatives were not to be precipitately taken over by state enterprises. All control stations established to check the movement of goods between rural areas and urban centers, which had virtually become bureaucratic bottlenecks and hunting ground for pilferers, profiteers, bribe takers and black marketeers were abolished. The Party agreed that in some fields of industry and trade private management would be more capable than government control in meeting consumer needs. It acknowledged that there were severe problems in the public sector undertakings: poor management skills, inadequate technological know-how and insufficient worker enthusiasm. The Party, therefore, resolved to rescind the government orders nationalizing private business and trade and restore small-scale enterprises and retail trade to the private sector. Additionally, the Party unhesitatingly adopted the capitalist practice of increasing productivity through manipulation of economic incentives. Workers were given bonuses and other rewards to improve production and to accentuate their morale.

Despite such clear directives, the Plan failed in its last year, 1980, to move the country economically forward. As the Ninth Plenum observed, in December 1980, the failure was owed to bureaucratic reluctance to implement those "capitalist" directives for fear that the creation of a socialist state would be thereby jeopardized. The Ninth Plenum endorsed the Sixth Plenum's resolutions on flexible application of policies. Additionally, it resolved to decentralize management from the central to the local level, clearly defining the rights of major industrial and economic establishments to take their own decisions in most matters including wage schemes, bonuses and worker welfare. Altogether the pragmatic liberalization implicit in the decisions of the Sixth and Ninth Plenums countered the overly rigid and dogmatic tenor of the Fourth Congress of the Party (1976) thereby providing a better base for the Third Five Year Plan.

Government and Politics in the New Vietnam

Reunification

After the Communist takeover of South Vietnam, it was expected that some decent interval would be allowed before the political, economic and administrative integration of the two halves of the country was taken up because of traditional Southern fears of North's domination. To be sure, such assurances had been given by the DRV to the NLF during the protracted war in the South. However, in the wake of the victory in the South, the Northern leadership was overwhelmed by the counter-argument that the reunification and integration of the two halves of the country would be difficult if it were delayed. The South's economic and political interests would be well grounded if given the time. Also, the capitalist and corrupt way of life to which the Southerners were accustomed during the war would have a deleterious effect on the North. Therefore,

within a few months of the "fall" of Saigon, the leaders of
the North and the South decided on political and administrative integration within a year. In April 1976 elections
were held for the National Assembly for all of Vietnam. By
July 1976 the two Vietnams were formally unified, the
DRV dissolved and the Socialist Republic of Vietnam
(SRV) proclaimed with Hanoi as its capital. The NLF was
also disbanded, its numerous mass associations being
integrated into its counterparts in the National Fatherland
Front. The Vietnamese Workers' Party (Lao Dong) was
also dissolved as was the People's Revolutionary Party of
the South. The two were now combined into the Vietnamese Communist Party (VCP) in December 1976. Thus,
the year 1976 witnessed the culmination of the decades-long
dream of the Vietnamese to end the artificial divisions of
their country under the French and since 1954, under the
Geneva Agreements and to unify all the Vietnamese under
a common political banner.

The Party and Government

The Party and governmental structure of the Democratic
Republic of Vietnam was now extended to the Socialist
Republic of Vietnam. As in all Communist countries, two
parallel hierarchies from the highest down to the lowest
levels of the Party and government existed in the DRV, the
Party's Politburo having a primacy over the government
though there was considerable overlapping in their respective composition. The Political Committee of the Party
played the most crucial role. The Party itself grew from
about 1,000 members in 1941 to 5,000 in 1945 to a massive
500,000 in 1953. After the partition in 1954, the Party's
membership was kept relatively stable despite the fact that
several million people—men and women—were later
involved with the long war aimed at the reunification of the
country. The link between the Party and the general public
involved in the "People's War" was provided by numerous

mass associations organized mostly on a functional basis: workers, peasants, students, artistes, women and so on.

The party cadres were mostly recruited by Labour Youth Groups and the Young Pioneers. They were dominated by petit bourgeois and peasant leaders because the total number of factory workers were not large in Vietnam. Besides, the Party functioned for a long time in rural areas where there were hardly any factories, these being located mostly in the cities which were under effective French control.

At the apex of the Party structure is the Politburo, presently consisting of 13 members and one alternate member, all key leaders of the Party. They execute the directives of the Central Committee, a large body of 115 to 120 members and 35 to 40 alternates. The Central Committee meets periodically to initiate and deliberate on Party policies. It draws its authority from the National Congress which meets infrequently, once in several years. Members of the National Congress represent Party organizations at all levels. Between the Party organization and the people stand the mass associations, serving as a link between the two.

The Leadership

The Vietnamese Communist leadership has been a remarkable, distinctive, stable gerontocracy. The average age of the members of the Politburo is a little over seventy. Barring a few purges and those called by death, the leadership remained the same for four or five decades as at the beginning of the 1940's. Thus, Ho Chi Minh, Pham Van Dong, Vo Nguyen Giap and Truong Chinh officiated at the birth of the Viet Minh in 1941. In 1946 the Central Committee of the Viet Minh was expanded to include Le Duan, Pham Hung and Nguyen Chi Thanh. Differences, ideological or otherwise, were not allowed to emerge to the surface, therefore, there were few changes in leadership. A major exception was in 1956 when the Party took note of the failure of the land reform movement and removed Truong Chinh from the post of General Secretary, though he was allowed to remain a member of the Politburo. The post of General Secretary remained vacant until 1960 when Le Duan, a "Southerner," was appointed to it to emphasize the decision of the Party to launch the movement that would end with the reunification of the country. All this does not mean that there was an entire lack of differences among the leaders. During the war, there were, in fact, two major factions led respectively by the strategist, Vo Nguyen Giap and the ideologue, Truong Chinh. There were also those who were influenced by the Sino-Soviet rivalry. Ho Chi Minh (until his death in 1969) and Le Duan thereafter successfully struck the middle path and closed the ranks in the name of the movement for the country's reunification.

Since the passing of Ho Chi Minh, Le Duan held the reins of power (somewhat sharing it with Le Duc Tho after 1976) until his death in mid-1986. Born in 1908 in Central Vietnam, the son of a successful gentry, he obtained a high school diploma which was a substantial level of education in those days. He was a founder member, along with 210 others, at the birth of the Indochina Communist Party in 1930. During World War II and the First Indochina War, he was assigned to the South where he developed an effective Party base which is why he was elected General Secretary of the Party in 1960 when the movement for the liberation of the South was launched. Although he hailed from Central Vietnam, he was regarded a Southerner because of his work there and he generally represented Southern interests in the Politburo in the North. After Ho Chi Minh's death in 1969, Le Duan became the "first among equals" in a system of collective Politburo level leadership, mandated by Ho Chi Minh in his will.

In the aftermath of the war, the Party's solidarity suffered. First of all, the influence of heroes of the final stages of the Vietnam conflict in 1975 as well as of those of the wars in Kampuchea and with China in 1978-79 increased in the Party and the government. There have been at least three major purges since 1975. Five criteria have guided such purges in the last decade: pro-Maoist elements; advocates of softer approach toward China and the *Khmer Rouge*; critics of the management of economy particularly the collectivization program in South Vietnam; corrupt and inefficient Party members; and finally, the opponents of Le Duan-Le Duc Tho leadership of the Party.

At the Fourth Congress of the Party in 1976, four members of the Central Committee and a Politburo member, Hoang Van Hoan, former Ambassador to China and Le Duan's adversary, were purged. Three years later, Hoang defected to China and openly condemned the "Le Duan clique." Also in 1976, Le Duan, under immense pressure from China to choose sides in the Sino-Soviet rivalry, opted in favor of the Soviet Union. The decision led to a purge of several pro-Chinese members of the Party. In 1980, a major Cabinet shake-up involved nineteen changes. The most important of these were: Vo Nguyen Giap, Defense Minister since 1945 and the legendary hero of Dien Bien Phu, was replaced by General Van Tien Dung, the Commander of the Saigon offensive of 1975. Giap continued, however, to be a member of the Politburo and was later put in charge of the much insignificant portfolio of Family Planning. Another change involved Foreign Minister Nguyen Dan Trinh being replaced by Nguyen Co Thach. Le Trong Tran, a Soviet and East Germany-trained general who was also foremost in the 1975 offensive became the Chief of the General Staff. Pham Hung, one of the principal leaders of South Vietnam, replaced Tran Quoc Hoan as Minister of the Interior. Lieutenant-General Le Duc Anh, Commander of the forces in Kampuchea became a member of the powerful and prestigious Political Committee in April 1982. The Chairman of the Planning Commission was removed along with a number of officials in the economic ministries responsible for the lackluster performance of the economy. Such large-scale purges must have sent shivers down the spine of many leaders, some of whom moderated their stand to avoid being eased out. One such was Truong Chinh, who was made the Chairman of the newly-constituted Council of State in 1981.

At the time of the Fifth Congress of the Party in 1982, it was rumored that as many as 500,000 members may have been purged. In order to replace their ranks, a new recruitment drive was taken up involving as many as 325,000, ninety percent of them under thirty years of age, seventy percent being those who had served in the army. The soldiers of the revolution were now expected as Party cadres and leaders to direct peacetime reconstruction. Despite such a policy of infusing fresh blood in the Party, only the Central Committee was allowed to change, as one-third of its members were replaced by young persons drawn from the armed forces. As for the Politburo, it continued to be the old gerontocracy.

In the 1980's, disillusionment with the Le Duan-Le Duc Tho leadership steadily intensified particularly among the provincial-level Party secretaries, younger persons who were frustrated with the massively troubled economy and the military stalemate in Kampuchea necessitating retention of and expenditure on the Vietnamese troops in that country. Considerable soul-searching seems to have taken place particularly during 1985–87 on how best to grapple with inflation, shortages of critical goods, unemployment and, above all, corruption. For a while it looked like the Party was headed for a clear schism between economic reformers within the Politburo like Pham Hung, Nguyen Van Linh and Vo Chi Cong opposing the doctrinaire hardliners like Truong Chinh, Le Duan, Pham Van Dong and Le Duc Tho, who believed in the purity of socialist principles and the correctness of Marxism-Leninism under all circumstances. Within certain limits, the Vietnamese leadership had already compromised and liberated the economy from the old strict controls. It had allowed personal incentives like cultivation of small, kitchen-garden plots by individuals and some amount of retail trading particularly in the South. What was now advocated was a system of production contracts, autonomy of state enterprises and capitalistic modernization along the lines of the experimentation in China, without of course any such attribution. The reformers had, however, to contend with a general preference for adherence to strict Party discipline and avoidance of a crude struggle for power and succession to the old leadership.

Such a sentiment and Le Duan's declining health due to a kidney ailment intensified the movement for change in early 1986 leading to a purge of several high level Party and government officials who were directly responsible for the economic reverses under Le Duan. Among them was Vice-Premier To Huu, Vietnam's Poet-Laureate, who was replaced by reformer Vo Chi Cong. Along with To, six other ministers in charge of finance, domestic and foreign trade and the Governor-General of the State Bank were removed. They were replaced by persons who had established their reputation for being innovative and reformative at the provincial and planning commission levels. In a counter move, in May 1986, a triumvirate of three Politburo members, Truong Chinh, Pham Van Dong and Le Duc Tho took over the duties of the ailing Le Duan who continued nominally to be the General Secretary of the Party. Le Duan died on July 10, 1986 and was officially replaced by the 79-year-old Truong Chinh as General Secretary while still continuing to hold the post of Chairman of the Council of State.

By the end of the year, at the Sixth Congress of the Party, the pendulum of power swung to the other side. The triumvirate of Truong Chinh, Pham Van Dong and Le Duc Tho resigned from the Politburo, marking for the first time in decades, a real shift of power within the Politburo, which with five new entrants, was now led by the reformer, Nguyen Van Linh as General Secretary. The new roster of the Politburo in December 1986 was more heavily weighted in favor of the reformers: Nguyen Van Linh, Pham Hung, Vo Chi Cong, Du Muoi, Vo Van Kiet, Le Duc Anh, Nguyen Duc Tam, Nguyen Co Thach, Dong Si Nguyen, Tran Xuan Bach, Nguyen Thai Binh, Doan Khue, Mai Chi Tho and alternate member, Dao Duy Tung. Renewal and renovation became the new rallying calls of the Party which seemed determined to root out corruption, streamline the administration and genuinely liberalize the economy in a substantial way.

The old guard had not, however, given up their government posts: Pham Van Dong continued in the office of the Prime Minister and Truong Chinh continued to be the Chairman of the Council of State, Vietnam's Collective Presidency. In order to test the rival strengths of the two groups, the Council of State decided, on January 3, 1987, to hold elections to the 496-member National Assembly in April, the third since the reunification of the country. The National Assembly would convene in June and elect the Prime Minister and Chairman of the Council. The struggle for power and moves to arrive at a compromise between the hardliners and reformers continued all through the first half of 1987. One such resulted in a major cabinet shake-up on February 17, 1987 when a hardliner and number two in the Politburo, Pham Hung, was relieved of his charge of the Ministry of the Interior. He continued, however, to be one of the Deputy Prime Ministers. Also removed were eleven of a total of thirty-five ministers.

The elections of the highest officials by the newly-elected National Assembly in June 1987 clearly showed that Vietnam was still far from passing the power to a brand new team of younger persons or entirely to the reformers willing to take risks in tackling the massive economic problems of the country. In a country where Confucian respect for seniority still persists, it was evidently impossible to ignore

the older generation completely. Instead of choosing reformers like Foreign Minister Nguyen Co Thach and Vo
Van Kiet, Head of the State Planning Commission, who are
at least in their sixties, the National Assembly elected a
hardliner, Pham Hung, 75, as Prime Minister in place of
Pham Van Dong, who had been in that post since 1955 and
a moderate reformer, Vo Chi Cong, 74, who had pioneered
pragmatic economic management in the seventies to the
largely ceremonial post of Chairman of the Council of State
replacing Truong Chinh. Even Giap, who had failed to get a
seat in the National Assembly, was made one of the Deputy
Prime Ministers. Vietnam's Party and Governmental hierarchy thus continues to be a gerontocracy.

Vietnam as a Military Power

With a population of 54 million, Vietnam does not figure
among the ten most populous countries of the world. Yet,
in terms of its military strength and proven capability, Vietnam must be ranked among the top five in the world. Even
before the reunification of Vietnam in 1976, North Vietnam
had the best trained army in all of Southeast Asia. At present its regular army numbers about 1.1 million, augmented
from 600,000 in the wake of the border war with China and
occupation of Kampuchea, making it the fourth largest
standing army in the world. Thanks to the naval craft and
military equipment left behind by the United States, Vietnam today has the fifth largest navy and one of the best
equipped armies in the world. Supplied by the Soviet Union
with MiG planes and SAMS, the Vietnamese have a fairly
respectable air capability. What is more important than all
the weapons and numbers of armed personnel is the excep-
tionally high morale of the Vietnamese defense forces, who
have drunk the potion of victory on the battlefield against a
superpower. Hanoi represents the capital of a successful
Communist revolution, potentially capable of becoming in
future the point of inspiration, guidance and assistance to

Communist parties in the other countries of Southeast Asia.

Does Vietnam have the economic capability and political ambition of supporting and leading Communist revolutionary movements in the neighboring countries? What would be a fair prognosis of Vietnam's international role in the next decade or so?

Vietnam's successful march into Kampuchea in a 17-day war that established a pro-Hanoi Government in Phnom Penh as well as the inconclusive war with China have confirmed the long-held view of military analysts of the high morale and efficiency of the Vietnamese military machine. In 1975, before the victory in Saigon, the North Vietnamese forces were estimated by the U.S. Defense Department at 583,000, the air and naval elements being responsible for 14,000 and the bulk belonging to the army. Estimates of the National Liberation Front (NLF) forces have varied by a wide margin; details of their integration into the reunified Vietnam's armed forces are sorely lacking. The usually well-informed London-based International Institute of Strategic Studies (IISS) places their figure at 615,000 (Navy 3,000, Air Force 12,000). These may have been underestimated by at least 100,000. Additionally, there are about 70,000 frontier, coast security, and People's Armed Security forces aside from Armed Militia of about 1.5 million.

The army is organized into 25 infantry divisions plus 2 training divisions, 1 artillery division (10 regiments), 4 armored regiments, 15-20 independent infantry regiments, 35 artillery regiments, 40 AA artillery regiments, 20 SAM regiments (each with 18 SA-2 launchers), with one engineering command. The army's equipment has been plentiful, varied and substantial, thanks to Russian supplies of heavy equipment, China's old supplies of light weapons, and a rich assortment of U.S. hardware that fell into Communist hands in April 1975. The IISS gives the details of equipment of the Vietnamese armed forces in 1978-79 as follows:

900 T–34, T–54 and T–59 med, PT 76, Type 60 1t tks; DTR–40/–50/–60 APC; 75–mm, 76–mm, 85–mm, 100–mm, 122–mm, 130–mm, 152–mm, 155–mm guns/how; SU–76, ISU–1PP, SP guns; 82–mm, 100–mm, 107–mm, 120–mm, 160–mm mor; 107–mm, 122–mm, 140–mm RL; Sagger ATOW; 23–mm, 37–mm, 57–mm, 85–mm; 100–mm, 130–mm towed; ZSU–57–2 SP AA guns; SA–2/–3/–6/–7 SAM.

The Air Force had 300 combat aircraft; one light-bomber squadron with 70 MiG–19/F–6, 70 MiG–21 F/PF; eight fighter bomber squadrons with 120 MiG–17, 30 SU–7. Transports included 20An–Z, 4 An–24, 12 Il–14, 4 Il–18, 23 Li–2 and 20 Mi–4, and 9 Mi–8 helicopters. There were about 30 trainers including Yak–11/18, MiG–15 UT 1/21 U.

An extremely important factor in evaluating the military strength of any country is, apart from its manpower and equipment, the proven fighting performance, discipline and morale of its troops. The Vietnamese score the highest points in all three categories, equalling the best anywhere in the world with a record of successive victories sometimes achieved ahead of schedule. In terms of the present armed strength of Vietnam, however, one has to keep in mind the actual stationing of about 160,000 of its armed forces in Kampuchea and 40,000–50,000 in Laos. Earlier, Vietnam planned to divert substantial numbers of its armed personnel to peacetime reconstruction tasks. Military involvement in Kampuchea and on its own northern borders with China have compelled Vietnam to revise such plans for use of the army in the country's economic development.

NOTES

1. Quoted in Huynh Kim Khanh, "Year One of Post-Colonial Vietnam," *Southeast Asian Affairs, 1977*, Singapore, Institute of Southeast Asian Studies, 1977, p. 290.
2. *Ibid.*, p. 291.

8
Vietnam's International Relations

In the post-Unification period, Vietnam's principal problems in external relations lay ironically with its Communist neighbors. Vietnam's march into Kampuchea in late 1978 and its continued occupation of that neighboring Communist country provides a focal point. Another is provided by the Sino-Soviet feud and the choice made by Vietnam in Soviet Union's favor. It is hard to say whether considerations of regional leadership or partisanship in the global Communist Sino-Soviet rivalry have dominated Vietnamese policies toward Kampuchea and Laos.

With the dramatic Communist victory in South Vietnam and Kampuchea in Spring 1975, and the "silent revolution" that pushed Laos fully into the Communist orbit in December of that year, it was assumed by most of the political observers that the Communists would regard the three victories as the culmination of the "liberation" movements in the Indochinese Peninsula and devote themselves to the tasks of domestic reconstruction. Even those anti-Communists who believed in the two-decades old "domino theory" and saw its practical fulfilment in the "fall' of the three capitals in rapid succession of each other, regarded the phenomenon as peculiarly applicable only to the states of the Indochinese Peninsula because of their common history of French rule. The initial feeling of panic and grave apprehension among the ASEAN states was replaced by the reassurance that there would be more than a "breathing spell" before the new Communist states would be ready or willing actively to assist the fraternal Communist movements in the other states of Southeast Asia. Hardly anyone, not even in the non-Communist world, expected at that time such fissures to develop among the new Communist states as would provoke large-scale interstate warfare culminating in the Vietnamese "blitzkrieg" into Kampuchea at the turn of 1978 and the Chinese "punitive" march across their southern border into Vietnam in February-March 1979. Nor was it expected that the new government of Vietnam would create an atmosphere in which an estimated one million of its people, mostly of Chinese ethnic origin, would prefer to take the risks of a clandestine, financially costly, departure by unsafe boats to indeterminate destinations. The question of the "boat people" aroused global concerns and helped revive tensions in Southeast Asia.

Recent events have also brought to the fore the political interdependence of the three Indochinese states—Vietnam, Laos and Kampuchea. The emergence of Communist regimes in all three countries in the same year, 1975, was no coincidence. The Pathet Lao and a segment of the *Khmer Rouge* had both received assistance from Hanoi, perhaps with the latter's expectation that they would seek guidance and direction after coming to power. Events in Vietnam over the last two decades had partly shaped and overshadowed the political developments in the two other Indochinese states. Are recent events a reflection of a Vietnamese plan to create an Indochinese Federation and a prelude to its domination of the entire Southeast Asian region? Is Vietnam militarily and economically capable of pursuing such alleged goals without external help and without provoking China more than it already has? If Southeast Asian nations lived in the shadow of Communist China for a quarter century, they have been apprehensive since 1975 of the rising power of Vietnam and its regional ambitions.

Vietnam and Kampuchea

Historical Hatred

Vietnam's Southeast Asian neighbors, notably Kampuchea, have reason to suspect Hanoi's expansionism. The
Khmers or Kampucheans, proud inheritors of a glorious
legacy of empire once extending over the southern belt of
mainland Southeast Asia, have historically hated the Vietnamese, who deprived them of the rich Mekong basin in the
eighteenth century and then shared with Thailand the suzerainty over what was left of the Khmer Empire. The French
conquest of Vietnam and Cambodia did not obliterate such
historical memories or fears of Vietnamese aggressiveness.
The prospect of withdrawal of the French in 1954 revived
Cambodian apprehensions. In that year at the Geneva Conference, the Cambodian delegation openly expressed its
fears and suspicions of domination by the Viet Minh, which
had already occupied portions of Cambodia in April 1954.
Cambodian diplomacy during 1954-55 was geared to en-
hancing their country's security against the Vietnamese first
through a military alliance with the United States. Such
moves were aborted quickly after Prince Norodom Sihanouk received assurances of non-interference from the
North Vietnamese Premier, Pham Van Dong, thanks to the
mediatory efforts of Nehru and Chou En-lai at Bandung in
1955. Tensions between Phnom Penh and the Saigon
governments continued all along even after a pro-United
States government was established in Cambodia in 1970
under General Lon Nol. Thus, in the wake of the
"friendly" U.S.-Vietnamese invasion of their country in
1970, Cambodian officials of the Lon Nol government
turned their eyes to the Cambodian massacre of thousands
of Vietnamese civilians on the pretext that they were all
Viet Cong. The hostility was mutual. The South Vietnamese forces treated Cambodia as a "military playground,
with any Kampuchean fair game." According to William

Shawcross, South Vietnamese air force pilots, "until then very lazy, actually paid bribes for the privilege" of flying bombing missions seven days a week over Cambodia.

Suspicions of Vietnamese were not limited to non-Communists or anti-Communists. As early as 1930, the Vietnamese Communists had betrayed their "imperialistic" ambitions. In January of that year, Ho Chi Minh succeeded in uniting the three Communist parties of Vietnam into the Communist Party of Vietnam. Later in October, the Party was renamed the Indochinese Communist Party (ICP) to include Cambodia and Laos, probably to suit Comintern convenience of treating all of Indochina as a national section of the Communist International. Until 1951, when the ICP technically divided itself into three national parties for the practical reason of organizing better resistance against the French, there was no separate Cambodian Communist Party as such. ICP early advocated a federation of Vietnam, Cambodia and Laos after the liquidation of French rule, although subsequently the ICP did pass resolutions leaving it to each nation to decide whether or not to join such a federation. Nevertheless, the Cambodian Communists did not abandon their fear that Vietnam would, by virtue of its size, numbers, educated manpower, economic and military strength, some day compel Cambodia and Laos into such a composite polity under Vietnamese domination.

The Khmer Rouge

Differences between *Khmer Rouge* and Vietnamese Communists originated in 1954 at the Geneva Conference on Indochina. There presumably under the pressure of Moscow and Beijing, which were eager to arrive at a settlement as part of their global policy of peaceful coexistence, the North Vietnamese did not press the cause of *Khmer Rouge* but instead agreed that it be disbanded and that its cadres retreat to Hanoi. The *Khmer Rouge* neither forgot nor forgave the Vietnamese Communists for this "betrayal." About 5,000 of the *Khmer Rouge*, to be later labeled "Hanoi-Khmers," withdrew to North Vietnam; the small band of the radicals that stayed behind, styled "Khmer Viet-Minh," were reinforced by individuals like Ieng Sary, Khieu Samphan, Hou Yuon, Hu Nam, and Saloth Sar (later known as Pol Pot). They had been trained in France, mostly in law or economics, and they organized and fought in the maquis against Sihanouk's government in the 1960's. They were all fiercely anti-Hanoi because of the latter's friendship with Sihanouk who had used force to all but eliminate the *Khmer Rouge* in the late 1950's. The North Vietnamese were quite content with Sihanouk's coopera- tion in allowing the flow of men and materiel along the Ho Chi Minh Trail across Eastern Cambodia and from the port of Sihanoukville (Kompong Som) into South Vietnam and, most importantly, in permitting the establishment of exten- sive secret base camps inside the Cambodian border for the Vietnamese National Liberation Front. By 1969 there were an estimated 40,000–50,000 North Vietnamese and NLF troops in the Cambodian sanctuaries.

This was, indeed, not the first time that a Communist state for tactical reasons and, even more so, for its own national interest, sought and received assistance from a non-Communist government at the expense of a "frater- nal" Communist Party. It was, therefore, only natural that the *Khmer Rouge* distrust of the North Vietnamese would continue even after a tactical alliance between the four regional Communist groupings of Pathet Lao, Lao Dong, NLF, and *Khmer Rouge* was established soon after Sihanouk's overthrow in early 1970. At this point in time, Hanoi needed the *Khmer Rouge's* cooperation in keeping the supply lines to South Vietnam open by harassing the forces of Lon Nol, the United States and South Vietnam in eastern Cambodia. The tension between the *Khmer Rouge* and Vietnamese Communists was such that the former in- sisted on having an upper hand in the operations and that too without Vietnamese manpower assistance. On the other hand, even as the North Vietnamese were contributing substantially to the growth and training of the *Khmer Rouge* during the early 1970's, they did not want the latter to develop independence and the ability to frustrate the long-term North Vietnamese ambitions to dominate all of Indochina. In order to ensure a pro-Vietnamese position, the North Vietnamese sent about 5,000 *Khmer Rouge* kept in reserve by them in Hanoi ever since their withdrawal from Cambodia in 1954. These "Hanoi-Khmers," as they came to be called, clashed with the homegrown *Khmer Rouge* under the leadership of Pol Pot and Khieu Samphan. In 1973, many Hanoi-Khmers were purged or killed by the Pol Pot group.

By 1972 the *Khmer Rouge* numbered well over 50,000, mostly young people, not necessarily Communist, with varying grievances against the U.S.-backed Lon Nol regime. The evidence of their superior training, discipline, fighting power and ability to handle Chinese, Soviet and American weapons supplied to them by the North Vietnamese, was noted in the successive skirmishes with Lon Nol's troops but also in the successful maintenance of the supply lines to South Vietnam. In early 1973 the *Khmer Rouge* were confirmed in their suspicions of the North Vietnamese when the latter repeatedly pressured them to accept a cease-fire that was presumably the precondition for American grant of reconstruction aid to Hanoi. It was the general impression that the *Khmer Rouge* were Hanoi's puppets, which could be made to dance to its master's will. Despite Hanoi's cutting off of military assistance and the U.S. saturated bombardment, the *Khmer Rouge* continued the offensive that brought the downfall of the Lon Nol regime, a full fortnight before Hanoi's victorious march into Saigon.

The *Khmer Rouge* would not easily forget the North Vietnamese subordination of Khmer interests to their own in 1973 in repetition of their previous experience in 1954. Equally, they would not forget the timely, massive military assistance they received from Beijing starting in mid-1974. The Chinese leaders had attempted unsuccessfully to encourage an American dialogue with Prince Sihanouk, who since his ouster in 1970 had been in exile in Beijing. Finally, they threw in their lot with the *Khmer Rouge* and in place of the North Vietnamese became the principal suppliers of automatic weapons, ammunition and mines. This equipment was used in the final siege of Phnom Penh and its capitulation, achieved partly through mining the waterways and cutting off the capital's food supply.

Tension between the *Khmer Rouge* and the Vietnamese Communists continued after the overthrow of the Lon Nol regime in March 1975. In addition, the Kampuchean government remained divided at least into four factions, one of which was certainly—though clandestinely—linked with Hanoi while yet another advocated rapprochement with Vietnam on pragmatic grounds. The government was a coalition, the core of which consisted of the Khmer Viet Minh and the student groups which had produced leaders like Pol Pot, Ieng Sary, and Khieu Samphan. They allied with moderates led by Prince Sihanouk and other non-Communists who were intensely nationalist, suspicious of Vietnamese expansionism, pro-Beijing and favoring rapprochement with the United States. Foremost in their links with Vietnamese Communists were obviously the "Hanoi-Khmers," the ICP group led by Chea Sim, the then minister for the interior. Last was a smaller group who styled themselves constructionists and advocated for pragmatic reasons accommodation with Vietnam. Its leader, Heng Samrin, became the clandestine conduit of top secret decisions of the Phnom Penh government to his allies in Hanoi.

Pol Pot's Regime — The Crisis Deepens

The leadership of the 1975 revolution told the world through Premier Pol Pot's five-hour speech in September

1977 that Hanoi had all along harbored plans to compel Kampuchea into an Indochinese federation as the first step toward its annexation. The Pol Pot regime was certainly justified in attempting every means to avert Kampuchea's conversion to a Vietnamese satellite. But it should have been realistic enough to appreciate the immensely superior Vietnamese military machine and should have, therefore, acted in such a way both domestically and internationally so as not to give an excuse for the alleged Vietnamese expansionism to succeed. As it was, Kampuchea launched the most brutal, insensate, domestic programs which had the effect of dislocating, decimating, and alienating the bulk of the population to the shock and dismay of the entire civilized world. The shocking excesses of the Pol Pot regime amounting to a gross genocide made any aggression by an external power to terminate the horrible condition prevalent in the pre-1979 Kampuchea look less culpable than otherwise. Further, it did create a large exodus of Khmer people into Vietnamese sanctuaries in Eastern Kampuchea spilling into Vietnamese borders where they could be organized by the Vietnamese into an alternative rallying point for overthrowing the anti-Hanoi Pol Pot regime. And internationally, instead of playing the Vietnamese against the Chinese so as to maximize their own diplomatic maneuverability, the Phnom Penh government chose to adopt adventurist policies which were certain to provoke Vietnam to an eventual showdown. First, they took the initiative to attack the border provinces, beginning in April 1977 and particularly the New Economic Zone in Tay Ninh with a view to bring pressure on the Vietnamese to vacate the sanctuaries inside Kampuchea. And secondly, they allied themselves with Vietnam's enemy, China, and invited several thousand Chinese military and technical personnel in what Vietnam called a bid to encircle it. Such policies, internal and international, could ensure neither Kampuchea's domestic stability nor reduce its vulnerability to Vietnamese aggression. The Vietnamese march into Kampuchea at the back of the newly-born Kampuchea United Front for National Salvation occurred at a time when Vietnam could not have chosen to do so but for the Pol Pot government's ill-conceived and compelling tactics.

The new leadership of Kampuchea felt that its fears of Vietnamese expansionism had been confirmed by the Vietnamese refusal to quit the sanctuaries on Kampuchean soil allowed them by Prince Sihanouk since the late 1960's. In addition, within two weeks of the Communist victory in Saigon, the new government opened an old sore between the two countries by claiming some islands in the Gulf of Thailand. That led to the first clash between the two Communist governments and although Hanoi recognized Phnom Penh's claim to Puolo Wai, the Vietnamese questioned at the May 1976 bilateral meetings the entire maritime boundary with Kampuchea that had been settled by the Brevie Line in 1939 during the French rule. The incident helped to strengthen Kampuchea's apprehensions of Vietnamese expansionist aims. An attempted coup in September 1976, sparked in all likelihood by the government's domestic policy excesses, was alleged to be a Vietnamese plot to overthrow the government through "Hanoi-Khmer" army units. The Pol Pot regime took advantage of the situation to liquidate the remnant of the Hanoi-Khmers, which included five members of the 20-member Party Central Committee. The regime's attitude toward Vietnam hardened. The Phnom Penh government refused to hold talks with Vietnam until the latter completely moved out of all territories claimed by Kampuchea.

The Conflict

Thereafter, Kampuchea obviously decided that offense was the best form of defense, an attitude for which it did not initially receive the full support of its Chinese allies. Beginning in January 1977 and escalating their activities between April and September 1977, Kampuchean forces moved into the old Vietnamese sanctuaries where an NEZ was being established. The attack would achieve the multiple purpose of weakening Vietnam's economy, keeping military pressure on Vietnam so as to secure the complete evacuation from the sanctuaries and frustrating an alleged Vietnamese plan to integrate Kampuchea into a Vietnamese-dominated Indochinese federation.

If the Vietnamese indeed had any such plans, they were not in a hurry to implement them because of their preoccupation with problems of economy and domestic dissidence. Their policy of conciliation with Thailand since 1977 and their apparent readiness to endorse the ASEAN concept of a neutral zone in Southeast Asia free of any big power influence were indicative of their desire to demonstrate even to their non-Communist neighbors that Vietnam sought peace and had no plans of military intervention in other states at least for several years.

If Vietnam wanted to live within its self-imposed constraints, China and Kampuchea seemed determined not to allow it that kind of luxury. Since the conclusion of the Vietnam war, China had emphasized in its relations with Southeast Asian nations that the Soviet Union represented the "present strategic danger to Southeast Asia," and cautioned them to beware of "the tiger at the back door while repelling the wolf through the front door." Therefore, China began to exert pressure on Vietnam from mid-1977 to condemn Soviet hegemonism by holding back further economic aid and building up Kampuchea's military strength. Thus, between 1975 and 1978, China supplied Kampuchea with 130-mm mortars, 107-mm bazookas, automatic rifles, transport vehicles, gasoline and various small weapons, enough to equip 30-40 regiments totaling about 200,000 persons. There is no way of knowing how much economic assistance was additionally provided by China beyond the initial gift of $ 1 billion made at the time of Sihanouk's return to Phnom Penh in 1975. An estimated 10,000 Chinese military and technical personnel were sent

to Kampuchea to improve the latter's military preparedness, which in the political circumstances of the time could
have been directed only against Vietnam since China had
bent over backward in the postwar period to become
friendly with Thailand, the only other neighboring country
that could be a threat to Kampuchean security. Critical of
these Sino-Kampuchean measures, Vietnam alleged that
they were designed to destroy the Vietnamese economy and
encircle the country militarily.

An all-out war with Kampuchea was not suited to Vietnam at that point for several additional reasons. Apart from
the diplomatic damage it would cause by destroying the new
self-image of sweet reasonableness Vietnam was attempting
to create among its Southeast Asian neighbors, a bellige-
rent act of those dimensions would certainly frustrate
efforts to secure economic aid from other countries.
Secondly, in the absence of a militarily strong anti-Pol Pot
movement, sizable Vietnamese forces would be locked up
in direct combat with Kampuchea's army, supported by
China. The Vietnamese leadership, therefore, attempted to
negotiate with the Khmers but to no avail. They then
resorted to large-scale fighting for three months beginning
in October 1977 with the limited purpose of securing a
Khmer-Vietnamese border treaty. In January 1978, Vietnam proposed that both sides withdraw their troops to five
miles from the existing border and submit themselves to an
internationally supervised truce commission. In May 1978,
Kampuchea agreed to peace talks that would begin in 1979
after Vietnam had demonstrated its genuine desire not to
integrate Kampuchea into an Indochinese federation under
Vietnamese control. Vietnam doubted the genuineness of
Kampuchea's offer, particularly because of the inter-
nationalization of the conflict, brought about by Beijing's
overt and firm commitment to Phnom Penh and the general
deterioration in Sino-Vietnamese relations.

Vietnam-China Relations

Historical Backdrop

The recent phase of Vietnam-China relations is best understood in terms of their rival long-term ambitions in Southeast Asia. Communist China has over the last three decades periodically published maps showing most of Southeast Asia as lying within China's historical sphere of influence. On the other hand, Vietnamese Communists have at least since the establishment of Indo-Chinese Communist Party (ICP) in 1930 indicated their plans to dominate the territories formerly under French rule. And although there is no evidence to support the allegation, Hanoi, in all likelihood, harbored ambitions to control Communist movements in the rest of Southeast Asia. Vietnam's ambition for a regional leadership through assistance to Communist movements and domination of governments could be attributed to reasons other than purely ideological. Its desire to create a strong independent center of power is partly a quest for enhanced security born of a traditional fear of Chinese domination of Vietnam. Historically, Vietnam has been a fiercely freedom-loving country apprehensive of its northern neighbor's expansionism. Vietnam's several revolts during the thousand-odd-year Chinese rule extending over the first millenium (111 B.C.-A.D. 939), its successful overthrow of the Chinese rule again in the fifteenth century (1407-28), its readiness to sign an agreement to allow the return of the French only to get the Chinese occupation troops out in 1946, and its reluctant acceptance of the cease-fire along the 17th parallel in 1954 at Geneva thanks to Chinese insistence, demonstrate Vietnam's intense distrust and suspicion of China, whether under imperial, nationalist, or Communist governments.

During the greater part of the three-decade-long struggle which ended in 1975, the Viet Minh and later the DRV and the NLF had to maintain cordial relations with China because of the much-needed military assistance. While no reliable figures of Chinese aid to North Vietnam exist— even official Chinese estimates vary from 14 to 21 billion dollars—there is no doubt that the Chinese economic and military assistance was crucial for the Communist success in South Vietnam. Despite such dependence, Hanoi retained its political independence; it refused, for instance, to enter into a formal military alliance with China and politely declined to "invite" Chinese Volunteer Forces to aid the Vietnamese liberation movement. Until 1965 there was a greater commonality in Sino-Vietnamese thinking on strategy and tactics, the Vietnamese being more appreciative of the Chinese than of the Soviets because of the former's support to wars of national liberation. Also, the Chinese aid to Vietnam up to that time was far more, almost double the amount proffered by the Soviet Union. The situation changed though in early 1965 with the U.S. strategic bombing of North Vietnam and the latter's need of more sophisticated defense equipment including surface-to-air missiles (SAMs) which could be supplied only by the Soviet Union. Thus far, the North Vietnamese had relied more on guerrilla warfare and much less on mobile warfare to carry on the struggle in the South. In mid-1965, the North Vietnamese strategists judged the time had come to switch to mobile warfare and in some instances even to positional warfare. Such an advanced war strategy was not appreciated by the Chinese, who preferred a protracted warfare in which the Vietnamese would depend for indefinite periods of time on Chinese assistance in the form of small weapons. Lin Piao's celebrated doctrine of the "wars of national liberation" launched on September 3, 1965 emphasized a policy of self-reliance and less external military aid, an indirect exhortation to Vietnam to reduce its dependence on the Soviet Union.

During the years of the Cultural Revolution, the Chinese authorities acted deliberately to impede the flow of Soviet military aid to North Vietnam. For example, the Soviet Union was asked to pay in U.S. dollars the freight for transporting armaments by Chinese rail-road wagons; their availability would be inordinately delayed. The Soviet Union had consequently to supply by sea both large and small weaponry which included SAM, MiG aircraft, bombers, helicopters, anti-aircraft batteries, a radar defense system, and all kinds of transport vehicles and heavy weapons from 1967 until the end of the war. The annual Soviet military aid to North Vietnam soon surpassed the Chinese figure.

Vietnam and Sino-Soviet Rivalry

The more recent phase of Sino-Vietnamese differences began in 1971 with Sino-American moves toward a rapprochement. American efforts to end the Vietnam conflict by asking the Chinese to cease assisting the North Vietnamese, and subsequent Chinese emphasis on a struggle against revisionism rather than Western imperialism, were regarded by Hanoi as a Chinese game to subordinate Vietnamese interests to those of China. In 1954, at the Geneva Conference, the North Vietnamese had reluctantly agreed to the partition of their country at the instance of China as a part of the global Communist policy of peaceful coexistence. Now in the early 1970s, the Vietnamese suspected that China did not want to see a strong, reunified Vietnam to emerge as a potential competitor for influence in Southeast Asia. Additionally, they found themselves on the opposite side of the Chinese in regard to the U.S. presence in Asia, which China regarded as a desirable counterbalance to Soviet ambitions in the area.

With the end of the war in South Vietnam, it was only a matter of time before the two halves of the country would unite to make one state. China was certainly not happy over the prospect of the emergence of a strong state on its southern borders. It would certainly not be a spectator to

Hanoi's suspected ambitions to dominate Laos and Kampuchea and lend assistance to fraternal Communist parties generally all over Southeast Asia, traditionally an area of China's political influence. In order that Vietnam itself assume the historical role of China's "vassal" state, the Beijing leaders insisted that Hanoi join them in condemning the Soviet Union of "hegemonism." China also threatened not to make any loans to Vietnam. When the Vietnamese gently pointed out that the late Premier Zhou En-lai had made a commitment in June 1973 to continue economic and military aid at the then existing level for five years, the Chinese "explained" that a prior agreement between Zhou En-lai and Ho Chi Minh called for termination of aid after the Vietnamese war ended. China did not make an exception even on humanitarian grounds. Thus, when Vietnam was hit by severe food shortages during 1976-77 because of adverse weather conditions, China did not choose to alleviate human misery by sending foodgrains across its southern borders. In contrast, the Soviet Union supplied 450,000 of the 1.6 million tons of food rushed to the country.

Vietnam alleged that China thereafter attempted to "contain" it by organizing a coalition of U.S., Thailand, Kampuchea and China as a "counter-weight" to Vietnamese influence on mainland Southeast Asia. Until late 1977, China continued to apply pressure on Vietnam in an effort to obtain the latter's loyalties in its conflict with the Soviet Union. That interregnum witnessed the steady deterioration of Sino-Vietnamese relations apparently because of three specific issues: the offshore islands, Vietnamese of Chinese ethnic origin and border claims. The real issues were political, centering around the question of political hegemony, in the short run, over Indochina and eventually over all of Southeast Asia.

The Islands Issue

Soon after the Provisional Revolutionary Government

assumed authority in Saigon it attempted to occupy the offshore Spratly Islands, located only 280 miles North-East of the Cam Ranh Bay, thereby coming into conflict with the People's Republic of China. The Spratly and Paracel Islands had been the subject of rival claims between China and Vietnam in the 19th century. Apart from their strategic location in the South China Sea on the maritime artery between the Indian Ocean and the Western Pacific, these uninhabited islands suddenly became valuable in the early seventies in the eyes of China, the Philippines (only the Spratly group) and South Vietnam because of some pre-liminary geological surveys indicating rich oil deposits. When the South Vietnamese government officially incor-porated the Spratly Islands through a special decree in September 1973, and China contested its claim, the DRV and the NLF had maintained silence although Hanoi had previously expressed territorial claims on the archipelago. Beijing took naval and air action in January 1974, interest-ingly enough, to occupy only the Paracel Islands closer to Chinese naval bases instead of the Spratlys, 550 miles further south. The Chinese short-range missile firing boats based on the naval base of Yulin on the Hainan Islands showed a clear superiority over South Vietnam's coast guard cutters, destroyer escorts and patrol boats in the engagements of January 19-20, 1974. The Spratlys were, in any case, beyond the range of Chinese air support which could be the reason why the Chinese took no action to prevent South Vietnamese occupation of these islands. Beijing's occupation of the Paracel group was important also because of the presence of a Chinese naval complex and sophisticated radar facilities on one of the islands since 1971.

Both the groups of islands—the Spratlys and the Paracels—continue to be an issue between Hanoi and Beijing. Vietnam's interests in the Spratlys are both strate-gic and economic. Hanoi is eager to continue the offshore oil exploration begun under the previous government and has sought external financial and technical assistance, among others, from Norway and India. There is no doubt the islands' worth is crucial for Vietnam's economic future and its plans for self-reliance in oil. Since 1975, however, Hanoi's efforts to negotiate the future of the islands with Beijing have been fruitless largely because of the latter's refusal even to answer Vietnamese communications on the subject which is, therefore, left for China to reopen at its convenience.

The Ethnic Chinese Issue

The "overseas Chinese" in Vietnam were as much hated by the local people as they were elsewhere in Southeast Asia because of their superior economic standing. Their loyalty to Vietnam was always suspect. Their unruly and disruptive behavior during the years of the Cultural Revolution was least appreciated in Vietnam. After the Communist victory in Saigon, its large Chinese population noted for its industry and wealth received special attention of the new government. The community's cooperation was vital for keeping the economy going until the government gradually moved to eliminate the private sector. By 1977, such cooperation was not as badly needed. The Vietnamese Chinese were then grouped along with intellectuals, devout Buddhists and Catholics as potential opposition to the spread of socialism. Although the Vietnamese Chinese were not specifically named as "capitalist" opponents of the new government, the frequent mention of the areas in which the Chinese predominantly lived as being the cesspool of black marketing and corruption was an indirect condemnation of the community. In the campaign for "ideological certification" of the "misfits," the Chinese were progressively moved to the New Economic Zones in the countryside which included the border province of Tay Ninh. There, the Chinese would serve additionally as a buffer between the Vietnamese and the Kampucheans.

In March 1978, the Vietnamese government came down most openly against the Chinese community. How far the Vietnamese Government's actions were inspired by Beijing's new initiative to win the loyalty and support of the overseas Chinese was not known. Beijing's campaign was perhaps launched with the twin objective of drumming up support for itself vis-a-vis Taipei and for securing technical and financial assistance from the overseas Chinese in Southeast Asia and the United States to help China's program to modernize its economy. The vigor of the campaign unnerved many of the Southeast Asian states with large Chinese minorities because of its political implications. Was the Vietnamese government's action against the ethnic Chinese a reaction to China's new policy towards the "overseas" Chinese or was it, as was more likely, a reaction to China's decision to help Vietnam's enemy, the Pol Pot regime, in Kampuchea? In any case, the Vietnamese government's policy toward the ethnic Chinese went far beyond being merely verbally vitriolic. It resulted in migration of a large number of Vietnamese Chinese providing the most visible and dramatic evidence of the growing gulf between Beijing and Hanoi governments.

In the name of official plans to carry out rapid socialization of the economy, the Vietnamese government raided the Cholon area of the twin city of Saigon where the Chinese lived and ordered their assets frozen. Of note was a change in the official reclassification of the Vietnamese Chinese in May 1978, as an ethnic minority abolishing the special category status the Chinese had enjoyed thus far. The change was to indicate the government's firm resolve to integrate the Chinese community along with other ethnic minorities in the national community. The Chinese community was thus faced with choosing one of the two alternatives: the obligations to the state that were implied in the acceptance of a Vietnamese citizenship or the handicaps of an alien status. The government saw in the largely urban Chinese community a partial but multifaceted solution to a

complex, depressing economic malaise. There was a shortage of financial resources with the government which
therefore planned to combat massive urban unemployment
by settling large numbers of city-dwellers in the countryside. The fact that the Chinese population was urban made
the new policy impact heavier on them than on others. The
jealousy aroused by the Chinese community's overwhelm-
ing grip over the trade and finance of the country and their
capacity to impede governmental economic policies were
no mean factors. Besides, there was the usual traditional
prejudice against the Chinese; a decision to move them to
the New Economic Zones close to the Kampuchean border
where their numbers might dwindle in the cross-fire of bi-
national conflict was not likely to arouse resentment among
the Vietnamese population. The large-scale hardship and
discontent the new policy caused to the Chinese led to a hue
and cry, many of them fleeing the country. A puzzling point
of this exodus was that a substantial number of Chinese
from North Vietnam also crossed the land border into
China, indicating that the causes of the feeling of insecurity
were political and had permeated the Chinese community
all over Vietnam.

It is doubtful if the Chinese government was genuinely
concerned over the plight of the "overseas Chinese" in
Vietnam. To be sure, China had all along maintained its
interest in the overseas Chinese but never enough to go to
war with any country in Southeast Asia. As for South
Vietnam, China had specifically protested against the South
Vietnamese government's legislation in 1955 compelling the
Chinese community to accept the Vietnamese citizenship.
In 1965 North Vietnam agreed with China to settle the
question in consultation with each other after the "liberation" of South Vietnam. In practice, the Chinese government had done little to protect the overseas Chinese,
whether in Indonesia during the second half of the sixties or
in Kampuchea before and after the Communist takeover.
The Vietnamese Government may have, therefore, as-

sumed that the "persecution" of the Vietnamese Chinese would not provoke Beijing. After all, of the 1.5 million Vietnamese Chinese, 90 percent had lived in the South, amassed fortunes by even exploiting the prolonged situation created by the Second Indochina War and had generally supported the capitalist way of life. The indignation of the Chinese government over the racially "discriminating" treatment to Vietnamese Chinese can be explained only in political terms as an attempt to find an additional excuse to attack Vietnam. This is reinforced by the half-hearted manner in which China tried to evacuate the Vietnamese Chinese. Thus, in June 1978, China sent two ships, "Minghua" and "Changli," to Saigon and Haiphong to evacuate the Chinese. The two ships remained off the coast during the six weeks of fruitless negotiations with Vietnamese officials over an acceptable evacuation procedure. On July 11, China closed its borders to the thousands of Vietnamese Chinese trying to enter China across the land frontiers. The Chinese authorities would accept across the land borders only those refugees who could produce exit visas issued by the Vietnamese government along the repatriation certificates from the Chinese embassy in Hanoi. Insistence on such documentation, particularly repatriation certificates, once again demonstrated that the Chinese government's concern for Vietnamese Chinese was not genuine.

Sino-Vietnamese Conflict

By mid-1978, the Sino-Vietnamese relations had sunk to such a precipitously low level that armed action against each other appeared imminent. China's actions since the turn of the year had shown that Beijing had decided to take sides in the growing Vietnam-Kampuchea dispute not because it was convinced of the rights of either party but because of the impact of the confrontation on the relative influence of the Soviet Union or China in the region. In January, Beijing dispatched Teng Ying Chao, a Central

Committee member and widow of former Premier Zhou
Enlai to Phnom Penh to show solidarity with the Pol Pot
regime. Again in early 1978, China made large-scale arms
shipments which included long-range 130-mm and 150-mm
artillery to Kampuchea even after the Vietnamese forces
had completely pulled back from the Kampuchean soil.
Hanoi's intelligence sources indicated a Chinese resolve at
this point to support Kampuchea in what Beijing expected
and perhaps hoped would be a protracted war.

At this point in mid-1978, Vietnam openly abandoned its
old policy of friendship with both the Communist giants.
Hanoi contemplated a quick military action to liquidate the
Pol Pot regime before it solidified itself further against
Vietnam with Chinese military assistance. In order to bolster its own security in the event of a Chinese attack across
the Sino-Vietnamese border to coincide with Vietnamese
action in Kampuchea, Hanoi decided to move clearly closer
to Moscow. On June 29, 1978, Vietnam joined the Moscow-
dominated COMECON, the Communist equivalent of the
Common Market and on November 3, signed with Moscow
a full-fledged twenty-five year Treaty of Friendship and
Mutual Cooperation. A partial price of Soviet assistance
was Vietnam's consent to Soviet use and development of
Da Nang and Cam Ranh Bay as missile bases.

China retaliated against the first of these actions by formally terminating on July 3, 1978 all its economic, military
and technical assistance to Vietnam ordering the Chinese
personnel there to head home. In the previous month,
Vietnam had rejected Chinese requests to open consular
offices in Saigon, Da Nang and Haiphong, while the
Chinese government asked Vietnam in a reciprocal action
to close its consular establishments in Canton, Nanning and
Kunming. Beijing alleged that the USSR and Vietnam had
a three part plan to "encircle" China: firstly, by removing
the Vietnamese Chinese from positions of authority;
secondly, by compelling Laos and Kampuchea through

military threats to join an Indochinese Federation nominally under Vietnamese control but, in fact, under Soviet domination; and lastly, by implementing the Brezhnev Plan for Asian Security system thereby bringing all of Southeast Asia into the Soviet sphere of influence. China accused Vietnam of being the "Cuba of Asia," a satellite of the Soviet Union helping the latter to achieve its strategic aims in Asia.

Vietnam and the Soviet Union

Towards the end of 1978, the only part that stood to gain from major conflicts in Indochina was the Soviet Union. Disturbing to the Soviet Union was the growing Sino-American friendship subsequent to the announced normalization of relations between the two countries. Moscow's actions to draw Vietnam closer to the Soviet Union politically, economically, and militarily should be seen in the context of its dual policy to weaken the Sino-American friendship and frustrate Chinese ability to augment its influence in Southeast Asia. The Soviet policy was in fact a continuation of its decade-long, diplomatic offensive to win all the countries of South and Southeast Asia to its side or at least wean them away from Beijing. Such efforts were supplemented by an increasingly military activity, particularly in the Indian Ocean, though decidedly on a low key.

The steadily increasing diplomatic and naval activity of the Soviet Union in South and Southeast Asia since 1968 must certainly be seen in the context of American withdrawal from the region and the growing Sino-American friendship. Traditionally, Southeast Asia had never figured importantly in the Russian ambitions for exercise of power. Yet the Soviet Union being partly an Asian country cannot countenance exclusive domination by any other major power, particularly China, over large parts of Asia. Additionally, Moscow has regarded it most important not to allow its ideological rival, Beijing, the "status and prestige of the standard bearer and protector of the ranks of revolution" not only in Southeast Asia but throughout the world.

However, the Soviet Union was and is far from being eager to become the "policeman" of Asia, an ambition any power geographically distant from the region should be able to desist after the glaring failure of the United States. Even during the Vietnam conflict, the Soviet Union grudged the heavy costs of assisting North Vietnam and the NLF in the form of war materials and sophisticated equipment. The Soviets were also far from happy over the Vietnamese situation impinging upon the progress of their talks with the United States, which were on a wide range of topics aimed at detente. Moscow was, therefore, most interested in pushing Brezhnev's system of collective security for Asia, first propounded in 1968 just a month before the Nixon Doctrine. Initially, the Brezhnev Plan aimed at some kind of a military alliance system in which the resources could be found locally and supplemented by the Soviet Union. No Southeast Asian nation, including North Vietnam, hurried to join the proposed system because none of them wanted to give the impression of ganging up against China, although Moscow denied its plan sought to contain the People's Republic of China.

Rationally speaking, the long-term interests of the superpowers, both of them geographically distant from the Southeast Asian region, would lie in denying all major powers including themselves an opportunity to dominate the area and to achieve such a goal through promotion of a regional balance of power. In the short run, however, the Sino-U.S. rapprochement, the almost complete withdrawal of American forces from Southeast Asia and the Sino-Soviet race to win the allegiance of the new Communist regimes in Indochina have been compelling factors in the acceleration of Soviet involvement in the region. Russia had no leverage with the Pol Pot regime which decried

Moscow's recognition of the U.S. backed Lon Nol regime up to its downfall in March 1975. In Vietnam, the leaders were forced by China to make a choice between Moscow and Beijing in October 1975 when the General Secretary of the Vietnamese Communist Party, Le Duan, was asked during his visit to China to condemn Soviet hegemonism. Le Duan had refused to comply with his host's wishes. Thereafter, China stopped any further aid to Vietnam, while Russia came forward generously to support the Vietnamese, whose dependence on the Russians was thereby even more enhanced. Already they were dependent on Moscow for supply of heavy, sophisticated, military hardware.

During 1978, Moscow apparently persuaded the Hanoi leadership to think that a continuing state of tension between a Chinese-backed Kampuchea and Vietnam would constitute a festering economic sore for Vietnam. The question should be resolved expeditiously at least in the interests of economy. In 1978-79, Vietnam was in dire need of food assistance amounting to 4.3 million tons because of successive crop failures. It was this desperate economic situation that made Vietnam finally succumb to Soviet pressures to join the Council on Mutual Economic Assistance (COMECON), the pro-Soviet Communist Common Market, in June 1978. After the U.S. announcement of normalization of relations with China, the Soviet Union stepped up its pressure on Vietnam for a formal military alliance against China. There is reason to believe that an overt anti-Chinese alliance was the price Moscow extracted for bailing Vietnam out of its economic crisis. The 25-year Russo-Vietnamese Treaty of Friendship and Mutual Assistance signed on November 3, 1978—barely six weeks before the Vietnamese march into Kampuchea—provided Vietnam a Soviet shield of protection from a Chinese attack. Article 6 of the Treaty clearly stated that in the event of an attack or a threat of an attack Vietnam and the Soviet Union would consult with each other and take "appropriate and effective measures" to "eliminate" that threat. The Treaty indeed marked a high point of Moscow's diplomatic success in Indochina.

Vietnam's Occupation of Kampuchea

Having thus armed itself with a treaty with the Soviet Union, Vietnam was ready for a brisk war aimed at toppling the Pol Pot regime and installing one favorable to itself. Hanoi had brought the Pol Pot regime's genocidal excesses to international attention through a publicity blitz. In order to make its planned march into Kampuchea politically palatable to the world, Vietnam helped the birth of the 14-member committee called the Kampuchean United Front for National Salvation (KUFNS), under the leadership of the dissident pro-Hanoi Khmer Communists like Heng Samrin and Chea Sim, but also including some exiled Kampuchean intellectuals and monks. An important element of the new front would be the support of Khmer Krom, the Cambodian minority of more than one-half million people resident in Cochin-China. Parenthetically, if that minority moved out of Vietnam, it would partly alleviate the food shortages in the country. Ostensibly, the Vietnamese forces were only helping the KUFNS in overthrowing the hated Pol Pot regime.

Unlike the NLF, the KUFNS did not command large-scale popular support because of its Vietnamese patrons. It was clearly a Vietnamese smoke screen created on the eve of the Vietnamese invasion to legitimize it in the eyes of the world. The success of the 17-day Vietnamese "blitzkrieg" into Kampuchea beginning Christmas Day, 1978, owed little to KUFNS or its few supporters inside that country. If the Heng Samrin government did not encounter serious opposition it was because of the public relief over the extinction of the oppressive Pol Pot regime with its vexations of regimented life, communal kitchens, broken families, and hard, unending labor. The Heng Samrin regime's success in establishing control over most of Kampuchea (except the Western region) owed not a little to the presence of an estimated 160,000 Vietnamese occupation troops who would not brook any measures to crush a serious public opposition.

Pol Pot and his cohorts fled to Western Kampuchea. For a while, China was able to continue making military and economic aid supplies to the anti-Heng Samrin guerillas thanks to the air strip at Siem Reap, passages through Laos and Thailand and smuggling along the 450-mile Kampuchean coastline. The Laotian corridor was soon plugged by the pro-Vietnam government which also expelled Chinese technical and military personnel from the country. With such handicaps, the Pol Pot group was obliged to join hands with other foes of the Heng Samrin regime including Sihanouk moderates and Khmer Serei who had ironically enough been pushed either across the Thai border or into the hideouts of the Cardamom mountains by the Pol Pot regime in 1975. The Khmer Serei's hatred of the military occupation of their motherland by the ancient enemy, Vietnam, far surpassed their antipathy toward the *Khmer Rouge*. Even so, it was doubtful if the anti-government resistance could achieve its aim of overthrowing the Vietnam-backed Heng Samrin government, a realization that may have been responsible for the precipitate Chinese invasion of Vietnam in February 1979. China expected Vietnam to withdraw substantial numbers of its troops from Kampuchea to move them to the Sino-Vietnamese frontier thereby relieving pressure on Pol Pot and his allies in Western Kampuchea.

Communists Clash in Indochina

The two wars—one at the turn of 1978 and the other in early 1979 in Indochina—in both of which Vietnam was a common factor, made that portion of Asia once more an area of instability and insecurity. Both China and Vietnam have had to keep their forces deployed on two different fronts since 1978-79; China on its borders with the Soviet Union and Vietnam; Vietnam on its Chinese borders and against the Chinese-backed Pol Pot forces in Kampuchea. All the regional states involved in those conflicts came out losers; only the Soviet Union, a non-regional nation, clearly succeeded in augmenting its influence in the region. Kampuchea was the greatest loser of all, its independence and integrity badly compromised, its domestic disorder worsened by a new civil war in which the two sides are supported by China and Vietnam. Vietnam lost on several grounds. Vietnam's military and political domination over the rest of Indochina has been achieved at tremendous costs to its own security, stability, economy and international image. Its Five Year Plan (1976–80) was practically scrapped as the government set new priorities in defense outlay and postponed the reconstruction projects. The country's military and diplomatic dependence on the Soviet Union and Eastern European countries became as complete as its isolation from most of the Third World. Moreover, its chances of getting developmental assistance from the United States, Western Europe, and Japan practically disappeared. Additionally, Hanoi's new stance drastically diminished its credibility among ASEAN states as a nation committed to carving a zone of peace in Southeast Asia. Finally, Vietnam's continued control and domination over Laos and Kampuchea became contingent on its own acute dependence on Soviet economic and military assistance, thus diluting its own hard-earned independence making it vulnerable to the charge of being Moscow's agent for acquisition of power and influence in Southeast Asia and for the containment of China.

Vietnam's successful overthrow of the Beijing-backed Pol Pot regime was a great blow to China. In February 1979, when Chinese forces marched across the border into Vietnam, Beijing's public posture was that it wanted to "teach a lesson" to Vietnam for its behavior toward Kampuchea and the ethnic Chinese. On neither count does Hanoi seem to have learnt the lesson. Vietnam did not withdraw its forces from Kampuchea. Additionally, it brought Laos fully into its orbit, ending the previously enormous Chinese influence there by asking all Chinese technical personnel to leave the country. Further, Vietnam stepped up its persecution of the ethnic Chinese, causing a mass exodus in the first half of 1979.

The month-long border hostilities did not by any measure establish China's military superiority over its much smaller southern neighbor. Hanoi did not even commit its crack regiments to the border war, most of the fighting being carried out by its militia forces. If anything, the conflict laid bare severe weaknesses in the Chinese military machine, which had not seen action since the border war with India in 1962, had not fully recovered from its severe discipline problems experienced during the Cultural Revolution and perhaps lacked certain categories of equipment previously supplied by the Soviet Union during the days of Sino-Soviet amity and alliance. The Chinese casualties were estimated at 20,000. The little war convinced the Chinese leaders that their defense expenses had to be enhanced even at the cost of their plans to modernize their economy. An additional strain on the economy arising from the conflict with Vietnam was the substantial expenditure on an estimated quarter million Vietnamese Chinese who had sought refuge in China.

In the short run, the Vietnamese ability to develop a third center of international Communism that would provide leadership to the Communist movements in all of Southeast Asia is most questionable. Hanoi's desire and ambition to establish itself as a regional power capable of standing against China are an outgrowth of its historical fears of Chinese domination and its desire to enhance its own national security. A long-term dependence on the Soviet Union to achieve such aims can hardly be a perma-

nent solution because of several reasons: geographical distance, alterations in Soviet international priorities, and
above all, the necessary consequence that Vietnam's hard-
won independence will be eroded. A fiercely independ-
ence-loving people like the Vietnamese cannot be expected
to play second fiddle to any country, even the Soviet
Union, for long. Vietnam's search for long-term security is
not likely to rest until it has discovered a self-reliant solution for extension of political influence in the region as a
means of bolstering its national defense against potential
Chinese aims to dominate it. Until then, Vietnam is likely
to follow its own prescription of 1946, at which time the
nationalist Ho Chi Minh agreed to welcome back the
French to North Vietnam only to get rid of the Chinese
army of occupation. He was rightly hopeful that he could
liquidate the French imperialism in his lifetime far more
easily than that of the historically dominant, geographically
close Chinese. Hanoi's recent behavior in helping Moscow
to acquire dominant political influence in Indochina may be
deemed such a temporary expedient to keep Beijing away
until the time when Vietnam can muster its own economic
and military strength enough to establish an independent
center of international communism.

The Boat People

Though not arising directly out of the Vietnam-China
conflict, the mass exodus of Vietnamese, principally of
Chinese ethnic origin, tarnished Vietnam's international
image. Soon after the fall of Saigon in 1975, a relatively
small number of people leaving Vietnam's shores in small
boats attracted international attention. In the subsequent
two years, the total remained below 20,000, mostly absorbed by Malaysia, Thailand and Hong Kong. In 1978, the
number rose sharply to 85,230. By the middle of 1979,
China alone had received 250,000 refugees, Hong Kong

62,000, France 61,000, and the United States 150,000, while more than 368,000 were awaiting resettlement in transit camps in Thailand, Malaysia and Indonesia. At least half that number were presumed to have died on the high seas due to starvation or drowning due to leaking boats. From the refugee accounts, it appeared certain that the Vietnamese government "officially" blessed the exodus but not before the refugees had each paid in gold the equivalent of 5,000 U.S. dollars, the government nettling nearly 4 billion dollars in the process.

The refusal of the Malaysian government (with 78,200 in transit camps) and Thailand (with 173,600) and Indonesia (47,000) to accept any more refugees, and, in fact, their decision to turn the new arrivals back to the seas created a crisis of conscience around the globe. The non-Communist Southeast Asian countries regarded the refugees not only as a heavy burden on their scarce economic resources but as a potential security risk. Malaysia, opposed to an increase in its Chinese population because of its impact on the delicate racial balance, was most reluctant to accept any more of the ethnic Chinese refugees.

The causes of the massive emigration from Vietnam were economic, social and political. During 1975–77, Vietnam suffered a series of bad harvests. The subsequent two years were marked by natural disasters like drought, floods and typhoons. The harvest in the Mekong delta suffered from the insect pests and in the Tonking delta from a fungus disease. The non-availability of foodstuffs and their exhorbitant prices caused great hardship. Both in the North and in the South, the urban population had swelled enormously during the long war. It suffered both from inadequate food and large-scale unemployment. The government attempts, particularly in the South to settle the surplus population compulsorily in the NEZs, so as to increase the production, were most unsettling to persons reluctant to leave the towns. The economic situation was worsened by the war in Kampuchea and with China. Additionally, the conscription was extended in 1978 from 18-25 to 16–35 and the period of mandatory service from 3 to 5 years. The war itself produced a large number of refugees willing to try their fortunes on the high seas or across the land frontier into Thailand. Finally, the exodus of Hoa, ethnic Chinese, from South Vietnam was prompted by the government's policy of abolition of private trade in April 1978, and by the growing tension between Vietnam and China in early 1979. About 250,000 Hoa fled from North Vietnam across the land border into China. Many of them had acted as "fifth columnists" in guiding the Chinese invaders along back trails to attack the Vietnamese defenders in the rear. The statement of China's Deputy Premier, Deng Xiaoping to the U.N. Secretary-General, Kurt Waldheim, in April 1979, that China might teach Vietnam "another lesson" made the Vietnamese apprehensive of the remaining Hoa particularly those in the strategic port city of Haiphong and the coastal coal mining towns of Hongay-Campha further north. They did not want to take chances and, therefore, expelled ethnic Chinese from those areas and also from Hanoi-Haiphong region. Of all the refugees and "boat people," 80 percent were of Chinese origin.

Several international conferences, in which the office of the United Nations High Commissioner of Refugees (UNHCR) was involved, discussed the crisis in 1979. In May, at the ASEAN-sponsored meeting in Jakarta, attended by representatives of 25 countries including Vietnam, Malaysia proposed that a refugee processing center for 200,000 be established in the U.S. or a U.S.-controlled territory "because the problem of the boat people is the hangover of the US involvement in South Vietnam." In response to calls for organized emigration, Vietnam agreed to send the emigrants directly to the countries of resettlement at the rate of 10,000 a month "to reduce the pressure on neighboring countries." It would allow anyone who wished to leave the country, except those who were of age for military conscription, or in the know of or possession of state secrets or those awaiting trial on criminal charges. At the U.N.-sponsored conference at Geneva in July, attended by representatives of 65 countries and international agencies, most Western countries and Japan announced their financial contributions as well as quotas for resettlement of refugees. The U.S. accepted the bulk of the responsibility. Of the more than 200 million dollars committed by numerous nations, the U.S. contributed 125 million dollars. The Geneva–based Inter-Governmental Committee for Migration declared in May 1982 that of the almost 700,000 refugees who had been resettled since 1975, over two-thirds, 477,000, were accepted by the U.S., 82,000 by France and 60,000 by Canada. At the same time, it revealed that over 200,000 were still awaiting resettlement in camps in Southeast Asian countries. From April 1982, the U.S. had declared new criteria for immigration of Indo-Chinese refugees. These included those with close relatives in the U.S., former U.S. Government employees and those formerly connected with the U.S. activities or with a former non-Communist government in Indo-China and who had a specific reason to fear of persecution. By that time, emigration by small boats had declined sharply but was still around, 30,000 annually.

The worldwide publicity the problem and plight of the refugees received has not helped Vietnamese acceptance in the comity of nations. It has been one of the factors causing tension between it and its ASEAN neighbors. There are an estimated 150,000 Laotians, Kampucheans and Vietnamese refugees languishing in camps in Thailand alone. About 25,000 to 30,000 "boat people" still arrive in different countries of Southeast Asia annually. The ASEAN nations have complained of a "compassion fatigue" on the part of Western nations in accommodating the Vietnamese "boat people" in their countries. Until the basic economic and social adjustment problems are solved in Vietnam, the problem of the emigration by desperate people will not simply go away.

Bibliography

General

Betts, R.F., *Assimilation and Association in French Colonial Theory, 1890-1914*, New York, 1961.

Blet, Henri, *France d'Outre Mer*, Paris, Arthaud, 1950.

Brimmell, J.H., *Communism in Southeast Asia*, London, OUP, 1959.

Butwell, Richard, *Southeast Asia: A Political Introduction*, New York, Praeger, 1975.

Cady, John F., *The History of Post-War Southeast Asia*, Athens, Ohio University Press, 1974.

Cady, John F., *Southeast Asia, Its Historical Development*, New York, McGraw Hill, 1964.

Chawla, S., Gurtov, M. and Marsot, A., Eds., *Southeast Asia under the New Balance of Power*, New York, Praeger, 1974.

Coedes, Georges, *The Indianized States of Southeast Asia*, Honolulu, East-West Center Press, 1968.

Coedes, Georges, *The Making of South East Asia*, Berkeley, University of California Press, 1966.

Cressey, George B., *Asia's Lands and Peoples*, Third Edition, New York, McGraw Hill, 1963.

Dobby, E.H.G., *Southeast Asia*, Seventh Edition, London, University of London Press, 1960.

Elsbree, Willard H., *Japan's Role in Southeast Asian Nationalist Movements, 1940-1945*, Cambridge, Mass., Harvard University Press, 1953.

Emerson, Rupert, Ed., *Government and Nationalism in*

Southeast Asia, New York, Institute of Pacific Relations, 1942.

Fifield, Russell H., *Americans in Southeast Asia: The Roots of Commitment*, New York, Thomas Crowell, 1973.

Fifield, Russell H., *Southeast Asia in United States Policy*, New York, Praeger, 1963.

Hall, D.G.E., *A History of South-East Asia*, Third Edition, London, Macmillan, 1968.

Hall, D.G.E., *Atlas of South-East Asia*, New York, St. Martin's Press, 1964.

Hall, D.G.E., *Historians of South-East Asia*, London, OUP, 1961.

Hanna, Willard A., *Eight Nation Makers: Southeast Asia's Charismatic Statesmen*, New York, St. Martin's Press, 1964.

Holland, William L., Ed., *Asian Nationalism and the West*, New York, Macmillan, 1953.

Kahin, George M., Ed., *Governments and Politics of Southeast Asia*, Second Edition, Ithaca, Cornell University Press, 1964.

Le May, Reginald, *The Culture of South-East Asia*, London, Allen & Unwin, 1954.

McVey, Ruth T., *The Calcutta Conference and the South East Asian Uprisings*, Ithaca, Cornell University, mimeo.

Morrison, Charles and Suhrke, Astri, *Struggles of Survival, the Foreign Policy Dilemmas of Smaller Asian States*, New York, St. Martin's, 1978.

Osborne, Milton O., *Region of Revolt: Focus on Southeast Asia*, Rushcutters Bay, New South Wales, Pergamon Press, 1970.

Panikkar, K.M., *Asia and Western Dominance*, London, Allen & Unwin, 1953.

Power, Thomas F., *Jules Ferry and the Renaissance of French Imperialism*, New York, King's Crown Press, 1944.

Priestley, H.I., *France Overseas, A Study of Modern Imperialism*, New York, Appleton-Century, 1938.

Purcell, Victor, *The Chinese in Southeast Asia*, London, OUP, 1965.

Pye, Lucian W., *Southeast Asia's Political Systems*, Englewood Cliffs, New Jersey, Prentice-Hall, 1967.

Quaritch-Wales, H.G., *The Making of Greater India*, Second Edition, London, Bernard Quaritch, 1961.

Roberts, Stephen H., *The History of French Colonial Policy, 1870-1925*, London, P.S. King, 2 vols., 1929.

SarDesai, D.R., *Southeast Asia, Past and Present*, New Delhi, Vikas, 1981.

Silverstein, J., Ed., *Southeast Asia in World War II*, New Haven, Yale University Press, 1966.

Steinberg, David J., *In Search of Southeast Asia*, New York, Praeger, 1971.

Tilman, Robert O., *Man, State and Society in Contemporary Southeast Asia*, New York, Praeger, 1969.

Trager, Frank N., Ed., *Marxism in Southeast Asia*, Palo Alto, Stanford University Press, 1960.

U.S. Foreign Policy for the 1970's: A New Strategy for Peace, A Report to the Congress by Richard Nixon, February 18, 1970, Washington, D.C., Government Printing Office, 1970.

U.S. Department of State, *A Threat to the Peace*, Washington, D.C., Government Printing Office, 1961.

Von der Mehden, *Religion and Nationalism in Southeast Asia*, Madison, University of Wisconsin Press, 1963.

Williams, Lea, *The Future of the Overseas Chinese in Southeast Asia*, New York, McGraw Hill, 1966.

Vietnam: Books

Ashmore, Harry S. and Baggs, William C., *Mission to Hanoi*, Berkeley, G.P. Putnam, 1968.

Bailey, Lois E., *Jules Ferry and French Indo-China*, Madison, University of Wisconsin Press, 1946.

Barron, John and Paul, Anthony, *Murder of a Gentle Land; The Untold Story of Communist Genocide in Cambodia*, New York, Reader's Digest Press, 1977.

Bator, Victor, *Vietnam: A Diplomatic Tragedy*, New York, Oceana Publications, 1965.

Bodard, Lucien, *The Quicksand War: Prelude to Vietnam*, Boston, Little Brown, 1967.

Brown, Sam and Akland, Len, Eds., *Why Are We Still in Vietnam?*, New York, Random House, 1970.

Buttinger, Joseph, *A Dragon Embattled, A History of Colonial and Post-Colonial Vietnam*, 2 vols., New York, Praeger, 1967.

Buttinger, Joseph, *The Smaller Dragon: A Political History of Vietnam*, New York, Praeger, 1958.

Cady, John F., *The Roots of French Imperialism in Eastern Asia*, Ithaca, Cornell University Press, 1954.

Carney, Timothy M., Ed., *Communist Party in Kampuchea, Documents and Discussion*, Ithaca, Cornell University Southeast Asia Program Data Paper, 1977.

Chen, King C., *Vietnam and China, 1938-1954*, Princeton, Princeton University Press, 1969.

Chesneaux, Jean, *Contribution a l'histoire de la nation Vietnamienne*, Paris, Editions Sociales, 1962.

Cooper, Chester L., *The Lost Crusade: America in Vietnam*, New York, Dodd Mead, 1970.

Devillers, Philippe and Lacouture, Jean, *End of a War: Indochina, 1954*, New York, Praeger, 1969.

Duiker, William J., *The Rise of Nationalism in Vietnam, 1900-1941*, Ithaca, Cornell University Press, 1976.

Duncanson, D.J., *Government and Revolution in Vietnam*, London, OUP, 1968.

Duong Dinh Khue, *Les Chefs d'Ouvre de la Litterature Vietnamienne*, Saigon, 1966.

Dutreb, M., *L'Admiral Dupre et la Conquete du Tonkin*, Paris, E. Leroux, 1924.

Ennis, Thomas E., *French Policy and Development in Indochina*, Chicago, University of Chicago Press, 1936.

Falk, Richard A., Ed., *The Vietnam War and International Law*, Princeton, Princeton University Press, 1968.

Fall, Bernard B., *Hell in a Very Small Place: The Siege of Dien Bien Phu*, New York, Lippincott, 1967.

Fall, Bernard B., Ed., *Ho Chi Minh on Revolution: Selected Writings, 1920-1966*, New York, Praeger, 1967.

Fall, Bernard B., *Last Reflections on a War*, New York, Doubleday, 1963.

Fall, Bernard B., *The Two Vietnams: A Political and Military Analysis*, Third Edition, New York, Praeger, 1967.

Fitzgerald, Frances, *Fire in the Lake*, Boston, Little Brown, 1972.

Fulbright, J. William, *The Arrogance of Power*, New York, Random House, 1967.

Galloway, John, *The Gulf of Tongking Resolution*, New Jersey, Associated University Press, 1970.

Garnier, Francis, *Voyage d'Exploration en Indochine*, Paris, Librairie Hachette, 1885.

Gettleman, Marvin E., Ed., *Vietnam: History, Documents and Opinions on a Major World Crisis*, Greenwich, Conn., Fawcett Publications, 1965.

Gheddo, Piero, *The Cross and the Bo Tree*, New York, Sheed and Ward, 1970.

Goodwin, Richard N., *Triumph or Tragedy: Reflections on Vietnam*, New York, Random House, 1966.

Gourou, Pierre, *The Peasants of the Tongking Delta*, 2 vols., New Haven, Human Relations Area Files, 1955.

Grauwin, Paul, *Doctor at Dien Bien Phu*, London, Hutchinson, 1955.

Great Britain, Foreign Office, *Further Documents Relating to the Discussion of Indochina at the Geneva Conference, June 16-July 21, 1954*, Cmd. 9239, London, HMSO, 1954.

Gruening, Ernest and Herbert W. Beaser, *Vietnam Folly*, Washington, D.C., The National Press, 1968.

Gurtov, Melvin, *The First Vietnam Crisis*, New York, Columbia University Press, 1967.

Halberstam, David, *The Best and the Brightest*, Greenwich, Conn., Fawcett Publications, 1969.

Halberstam, David, *Ho*, New York, Vintage Books, 1971.

Halberstam, David, *The Making of a Quagmire*, New York, Random House, 1965.

Hammer, Ellen J., *The Struggle for Indochina*, Palo Alto, Stanford University Press, 1956.

Hickley, Gerald C., *Village in Vietnam*, New Haven, Conn., Yale University Press, 1964.

Hinton, Harold C., *China's Relations with Burma and Vietnam*, New York, Institute of Pacific Relations, 1958.

Ho Chi Minh, *Prison Diary*, Tr. Aileen Palmer, Hanoi, Foreign Languages Publishing House, 1961.

Hoang Van Chi, *From Colonialism to Communism*, New York, Praeger, 1966.

Honey, P.J., *Communism in North Vietnam: Its Role in the Sino-Soviet Dispute*, Cambridge, Mass., M.I.T. Press, 1963.

Huyen, N. Khac, *Vision Accomplished? The Enigma of Ho Chi Minh*, New York, Macmillan, 1971.

Kahin, George M. and John W. Lewis, *The United States in Vietnam*, New York, Dial Press, 1967.

Kelley, Gail Paradise, *From Vietnam to America: A Chronicle of the Vietnamese Immigration to the United States*, Boulder, Colorado, Westview Press, 1977.

Kurland, Gerald, Ed., *Misjudgment or Defense of Freedom?, The United States in Vietnam*, New York, Simon & Schuster, 1975.

Lacouture, Jean, *Ho Chi Minh, A Political Biography*, New York, Random House, 1968.

Lacouture, Jean and Philippe Devillers, *La Fin d'une Guerre, Indochine, 1954*, Paris, Les Editions du Seuil, 1960.

Lacouture, Jean, *Vietnam Between Two Truces*, New York, Vintage Books, 1966.

Lam, Truong Buu, *Patterns of Vietnamese Response to Foreign Intervention, 1858-1900*, New Haven, Yale University Southeast Asia Studies, 1967.

Lancaster, Donald, *The Emancipation of French Indochina*, London, OUP, 1961.

Laniel, Joseph, *Le Drame Indochinois: de Dien Bien Phu au Paris de Geneve*, Paris, Plon, 1957.

Le Duan, *On the Socialist Revolution in Vietnam*, 2 vols., Hanoi, Foreign Languages Publishing House, 1965.

Le Thanh Khoi, *Viet-Nam*, Paris, Les Editions de Minuit, 1955.

Marr, David G., *Vietnamese Anti-Colonialism, 1885-1925*, Berkeley, University of California Press, 1971.

Masson, Andre, *Histoire de l'Indochine*, Paris, Presses Universitaires de France, 1950.

Maybon, Charles, *Histoire Moderne du Pays d'Annam, 1592-1820*, Paris, Typogralphie Plong-Nourrit, 1919.

McAlister, John T., Jr., and Paul Mus, *The Vietnamese and Their Revolution*, New York, Harper & Row, 1970.

Mus, Paul, *Viet-Nam, Sociologie d'Une Guerre*, Paris, Les Editions du Seuil, 1952.

Navarre, Henri-Eugene, *Agonie de l'Indochine, 1953-54*, Paris, Plon, 1956.

Neumann-Hoditz, Reinhold, *Portrait of Ho Chi Minh*, Berlin, Herder and Herder, 1972.

Nghiem Dang, *Viet-Nam, Politics and Public Administration*, Honolulu, East-West Center Press, 1966.

Nguyen Duy Thanh, *My Four Years with the Viet Minh*, Bombay, Democratic Research Service, 1950.

Nguyen Phut Than, *A Modern History of Viet-Nam*, Saigon, 1964.

Nguyen Van Long, *Before the Revolution: The Vietnamese Peasants under the French*, Cambridge, Mass., Harvard University Press, 1973.

Norman, C.B., *Tonkin or France in the Far East*, London, Chapman & Hall, 1884.

Osborne, Milton E., *The French Presence in Cochin-China and Cambodia, Rule and Response, 1859-1905*, Ithaca, Cornell University Press, 1969.

Pentagon Papers, New York, Bantam Books, 1971.

Pham Van Dong and the Committee for the Study of the History of the Vietnamese Workers' Party, *President Ho Chi Minh*, Hanoi, Foreign Languages Publishing House, 1960.

Pike, Douglas, *History of the Vietnamese Communism, 1925-1976*, Palo Alto, Hoover Institution Press, 1978.

Pike, Douglas, *Viet Cong*, Cambridge, Mass., M.I.T. Press, 1966.

Ponchaud, Francois, *Cambodia, Year Zero*, New York, Holt & Rinehart, 1977.

Porter, D. Gareth, *The Myth of the Bloodbath: North Vietnam's Land Reform Considered*, Ithaca, Cornell University International Relations of East Asia Project, 1972, mimeo.

Porter, D. Gareth, *A Peace Denied: The United States and the Paris Agreements*, Bloomington, Indiana University Press, 1975.

Race, Geffrey, *War Comes to Long An*, Berkeley, University of California Press, 1972.

Robequain, Charles, *The Economic Development of French Indo-China*, London, OUP, 1954.

Roy, Jules, *The Battle of Dien Bien Phu*, Tr. Robert Baldick, New York, Harper & Row, 1965.

Sainteny, Jean, *Histoire d'Une Paix Manquee Indochine*, Paris, Aniot Dumont, 1953.

Sainteny, Jean, *Ho Chi Minh and his Vietnam: A Personal Memoir*, Chicago, Cowles Book Company, 1970.

SarDesai, D.R., *Indian Foreign Policy in Cambodia, Laos and Vietnam, 1947-1964*, Berkeley, University of California Press, 1968.

Scigliano, Robert, *South Vietnam: Nation under Stress*, Boston, Houghton Mifflin, 1963.

Schlesinger, Arthur M., Jr., *The Bitter Heritage: Vietnam and American Democracy, 1941-1966*, Boston, Houghton Mifflin, 1967.

Shaplen, Robert, *The Lost Revolution, 1946-1966*, New York, Harper & Row, 1965.

Sihanouk, Prince Norodom, *My War with the CIA*, Harmondsworth, Penguin Books, 1973.

Smith, Ralph, *Viet-Nam and the West*, London Heinemann, 1968.

Starobin, Joseph R., *Eye-Witness in Indo-China*, New York, Cameron and Kahn, 1954.

Stoessinger, John G., *Henry Kissinger: The Anguish of Power*, New York, W. W. Norton, 1976.

Taboulet, Georges, *La Geste Francaise en Indochine*, 2 vols., Paris, Adrien-Maisonneuve, 1955-56.

Tanham, George K., *Communist Revolutionary Warfare: The Vietminh in Indo-China*, New York, Praeger, 1961.

Thompson, Virginia, *French Indochina*, New York, Macmillan, 1937.

Tran Dan Tien, *Glimpses of the Life of Ho Chi Minh*, Hanoi, Foreign Languages Publishing House, 1958.

Truong Chinh, *The August Revolution*, Hanoi, Foreign Languages Publishing House, 1958.

Truong Chinh, *Resolutely Taking the North Vietnam Countryside to Socialism through Agricultural Cooperation*, Hanoi, Foreign Languages Publishing House, 1959.

Truyen, Mai Tho, *Le Bouddhisme au Viet-Nam*, Saigon, 1952.

Vo, Nguyen Giap, *People's War, People's Army*, New York, Praeger, 1962.

Warbay, William, *Ho Chi Minh and the Struggle for a Free Vietnam*, London, Merlin Press, 1972.

Westmoreland, William C., *A Soldier Reports*, New York, Doubleday, 1976.

Woodside, Alexander B., *Community and Revolution in Modern Vietnam*, Boston, Houghton Mifflin, 1976.

Woodside, Alexander B., *Vietnam and the Chinese Model*, Cambridge, Mass., Harvard University Press, 1970.

Warner, Denis, *The Last Confucian*, New York, Macmillan, 1963.

Zagoria, Donald, *Vietnam Triangle: Moscow, Peking, Hanoi*, New York, Pegasus, 1967.

Vietnam: Articles

Adams, J. and N. Hancock, "Land and Economy in Traditional Vietnam," *Journal of Southeast Asian History*, I, 2 (1970).

Aurousseau, Leonard, "La premiere conquete chinoise des pays annamites," *Bulletin de l'Ecole Francaise d'Extreme-Orient*, XXIII (1923).

Briggs, L.P., "Aubaret and the Treaty of July 15, 1867, Between France, and Siam," *Far Eastern Quarterly*, IV (1947), pp. 122-138.

Cadiere, L., "Le Mur de Dong-Hoi, Etude sur l'Etablissement' des Nguyen Cochinchine," *Bulletin de l'Ecole Francaise d'Extreme-Orient*, VI (1906).

Chen, King, "North Vietnam in the Sino-Soviet Dispute," *Asian Survey* (September 1964).

Clifford, Clark, "A Vietnam Reappraisal," *Foreign Affairs*, XLVII (July 1969), pp. 601-622.

Cotter, M.G., "Towards A Social History of the Vietnamese Southward Movement," *Journal of Southeast Asian History*, IX, 1 (1968).

Coughlin, M., "Vietnam in China's Shadow," *Journal of Southeast Asian History*, VI, 2 (1967).

Devillers, Philippe and Jean Lacouture, "The Struggle for the Unification of Vietnam," *China Quarterly* (January-March 1962), pp. 2-23.

Fall, Bernard B., "The Political-Religious Sects of Vietnam," *Pacific Affairs*, XXVIII (September 1955), pp. 235-253.

Fall, Bernard B., "Power and Pressure Groups in North Vietnam," *China Quarterly* (January-March 1962), pp. 37-46.

Fischer, Ruth, "Ho Chi Minh: Disciplined Communist," *Foreign Affairs* (October 1954).

Gilbert, Stephen P., "Implications of the Nixon Doctrine for Military Aid Policy," *Orbis*, XVI, 3 (Fall, 1972).

Gittinger, J. Price, "Communist Land Policy in North Vietnam," *Far Eastern Survey*, XXVII (August 1959), pp. 113-126.

Henderson, William, "South Vietnam Finds Itself," *Foreign Affairs*, XXXV (January 1957), pp. 283-294.

Honey, P.J., "French Historiography and the Evolution of Colonial Vietnam," in D.G.E. Hall, Ed., *Historians of Southeast Asia*, London, OUP, 1961.

Huynh, Kim Khanh, "Year One of Post-Colonial Vietnam," *Southeast Asian Affairs*, Singapore, Institute of Southeast Asian Studies, 1977.

Kalgren, B., "The Date of the Early Dongson Culture," *Bulletin of the Museum of Far Eastern Antiquities*, XLV|(1942), pp. 1-29.

Lacouture, Jean, "From the Vietnam War to an Indochina War," *Foreign Affairs*, XLVIII, 4 (July 1970), pp. 617-628.

Laffey, Ella S., "French Adventurers and Chinese Bandits in Tongking: The Garnier Affair in its Local Context," *Journal of Southeast Asian Studies*, VI (March 1975), pp. 38-51.

Mus, Paul, "Cultes Indiens et Indigenes au Champa," *Bulletin de L'Ecole Francaise Extreme-Orient*, XXXIII (1933), pp. 367-410.

Mus, Paul, "The Role of the Village in Vietnamese Politics," *Pacific Affairs* (September 1949).

Nguyen Thai, "The Two Vietnams and China," *The Harvard Review*, II, 1 (Fall-Winter, 1963).

Pelliot, Paul, "Les Grands Voyages Maritime Chinois au debut du XV siecle," *T'oung Pao*, XXX (1933).

Porter, D. Gareth, "Vietnam's Long Road to Socialism," *Current History* (December 1976), pp. 209-218.

Shabad, Theodore, "Economic Development in North Vietnam," *Pacific Affairs* (March 1958).

Thayer, Carlyle A., "Vietnamese Foreign Policy Orientations," *Southeast Asian Affairs, 1977*, Singapore, Institute of Southeast Asian Studies, 1977.

Tran Van Giap, "Le Bouddhisme en Annam," *Bulletin de l'Ecole Francaise Extreme-Orient*, XXXII (1932).

Index

ARVN (Army of the Republic of Vietnam), 108, 118, 122
ASEAN (Association of Southeast Asian Nations), 160, 169, 186, 190-191
Acheson, Dean, 86
Admiral La Touche Treville, 70
Adran, Bishop of, 46
Africa, 26, 45, 57
Afro-Asian Conference, 124
Agent Blue, 137
Agent Orange, 133, 137
Agriculture, 2, 12-13, 30, 61, 77, 80, 116, 118-119, 136, 141, 143, 145, 147
Cooperatives, 98-99
Collectivization of, 142, 148, 153
Ai Lao Pass, 2
Allies, 76, 77, 79, 80
Amaravati School of Art, 8
An Duong Vuong, 14
Ang Duong, 52
Angkor, 9
Animism, 109
Annam, 2-3, 7, 15, 22, 27, 36, 39-40, 42, 46, 50, 58, 62, 83, 96
Annamite Cordillera, 2
Asia, 24, 26, 45, 48, 57, 62, 76, 85-86, 91, 109, 181-182, 185
Asian Development Bank, 140
Association for the Restoration of Vietnam, 64-65, 70
Association of Vietnamese Revolutionary Youth, 72
Au Co, 12
Au Lac, 14-15, 27
Australia, 85, 91
Austro-Hungarian Empire, 71

Austro-Indonesian, 4, 14
Au Viet, 14-15
Avignon, 45
Ayuthaya *see* Thailand

Bac Kan, 78
Bac Viet, ?
Bahnar, 5
Bandung, 124, 162
Bangkok, 52, 73
Bao Dai, 74, 79-80, 84, 92-94, 100
Bastille, 42
Ba Trieu, 20-21
Bazin, Rene, 68
Beijing, 31-32, 34, 85, 109, 122, 127, 163, 166, 170, 174-177, 179-183, 186, 188
Belgium, 93
Benedictine Monastery, 93
Betel-nut, 61
Bhadravarman, 7
Bhadreshwara, 8
Binh Xuyen, 94, 100
Black Flags, 54, 56, 58
Black marketing, 118, 148, 176
Blank Zones, 137
Boat people, 10, 161, 188-191
Bolshevik, 100
Borodin, Mikhael, 72
Boxer Uprising, 63
Brevie Line, 168
Brezhnev Plan for Asian Security, 181-182
Bronze, 12-13, 15
Brussels, 67
Buddhism, 17, 95-96, 101-102, 109-113, 176

Mahayana Buddhism 17, 36
Buddhists, 95, 101-102, 109-112, 176
Buddhist Crisis, 109-113
Buddhist Institute for Secular
  Affairs, 110
General Buddhist Association, 110
Unified Buddhist Church, 110
Burma, 9, 30, 51, 62, 91
Buttinger, Joseph, 24, 48

Cady, John F., 48
California, 43
Ca Mau peninsula, 41, 107
Cambodia see Kampuchea
Cam Mon plateau, 2
Cam Ranh Bay, 7, 175, 180
Canada, 90, 191
Canh (Prince), 42, 46
Canton, 10, 15, 64, 72, 180
Cao Bang, 78
Cao Dai, 94, 100
Cape Varella, 8
Cardamom Mountains, 185
Carleton Hotel, 70
Carter, President Jimmy, 141
Catholics (Catholicism), 45-51, 92, 94-
  97, 102, 110-111, 176
  Catholic Digest, 48
Censorship, 96, 101
Central Highlands, 129
Central Office of South Vietnam
  (COSVN), 123, 126-127
Champa, 3, 6-9, 21, 27, 31-35, 38, 40
  Chams, 3, 6-9
Changli, 179
Chea Sim, 166, 184
Che Bong Nga, 33
Chemical defoliation, 117, 137
Chen, King, 23
Chenla, 9
Chiang Kai-shek, 70, 76
Chiao Chih, 3, 15, 20
Ch'ien-lung (Emperor), 60
China, 1, 3-4, 6-24, 26-43, 46-49, 53-55,
  58, 60, 63-64, 66, 68-70, 76, 80, 85,
  92, 97, 116, 122, 124-127, 129, 134,
  138, 141-142, 144-145, 147, 155, 158,
  161, 165-167, 169-191; Aid to

Vietnam, 170-172, 174, 180, 183;
  Border with Vietnam, 144, 159, 179-
  180, 186; Chinese Volunteer Forces,
  172; Cultural Revolution, 172, 176,
  187; Ethnic Chinese, 161, 174, 176-
  179, 187-191; Nationalist China, 76,
  80; Regional power, 124; Revolution
  (1911), 65-66; Sino-U.S. relations,
  181, 183; Trade routes to, 53-57; War
  with Vietnam, 10, 144, 147, 153, 161
Ch'ing monarchy, 63, 66
Chiu Chen, 15
Cholon, 10; see Saigon-Cholon
Chou En-lai see Zhou Enlai
Christianity, 45-51, 92, 110
Chu Dat, 20
Civil Service Examination, 23-24, 30,
  34, 36-37, 43, 51, 63, 70
Clifford, Clark, 120
COSVN see Central Office for South
  Vietnam
Coal, 97, 140, 146-147
Cochin-China, 3, 40, 43, 46-47, 49-50,
  52, 55, 62, 65, 81, 102, 104, 184
Code of Hong-Duc, 37
Coedes, Georges, 8
Col des Nuages, 32
Cold War, 85, 121
Collins, General J. Lawton, 95
Co Loa, 14-15, 22, 27
COMECON, 140, 180, 183
Communism (Communists), 10, 64, 66,
  68, 70-73, 77, 82-92, 94-95, 100-112,
  123-131, 135-136, 138, 157-158, 160-
  161, 163; Comintern (Communist
  International), 72, 74, 85, 163, 187-
  188; Comintern South Sea Bureau,
  73. Historians, 42-43
Confucius, 19, 23-24, 27, 29-30, 36-37,
  43, 47, 51, 92, 109, 112, 156;
  Confucian Temple of Literature, 29
Corruption, 118, 134, 145, 149, 153-154,
  156, 176
Council of Reconciliation and Concord,
  128
Counter-insurgency, 117
Cua Rao, 2
"Cuba of Asia," 181

Cultural Revolution *see* China
Cuong De (Prince), 63
Currencies, 139, 143
Cuu Chan, 20-21
Cuu Quoc, 62, 76

DRV *see* Democratic Republic of
  Vietnam
Dai-co-Viet, 3, 28
Dai-la, 30
Dai Viet, 30-32
Da Nang, 7, 42, 45, 48, 180
Dao Duy Tung, 156
Dao Lang, 21
Da Trach, 21
De Behaine, Pigneau, 42, 46
Defoliation, 137
De Gaulle, General, 80
  Gaullists, 78
De Lagree, Doudart, 51-53
Democracy, 62, 68, 77, 79
Democratic Republic of Vietnam
  (DRV), 73, 79-82, 97-100, 116, 124,
  128-129, 140, 149-150, 171, 175
Deng Xiaoping, 190
De Rhodes, Alexandre, 5, 45
De Tham, 62
Diem, Ngo Dinh, 42, 75, 80, 84, 89, 91-
  113, 130
Dien Bien Phu, 77, 87-88, 153
Di Lao, 21
Dinh Bo Linh, 28
Dinh Dynasty, 35, 38
Doan Khue, 156
Domino Theory, 160
Dong Dau, 12
Dong Duong, 7
Dong Hoi, 39-40
Dong Minh Hoi, 81
Dong Si Nguyen, 156
Dong-Son Culture, 12-14, 23
Douglas, William O., 93
Dravidian Art, 8
Dulles, John Foster, 88, 91
Du Muoi, 156
Duong Dinh Nghe, 22
Duong Van Gieu, 67
Duong Van Minh, 114, 129

Dupleix, 52
Dupre, Marie-Jules, 53-57
Dupuis, Jean, 53-56
Dutch raids, 44
Duy Tan (emperor), 65-66
Duy Tan Hoi, 63

East Europe, 186
East Germany, 153
East India Company, 44
Ecology, 136-137
Eisenhower, President Dwight, 95, 100
Elysee Agreements, 84, 86
Escoffier, 70
Ethnic Chinese, 161, 174, 176-179,
  187-191
Europe, 47, 49, 58, 71, 76, 86, 123, 186
European Economic Community, 140

Fai Fo, 45
Farmers Liberation Association, 108
Ferry, Jules, 57-58
"Fifth Columnists," 190
First Indochina War (1946-1954), 82,
  85, 101, 152
Five Dynasties, 22
Five Year Plan (1976-80), 140, 186
Flores, 13
Foochow, 58
Food Denial Program, 137
Ford, President, 129
Formosa *see* Taiwan
Fourteen Points, 66
France, 3-6, 8, 10, 26, 31, 42, 44-59, 62-
  89, 91-93, 97, 101, 111, 123, 140, 146,
  150, 160, 162-164, 168, 171, 188-189,
  191; French Union, 84; French
  withdrawal, 123, 154; Mission
  Civilisatrice, 53; Religion, 44-51;
  Society of Foreign Missions, 45;
  Trade, 44, 48, 50, 53-58; French
  Legionnaires, 74; French Socialist
  Party, 71; French Communist Party,
  72; Geographical Society, 57
Franco-Spanish Expedition, 49
Free enterprise, 135, 138
Fulbright, William, 119
Funan, 7, 9

Gandhi, Mahatma, 67
Garnier, Francis, 51-57
Geneva, 191
   Geneva Agreements, 40, 88-89, 94,
   97, 103, 106, 128, 133, 150
   Geneva Conference, 88-89, 93, 107,
   162-163, 171, 173
Genocide, 167, 184
Germany, 78
Gerontocracy, 151, 154, 157
Gia Dinh, 42, 142
Gia Long, 3, 41-43, 46-47
Giap, General, 75, 77, 87-88, 151-153,
   157
Goa, 45
Go Mun, 12
Gracey, General, 80
Great Britain, 1, 55, 62, 67, 70, 80, 88,
   91, 96
Great Wall of China see China
Gross National Product, 119, 155
Guerrilla Warfare, 31-32, 35, 77, 79,
   106-109, 115, 120, 125-126, 129, 137,
   172
Gulf of Thailand see Thailand
Gulf of Tongking see Tongking
Gupta influence, 8

Hai Ba Pagoda, 19
Hainan, 175
Haiphong, 56, 83, 123, 136, 144, 179-
   180, 190
Han dynasty, 7, 15, 22, 35
Hankow, 53-54
Han-lin Academy, 29
Hanoi, 3, 11, 14, 17, 19-20, 27, 29, 33,
   35, 38-40, 42-43, 55-56, 58, 64, 68, 72,
   80, 83, 96-97, 99, 104-107, 114-115,
   126-127, 130, 136, 141-142, 150, 157,
   161-166, 168, 171-173, 175-177, 179-
   180, 183-184, 186-187
Hanoi-Khmers, 126, 129-130, 164-170,
   184
Hanoi-Langson, 136
Hanoi-Vinh, 136
Han people, 14
Ha Tay, 22
Ha Tinh, 21, 74

Hat Mon, 19
Ha Trai pass, 2
Hegemonism, 169
Heng Samrin, 166, 184-185
Herrick, Captain, 116
Hinduism, 7-8
History of the Loss of Vietnam, 64
Ho dynasty, 33-34
Hoa see Ethnic Chinese
Hoa Lao, 94, 100
Hoa-Lai, 8
Hoa-Lu, 38
Hoanh Son, 2
Hoang Van Hoan, 153
Ho Chi Minh, 64-66, 70-74, 76, 78-79,
   85, 93-96, 100, 106, 129, 151-152, 163,
   174, 188; Death, 152
Ho Chi Minh City, 10, 129
Ho Chi Minh Trail, 115, 125, 164
Hongay-Campha, 190
Hong Kong, 49, 73-74, 76, 93, 168
Hong River, 12
Ho Quy Ly, 34
Hou Yuon, 126, 164
Hre, 104
Hue, 3, 7, 32, 38-40, 42-43, 47, 58, 70,
   96, 111, 121
Hu Nam, 164
Hunan, 13
Hung kings, 12, 14, 19
Huynh Kim Khanh, 137

ICP (Indochina Communist Party), 73-
   76, 81, 126, 152, 163, 166, 171
I Ching, 17
Ieng Sary, 126, 164, 166
India, 7-9, 11, 13, 17, 42, 67, 81, 90-92,
   140, 176, 187; Sino-Indian relations,
   91, 187; Indian National Congress, 67
Indian Ocean, 175, 181
Indochina Communist Party see ICP
Indravarman V, 31
Indochina, 1, 46, 74, 76, 78, 80, 87, 115,
   123, 128, 130, 160-161, 163, 165, 181-
   182, 184, 186, 191; Indochinese
   Federation, 161, 169-170, 181
Indonesia, 7, 9, 44, 76, 91, 178, 189
Information Catholique

Internationales, 111
Inter-Governmental Committee for Migration, 191
International Control Commission 90-91
International Institute of Strategic Studies (IISS), 158
International Monetary Fund (IMF), 140
Iron Age, 15
Irrigation, 16, 43
Islam, 9

Jakarta, 190
Japan, 45, 62-64, 76, 78-79, 140, 146, 186
Jenan, 15
Jerai, 5
Jesuits, 45
Johnson, President L.B., 115-116, 121, 123

Kahin, George McTurnan, 107
Kampuchea, 1, 2, 5, 7-10, 40, 52-53, 73, 79, 84, 91, 107, 115, 119, 123-128, 130-131, 134, 142, 144-145, 147, 153-154, 159-170, 174, 176, 180, 183-186; Communist Party, 126; Sanctuaries, 164-165, 167-169; War and Occupation of, 144-145, 157-160, 180, 183-186, 189
Kampuchean United Front for National Salvation (KUFNS), 168, 184
K'ang Yu-wei, 63
Kar, 104
Kautilya, 124
Keelung, 58
Kemmarat Rapids, 2
Kennedy, John F., 93, 109, 113
Keo Nua Pass, 2
Khieu Samphan, 126, 164-166
Khmers, 7-9, 39-40, 124, 162
Khmer Rouge, 126-127, 129-130, 153, 161, 163-166, 185
Khmer Serei, 185
Khmer Viet-Minh, 164, 166
Khoi Nghia, 108

Khuc Hao, 22
Khuc Thua Du, 22
Khuc Thua My, 22
Kim-lien, 70
Kissinger, Henry, 109, 121, 128
Krestintern, 72
Kublai Khan, 31-32
Kudu, 8
Kunming, 58, 180
Kuomintang (KMT), 66, 68, 72-73
Kwangsi, 4, 15
Kwantung, 4, 14-15, 22
Kweichow, 4

Labour Youth Groups, 151
La Cloche Felee, 65
Lac Long Quan, 11-12
Lac Viet, 14-15
Lakewood, 93
Lambat, Chasseloup, 51
Lamson, 38
Lan Chang, 35
Lang Son, 21, 27, 58, 78
Lao Dong, 104-105, 108, 150, 164
Laos, 1, 2, 5, 7, 21, 35, 38, 53, 73, 79, 84, 87, 91, 107, 115, 119, 123, 128, 159-161, 163, 174, 180, 185, 187
League Against Imperialism, 67
Le Chieu-tong, 38
Le Duan, 104, 151-157, 183; Le Duan Clique, 153
Le Duc Anh, 153, 156
Le Duc Tho, 128, 152-157
Le dynasty, 34-38, 40, 50
Lefevre, Dominique, 48
Le Hoan, 28
Le Loi, 35
Lenin, 71, 154
Le Quy Ly, 33-34
Le Thanh Khoi, 50-51
Le Thanh Ton, 35-37, 43
Le Trong Tran, 153
Le Van Duyet, 47
Le Van Khoi, 47
Lewis, John, 107
Liang (Emperor), 21
Liang Ch'i-ch'ao, 63-64
Lin Piao, 172

Lin-yi, 7
Liu Shao-chi, 85
Locke, 63
London, 70, 158
Lon Nol, 127, 129-130, 162, 164-165
Losing one's Country (*mat nuoc*), 62, 131
Louis XVI, 42
Luong Long, 20
Ly Bi, 21
Ly dynasty, 29
Ly Thien Bao, 21

Macao, 45
Mac Dang Dung, 38
Mac dynasty, 38-39
McNamara, Robert, 119-120
Maddox, U.S.S., 115
Mai Chi Tho, 156
Mai Thuc Loan, 21
Malacca, 45
Malaya, 13, 76
Malayo-Indonesian, 4
Malay-Polynesians, 5, 12
Malaysia, 188, 190
Mandarin Road, 43
Mandate of Heaven, 37, 41
Manila Pact, 91-92
Mansfield, Mike, 93, 95
Mao Zedong (*also*, Maoists), 139, 153
Marchand, Father, 47
Marr, David, 11, 60
Marxism, 66, 68-69, 71-73, 154; *also see* Communism
Maryknoll Seminary, 93
Marshall Plan, 86
Mat Nuoc see Losing one's Country
Maybon, Charles, 46
Ma Yuan, 18-19
Mekong, 1, 3, 7, 9-10, 35, 40, 42, 50-53, 101-102, 138, 142, 162, 189; Mekong Expedition, 51-53
Mendes-France, Pierre, 87-88
Meo, 5
Mexico, 49
Michigan State University, 101
MiG planes, 157, 172
Ming dynasty, 33-34, 38

Minghua, 179
Minh Mang, 43, 46-47
Missing-in-Action (MIA), 141
MIT, 119
Moluccas, 13
Mon Kay, 85
Mon-Khmer, 4-5
Mongolian, 4-5, 12, 14
Mongols, 8, 30-33
Mons, 9
Monsoon, 16, 116
Montagnards, 5-6, 54, 102
Montesquieu, 63
Moscow, 73, 109, 127, 140, 163, 180-184, 188
Mount Tan Vien, 11
MuGia Pass, 2
Muong, 5, 12, 14, 21
Muslim rebellions, 54
My-son, 8

Nam Viet, 3, 15-16, 18-22
Nan Chao, 22, 27
Nanning, 180
Nan-yueh, 3, 15-16
National Bank of Vietnam, 139
National Fatherland Front, 150
National Liberation Front (NLF), 103-109, 115-119, 121-122, 124-125, 127, 131, 149-150, 158, 164, 172, 175, 182, 184
Nationalist China *see* China
Nationalization, 80, 139-140
Napoleon III, 49
Navarre, Henri, 87
Nehru, Jawaharlal, 67, 124, **162**
New Economic Zone (NEZ), **142-144,** 167, 169, 176, 178, 189
New Jersey, 93
New York, 93
New York Times, 130
New Zealand, 91
Nghe An, 2, 21-22, 70, 74
Ngo Dinh Diem *see* Diem
Ngo Dinh Kha, 92
Ngo Dinh Khoi, 92-93
Ngo Dinh Luyen, 93
Ngo Dinh Nhu, 96, 101, 103, 112-113

Ngo Dinh Thuc, 96, 110-111
Ngo Quyen, 22, 27-28
Nguyen Ai Quoc *see* Ho Chi Minh
Nguyen Anh *see* Gia Long
Nguyen, Chi Thanh, 151
Nguyen Co Thach, 153, 156-157
Nguyen Dan Trinh, 153
Nguyen Don, 105
Nguyen Duc Tam, 156
Nguyen dynasty, 38-43, 66
Nguyen Hoang, 39
Nguyen Huu Tho, 103-104
Nguyen Kao Ky, 117, 130
Nguyen Kim, 38-39
Nguyen Lam, 146
Nguyen Sinh Cung, 70
Nguyen Tan Tranh, 70
Nguyen Thai Binh, 156
Nguyen Thai Hoc, 68-69
Nguyen Trung To, 49
Nguyen Van Hue, 40-41
Nguyen Van Linh, 154, 156
Nguyen Van Lu, 40-41
Nguyen Van Nhac, 40-41
Nguyen Van Thieu, 117, 128-130
Nha Trang, 7-8
Nhan Dan, 146
Nhat Linh, 111
Nhu *see* Ngo Dinh Nhu
Nhu, Madame, 96, 112
Ninh Binh, 56
Nixon, Richard, 109, 121-123, 127;
    Nixon Doctrine, 182
Nobel Peace Prize, 128
Norodom, Sihanouk, 52
Norway, 176

Office of Strategic Services, 76
Off-shore Islands, 174-176
Oil, 175-176
Operation Rolling Thunder, 116
Opium War, 46
Osborne, Milton, 83
Ossining, 93
Overseas Workers' Union, 70

Pacificauon, 62
Pacific Ocean, 175

Pakistan, 91
Pallavas, 7-8
Palu, 46
Pan-chia *see* Census
Panduranga, 7-8
Paracel Islands, 175
Paris, 44-45, 53-56, 70-71, 93; Paris
    talks, 127; Paris Accords, 121, 127-
    128, 130, 141; Paris Chamber of
    Commerce, 52; Paris Geographical
    Society, 51-52
Pasquier, Pierre, 75
Passes, 2, 5
Pathet Lao, 161, 164
Peaceful coexistence, 88, 91, 105, 163,
    173
Peasants, 16, 23, 61, 68, 82, 98, 101-102,
    122, 151
Peasants' International, 72
Pentagon Papers, 116
People's Armed Security Forces, 158
People's Revolutionary Party, 103, 105,
    108
People's War, 120, 150
Pescadores Islands, 58
Pham Hung, 151, 153-154, 156-157
Pham Huy Thong, 41
Pham Quynh, 75
Pham Van Dong, 73, 75, 151, 155, 157,
    162
Phan Boi Chau, 63-64, 68, 72
Phan Chau Trinh, 63, 65
Phan Rang, 7-8
Phaulkon, Constance, 44
Philippines, 76, 81, 91, 175
Phnom Penh, 52, 123, 125, 127, 158,
    162, 166, 167-170, 180
Pho Bang, 70
Phu Cam, 92
Phu Loi, 101
Phung Hai, 22
Phung Hung, 22
Phung Nguyen, 12
Phung Thi Chinh, 18
Pike, Douglas, 106
Pleiku, 116
Poland, 90
Pol Pot, 126, 129, 164-168, 170, 177,

180, 183-184, 186
Polynesia, 45
Pondicherry, 42
Popular Front (France), 75
Population, 1, 4, 38, 119, 135-136, 138,
    141-142, 147, 178, 189
Potsdam, 80
Provisional Revolutionary Government
    (PRG), 128-129, 174
Prussia, 53
Psychological warfare, 117
Puolo Condore, 42, 74
Puolo Wai, 168

Quan Lang, 14
Quang Nam, 8, 33, 40
Quang Ngai, 40, 104
Quang Tri, 2, 7
Qui Nhon, 7, 130
Quoc Hoc College, 70
Quoc Ngu, 4, 17, 64

Railway, 58, 136
Rand Corporation, 107
Red River, 5, 15-17, 30, 35, 53-54, 56,
    58, 97, 142
Re-education, 138
Refugees, 94-95, 97, 101-102, 110, 118-
    119, 134, 137-138, 188-191
Revisionism, 173
Rhade, 5
Rice, 1, 6, 61, 79, 102, 135, 137, 142,
    147
Riviere, Henri, 58
Roglai, 5
Rome, 45
Rousseau, 63
Rumania, 140, 146
Russia *see* Soviet Union
Russian Revolution, 66
Ryukyu Islands, 63
Ryukyu's Bitter Tears, 63

SEATO (Southeast Asia Treaty
    Organization), 91
Saigon, 9-10, 42-43, 49-53, 56, 65, 80,
    91, 94-95, 100, 103, 112, 118-119, 122,
    128, 130-131, 134-136, 139, 150, 153,

158, 165, 168, 175-177, 179-180, 188;
    Fall of Saigon, 129, 150, 153, 158,
    162, 165, 188; Saigon-Cholon, 118,
    138, 142, 177; Saigon-Cholon Peace
    Committee, 103-104
Sailendra, 27
St. Andre les Druges, 93
St. Cyr, 84
Saloth Sar *see* Pol Pot
Salt, 18, 54-55
Sanskrit, 7, 9
Search and destroy operation, 117
Second Five Year Plan, 140-141, 143-
    144, 146-147
Second Indochina War (1964-1975), 90-
    114, 131, 135, 179
Sedang, 5
Shanghai, 55, 64
Shawcross, William, 163
Shih Huang Ti, 15
Siam *see* Thailand
Siem Reap, 185
Sihanouk, Norodom, 123-127, 162, 164,
    166, 168-169, 185
Sihanoukville, 125, 164
Singapore, 49
Si Nhiep, 20
Sino-Soviet rivalry, 105-106, 152-153,
    160, 169, 173-174, 182
Siva, 7
Socialism, 71, 146-147
Society of Foreign Missions, 45-46
Sogetu, General, 31-32
Song Ca, 2
Song Da, 2, 13
Song Chay, 13
Song Ma, 2, 13
Sontay, 18-19
South China Sea, 1, 48, 116, 175
Southeast Asia, 1, 9, 10, 17, 23, 31, 34,
    51, 57, 67, 85, 89, 91-92, 157-158,
    161-162, 169-171, 173-174, 176-178,
    181-182, 186-187, 189, 191
Southeast Asia Treaty Organization *see*
    SEATO
Soviet Union, 71-73, 76-77, 86, 88, 90,
    98, 106, 116, 122-123, 126, 129, 141-
    142, 145-146, 153, 157-158, 160, 165,

169, 172-173, 179-184, 186-187;
Economic aid, 141, 145-146, 180, 182-
183, 186; Hegemonism, 169, 174, 183;
Military aid, 171-173, 180, 182-183,
186; Treaty of Friendship and
Cooperation, 145-146, 180, 183-184
Spain, 49
Spratly Islands, 143, 175
Strategic Hamlet Program, 115
Suffren, 83
Sung dynasty, 28, 35
Sun Yat-sen, 63-64, 68
Surface-to-air missiles (SMS), 157-158,
172-173
Su Ting, 18
Sweden, 140
Szechuan, 13

Tai, 4-5
Tai Do, 33
Taipeh, 177
Taiping Rebellion, 46, 53
Taiwan (Formosa), 58, 122
T'ang dynasty, 20-22, 25, 35
Taoism, 109
Tay Ninh, 176
Tayson rebellion, 40-41
Teng, Ying Chao, 179
Tet festival, 121
Tet offensive, 121
Thai Binh, 21
Thailand, 1, 5, 7, 44, 47, 51-52, 91, 124,
162, 168-170, 174, 185, 188-190;
Thais, 4, 9, 22, 27; Gulf of Thailand,
168
Thai Nguyen, 136
Thanh Hoa, 15, 20-21, 33, 35, 38
Thanh Long, 29, 39, 42
Thanh Nien, 72-73
Than Thai, 65, 92
Thi Sach, 18
Thich Quang Duc, 111
Thieu *see* Nguyen Van Thieu
Thieu Tri, 46
Third Five Year Plan, 149
Third International, 71
Third World, 186
Tho tribe, 5

Tibet, 91
Tibeto-Mongolian,
Tientsin, 58
Toghani (Prince), 31-32
To Huu, 155
Tong Binh, 21-22
Tongking, 1, 4, 7, 12-17, 20, 27, 32-33,
38-40, 42-43, 47, 53-58, 65, 78, 80, 84,
115, 136, 189; Gulf of Tongking
Incident, 115-116; Tongking
Resolution, 116
Tourane *see* Da Nang
Tra Kieu, 7
Tran Anh-tong, 32
Tran dynasty, 29-30, 33, 35
Tran Du-tong, 33
Tran Hung Dao, 32
Tran Ninh, 2
Tran Quoc Hoan, 153
Tran Quoc Toan, 32
Tran Quynh, 146
Tran Thai Tong, 30
Tran Thanh Tong, 30
Tran Truong Kim, 79
Tran Xuan Bach, 156
Treaty of Nanking, 49
Treaty of Tientsin, 49
Trieu, 35
Trieu Da, 15
Trieu Quang Phuc, 21
Trieu Viet Vuong, 21
Trinh dynasty, 38-40
Trinh Tung, 39
Trinh Kiem, 39
Trotskyites, 75
Trung Nhi, 18
Trung sisters, 15, 18-20
Trung Trac, 18
Trung Viet, 3
Truong Chinh, 151-152, 154-157
Tsin dynasty, 7
Tu Do, 102
Tu Duc, 46, 48-49, 55-56
Tunghing, 85
Tung Mountain, 21
Turner Joy, 115
Two Tracks Plan, 121

Unified Buddhist Church, 110
United Kingdom *see* Great Britain
United Nations, 90, 136, 190-191
United Nations High Commissioner of
    Refugees, 190
United States, 4, 42-43, 48, 76, 78, 81,
    85-86, 88, 90-95, 97-98, 100, 106-107,
    109, 112-125, 131, 133-145, 148, 157,
    162-163, 169, 172-173, 177, 181-183,
    189-191; Aid, 85, 95, 118-119, 127-
    130, 141-143, 145; Bombing, 116-117,
    119, 121-123, 125, 128, 133, 136, 144,
    165, 172; C.I.A., 127; Declaration of
    Independence, 80; Geneva
    Agreements, 88, 90; Military
    Advisory Group, 42; Military bases,
    117, 119, 135; Mutual Assistance
    Program, 86; Office of Strategic
    Services, 76; Presidential elections,
    115, 120-121; Relations with China,
    181, 183; Refugees, 189-191; War
    protest, 120; Withdrawal, 136
University of Toilers of the East, 72
Uriyangadai, 30

VNQDD *see* Vietnam Quoc Dan Dong
Van An Thanh, 21
Van Lang, 12-14
Van Tien Dung, 153
Van Xuan, 21
Varenne, Alexandre, 64-65
Varman, 7
Vatican, 45
Vauban, 42
Versailles Conference, 66, 71
Ve Son, 21
Vichy Regime, 76
Vietnam, Census, 34; Vietnam
    Communist Party, 73, 163; Education,
    64, 67-68, 71; Language, 4-5, 24, 34,
    45; Nationalism, 4, 11, 17-19, 21, 24,
    27, 35, 60, 64-89, 101, 103; Partition,
    38-40, 90, 150; Reunification, 4, 88-
    90, 92, 94, 100, 103, 105-106, 128,
    130, 134, 147, 149-150, 156-157, 160;
    Revolts, 3, 17-23, 47; Script, 4, 17,
    36, 45, 64; Tribes, 5-8; Tributary
    relationship, 27, 31-33, 35-36, 58;

Unification, 39-43; Viet Minh, 6, 76-
    89, 104, 106, 126, 151, 162, 171;
    VNQDD, 68-70, 81-82
Central Vietnam, 2-3, 5-6, 13, 35, 39-
    40, 51, 92, 101, 137, 152; Fourteenth
    parallel, 89; Sixteenth parallel, 80;
    Seventeenth parallel, 40, 90-91, 171
North Vietnam, 11, 13, 50, 78-81, 83,
    90, 94, 97-101, 103-114, 122-123, 128-
    130, 135, 140, 143, 147-148, 157-158,
    163-165, 172, 178, 182; *also see*
    Democratic Republic of Vietnam;
    South Vietnam, 7-8, 40, 74, 79, 83,
    88, 90-100, 116-118, 120, 123, 130-
    131, 133-135; Central Office for
    South Vietnam (COSVN), 123;
    Elections, 90-91, 94, 105-106, 129;
    Government of, 88-92, 115, 122, 129,
    136-137, 139-140, 164; Republic of
    Vietnam, 94, 113; State of Vietnam,
    93; Vietnamization, 122; Viet Cong,
    116-117, 120
Socialist Republic of Vietnam: Birth,
    150; Boat people, 161, 188-191;
    Economy, 137-156, 164-188;
    Economic planning, 140-150;
    Economic problems, 130-131, 134,
    137-139, 156, 169; Elections, 150, 156;
    Ethnic Chinese, 161, 174, 176-179,
    187-191; Five Year Plans, 140-148;
    Foreign relations with China, 144-
    153, 171-191; with Kampuchea, 134,
    144-145, 157-161, 180-185; With U.S.,
    133-145, 148, 157, 162-163, 169, 172-
    174, 177, 181-183; With USSR, 173-
    174, 181-184, 186-188; Government,
    Council of State, 146, 154-157;
    National Assembly, 150, 156-157;
    Land reform, 97-99, 101-102, 152;
    Leadership, 134, 151-157;
    Nationalization, 80, 139, 148;
    Occupation of Kampuchea, 160-161,
    180, 183-185; Reconstruction, 138-
    140; Re-education, 138; Sino-
    Vietnam border, 144, 159, 179-180,
    186, War with China, 10, 144, 147,
    153, 157-159; War with Kampuchea,
    144, 147, 153, 157-159

Vinh, 32, 74
Vinh Phu, 13
Viet-Tri, 136
Vo Chi Cong, 155-157
Vo Nguyen Giap *see* Giap
Vo Van Kiet, 156-157
Vuong Van Dong, 104

Wang Mang, 17-18
Washington, 116, 121, 127-128, 130
Watergate, 129
Westernization, 24, 49
Western Powers, 24, 37, 51, 63, 66, 77,
  92, 94, 141, 145, 191
Whampoa Military Academy, 64, 73
Wilson, President Woodrow, 66, 71
Women's Liberation Association, 108
World Bank, 140
World Federation of Trade Unions. 85

World Health Organization, 119
World War I, 66
World War II. 70, 77, 89, 123, 133, 152
Wu Ti, 15

Yangtze, 14
Yellow Flags, 54
Yen Bay Uprising, 69
Yen Tre, 62
Young Pioneers, 151
Youth Liberation Association, 108
Yuan dynasty, 35
Yueh, 4
Yugoslavia, 140
Yulin, 175
Yung Lo, 34
Yunnan, 13, 22, 27, 30, 53-54, 58, 69

Zhou Enlai, 162. 174, 180